MEASURING
INEQUALITY

WITHDRAWN

MEASURING INEQUALITY

A METHODOLOGICAL HANDBOOK

Philip B. Coulter

Westview Press
Boulder • San Francisco • London

To Mignon

Copyright © 1989 by Westview Press, Inc.

Published in 1989 in the United States of America by Westview Press, Inc., 5500 Central Avenue, Boulder, Colorado 80301, and in the United Kingdom by Westview Press, Inc., 13 Brunswick Centre, London WC1N 1AF, England

Library of Congress Cataloging-in-Publication Data
Coulter, Philip B.
   Measuring inequality : a methodological handbook / by Philip B. Coulter.
      p. cm.
   Bibliography: p.
   Includes index.
   ISBN 0-8133-7726-9
   1. Equality. 2. Proportional representation. 3. Income distribution. 4. Social classes. I. Title.
JC575.C68   1989
323.42—dc19   89-5442
                                                                                                  CIP

Printed and bound in the United States of America

The paper used in this publication meets the requirements of the American National Standard for Permanence of Paper for Printed Library Materials Z39.48-1984.

10   9   8   7   6   5   4   3   2   1

CONTENTS

89-1473

viii

TABLES AND FIGURES

TABLES

x

FIGURES

PREFACE AND ACKNOWLEDGMENTS

The impetus to write this book grew out of curiosity and frustration. For a research project in which I was involved, I wanted to select an appropriate index to measure inequality, so I searched for a book that comprehensively reviewed the available indexes, identified their operational similarities and differences, and clarified their theoretical underpinnings. Discovering that no such book existed, I became increasingly frustrated and curious.

It became evident that I would have to undertake my own systematic review of the literature, presumably in my own discipline, in order to identify the alternative measures and choose an appropriate one on the basis of proper theoretical and methodological criteria. This effort led to additional frustrating discoveries. First, I encountered a bewildering abundance of inequality indexes—well over fifty distinguishable measures. Second, my review of the methodological literature on inequality measurement took me through the issues of literally scores of professional journals in five academic disciplines—economics, geography, political science, sociology, and statistics. Third, although I found some cross-disciplinary referencing of inequality measures, by and large each discipline's inequality measurement remained insulated from that of other disciplines.

Fourth, with few exceptions theory and technique remained separate. Methodologists who devised the measures seldom grounded them thoroughly in theory. Similarly, persons who wrote about inequality theory usually did not actually invent measures nor discuss their theoretical properties. And no comprehensive theoretical discussion could be found in the literature; inequality theory lay in bits and pieces in numerous journal articles. Fifth, the many researchers who used inequality measures to analyze actual data usually appeared to be unaware of either the theoretical or technical properties of their chosen index. Most chose an index on the basis of habit and convenience and made no effort to justify their choice.

What began as a decision to spend an afternoon reading up on a few things in one of the books on the subject turned out to be an extraordinary professional adventure over a period of several years. When it became patently clear that the multidisciplinary field of inequality measurement stood in a confusing state of disorganization, I decided to do something about it. This decision led me to create a new measure, the index of inequity, and to write this book. *Measuring Inequality: A Methodological Handbook* is the result of my attempt to organize the field, across several social science disciplines, in terms of its mathematical foundations, theoretical properties, and technical characteristics.

Because the field contains an astonishing array of unique indexes, establishing taxonomic order with reference to these three sets of fundamentals seemed to be the highest priority. The book's intended purpose, however, is very practical. Now, presumably, researchers who want to conceptualize inequality more skillfully and choose, use, and interpret an appropriate inequality index on the basis of theoretical and technical criteria can do so more easily.

I am grateful for the encouragement, advice, and help of numerous friends and colleagues, who read all or parts of the manuscript. In particular, I profited enormously from the help offered by Rick Hofferbert of the State University of New York at Binghamton; Dorothy James of American University; Majeed Alsakafi, Charles Leathers, and Martha Griffith of the University of Alabama; Chong-Hwa Leeper; and an anonymous reviewer for Westview Press. Lennie Schmandt converted the manuscript from ordinary typing to camera-ready with precision and dispatch. In addition, I want to thank the University of Alabama for providing me with a one-year administrative leave, which gave me the time to read, think, and write almost without interruption.

I also want to thank the Institute for Social Science Research at the University of Alabama for its support of this project and my colleagues at ISSR for their friendship and professionalism. The generous contributions of all these individuals and institutions made the book possible and better. Finally, however, I accept full responsibility for the book's flaws.

Philip B. Coulter

1

DISTRIBUTION IN SOCIAL SCIENCE

Distribution is one of the most important concepts in social science. It has been a fundamental concern in several academic disciplines for well over a century, and some contemporary social scientists argue that their disciplines actually originated in early philosophers' efforts to explain the origins of inequality in the distribution of valued resources. Naturally, social statisticians have devoted considerable effort to measuring this important concept.

The purpose of this book is to encourage the proper study of inequality. It explains the multidisciplinary inequality theory and careful conceptualization necessary to inequality measurement. It discusses specific techniques to operationalize inequality and stresses both their underlying mathematical logic and their statistical procedures. Most critically, it emphasizes the importance of carefully linking theory and measurement, conceptual definition and operational definition. What are the alternatives in conceptualizing inequality? How should we conceptualize inequality, given a specific research problem? Once we have appropriately conceptualized inequality, exactly how should we measure it? This book provides a virtual encyclopedia of the logic, procedures, performance characteristics, interpretation, and applications of inequality measures. It seeks to integrate the principles of inequality theory and statistical measurement techniques from several disciplines and, thereby, to facilitate more and better analysis of inequality.

This introductory chapter focuses on the importance, definition, and use of measures of inequality. The next section argues that distribution has been a major concern of several social science disciplines practically from their origins as disciplines one or more centuries ago. Then, the discussion turns to some basic definitions and standard analytical tools appropriate for measuring distribution in social science. Chapter one concludes with an overview of the remaining chapters and alerts the reader to the logic underlying their organization.

THE IMPORTANCE OF DISTRIBUTION

Distribution has been a perennial concern of political scientists, sociologists, and economists virtually since their origins. All three academic disciplines include reference to distribution in their definitions.

Probably the first scholar to examine inequality empirically and critically, Aristotle, in about 350 B.C., proclaimed that "in all states there may be distinguished three parts, or classes, of the citizen body—the very rich; the very poor; and the middle class which forms the mean" (Barker, 1958:180). Justice, he argued, "is found in the distribution of honors, of material goods, or of anything else that can be divided among those who have a share in the political system" (Ostwalt, 1962:116). Whether contemporary political scientists define political science as the study of "changes in the shape and composition of value distributions in a society" (Lasswell, 1935), "the authoritative allocation of values" (Easton, 1981:129), or the similarities and differences in the uneven distribution of political resources and political influence among members of a political system (Dahl, 1984:50-51; see also Brams, 1968), distribution and inequality are central concepts.

Among sociologists, Dahrendorf argued that "the first questions asked by sociology" were "why is there inequality among men? Where do its causes lie? Can it be reduced, or even abolished altogether?" (1968:152). He further claimed that the entire history of sociological thought could be written in terms of attempts to answer these questions. Since Marx (1963 and 1976) and Weber (Gerth and Mills, 1946), social stratification and class conflict based on economic class, social status, and political power have preoccupied contemporary sociologists. In fact, Blau argued that sociological theory "centers attention on the *distribution* of people among different positions either because they are members of different groups or because they differ in hierarchical status" (1977:1).

Classical economist Ricardo wrote that income distribution is the "principal problem" in economics and that economics should be devoted to "enquiry into the laws which determine the division of the produce of industry among the classes who concur in its formation" (Sraffa, I, 1926). Contemporary economists agree. For example, Samuelson, argued that the problems of distribution are "fundamental and common to all economies, but different economic systems try to solve them differently" (1970:16). Scott and Nigro defined economics as "the study of how people behave to allocate and distribute scarce resources among competing ends over time" (1982:18), clearly emphasizing the importance of inequality.

Distribution of valued resources is one of the most enduring practical problems of human societies and, not surprisingly, represents a strong confluence of theory from several social science disciplines. Leading thinkers in political science, sociology, and economics agree that distribution is a defining characteristic of polity, society, and economy. All polities, societies, and economies are similar in that they are characterized by inequality, but their most important differences are the extent and types of their inequality. Measuring inequality well, therefore, is a compelling enterprise.

CONCEPTUAL SPECIFICATIONS

By this time, general definitions of distribution and inequality are probably fairly clear. Their meaning is implicit in the way social scientists incorporate the concepts in definitions of their own academic disciplines. It is useful, nonetheless, to establish specific conceptual definitions of distribution and inequality at this point, so that our subsequent discussion will refer to a common core of meaning. I offer the following generic definitions to illuminate the meaning of the terms distribution and inequality in social science:

> Distribution is defined as the division of units
> among components of a social system. Inequality
> is defined as variation in that division.

Each of the major terms in these definitions requires explanation in order to convey the precise meaning of inequality. Variation refers to the process of changing in form, condition, or substance from a former or usual state or from an assumed standard. It can exist with respect to differences among components at a given point in time or within one component across periods of time. Division refers to separation of a whole into parts to be shared and resembles dispersion in statistics.

The term units refers to whatever is to be divided into parts to be distributed among or possessed by components. A component possesses a share of the units, some frequency and proportion of the total units. Components can be individuals, groups, or places among which units are distributed. Or components can be categories or classes among which people are distributed. The term system indicates an arrangement of things so interrelated as to form an organic whole separate from things outside the arrangement. It provides the reason that the components logically go together and form an identifiable and coherent arrangement of people, places, or groups.

A brief review of some of the units, components, and systems studied by social scientists will illustrate the definitions. Researchers have investigated the division of units such as federal aid, financial transactions, income, industrial productive capacity, market share, land, native languages, parliamentary seats, political party preference, population, war-making capacity, public services, minority group members, religious preferences, social status, students, unemployment, and wealth. Possessing shares of any of these units is a characteristic of the components. Some of these units are scarce and valuable resources, such as income, power, and status. Attitudes and language may be abundant and neutral.

Social scientists have studied the division of these units among numerous components. People studied as components include individuals and candidates for political office. Social groups that have been examined include business firms, communes, farms, households, income classes, occupational classifications, political parties, population groups, school classes, and sectors of the economy. Places that have been analyzed as components include legislative districts, nation states, urban neighborhoods, school districts, regions of a country, and American states. Some of the geographical places, such as communes and neighborhoods, have important social group characteristics and could be classified either way.

The primary, large-scale systems that give meaning and coherence to division of units among such components are, of course, society, polity, and economy. Social status (units) is divided among occupations (components) in a society (system). Votes (units) are divided among political parties (components) in a multiparty polity (system). Income (units) is divided among income classes (components) in an economy (system). All three can be combined. Power (units of social, economic, and political resources) is divided among nation states (societies/economies/polities) in the world (international system).

An important point emerges from this review of units and components. It is possible not only for an investigator to conceptualize the distribution of units among individuals or social groups, but also to conceptualize the distribution of individuals among components such as places or social groups. For example, dollars can be distributed among people, and individuals can be distributed among ethnic groups. The type of conceptualization that is appropriate depends on the problem at hand. Selecting an appropriate statistical technique to measure inequality, given the problem at hand, is critical.

Many studies of distribution have examined small subsystems of the national society, polity, or economy. Typical examples include division of (a) native language spoken among territorial units in a region, (b) police protection services among neighborhoods in a city, and (c) shares of the market among business firms competing in a particular type of business.

The type of variation determines the distributional property of the system. If all components possess the same number of units, the distributional property is equality. If all components do not have the same number of units, the system is characterized by some degree of inequality. But inequality is a generic concept with many variations and forms.

Investigators use the concept inequality for two purposes, description and explanation. Examples of description include describing inequality in one system, comparing inequality in two or more systems, and describing changes in inequality in one system over time. Examples of explanation include cross-sectional and time-serial analysis of inequality either as a cause or a consequence.

Researchers sometimes seek to explain inequality as a dependent variable across several systems at a single point in time. Similarly, they often use inequality as an independent variable to explain some other phenomenon cross-sectionally. At other times, analysts explain change in a single system's distribution across time, in which case inequality is a dependent variable in a dynamic or time-serial analysis. One can also use change in a distribution across time as an explanatory variable.

Researchers have given many different names to specific types of equality or inequality, for example, advantage, apportionment, concentration, deprivation, deviation, dissimilarity, diversity, entropy, fluctuation, fragmentation, heterogeneity, (hyper)fractionalization, imbalance, inequity, instability, polyarchy, unanimity, uniformity, and variation. These are names of some of the distributional properties that scholars have investigated as well as names of the indexes of distribution they have devised to measure these properties.

The actual number of identifiable, measurable concepts of inequality is not as overwhelmingly large as the list implies. As subsequent chapters will demonstrate, however, social scientists use many different conceptualizations and operationalizations of inequality. We turn next to three graphic techniques that aid conceptualization of distribution.

USEFUL ANALYTICAL TOOLS
    Three graphic analytical tools are essential to conceptualizing and measuring inequality: the frequency distribution, the cumulative frequency distribution, and the Lorenz curve. Each provides a different kind of visual analysis of distribution and serves as the basis of several inequality measures. Although I illustrate each through application to income distribution, remember that income is only one kind of unit that can be distributed among components. Social scientists have studied the distribution of many other important units, and we shall consider them throughout this book.

Frequency Distribution
    As the curve or frequency polygon in figure 1-1 demonstrates, the frequency distribution plots rank-ordered income classes or groups on the horizontal axis and number of income receivers on the vertical axis. The curve begins very low in the extreme left of the graph and ascends rapidly to a peak. The peak is the income category with the largest number of income recipients and is called the mode or modal category. At the peak, the curve descends rapidly at first, but at one point (called the arithmetic mean) it's downward slope becomes less radical until it actually parallels the horizontal axis. The area around the mode is graphically well displayed; these are the middle-income recipients. The right-hand "tail" of the distribution, however, conceals much of what is happening to the

Figure 1-1
Frequency Distribution

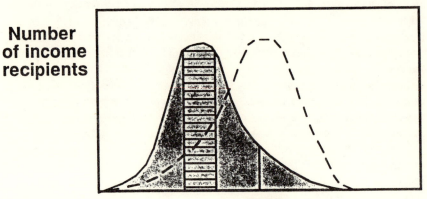

**Number
of income
recipients**

mean

Income classes

Figure 1-2
Cumulative Frequency Graph

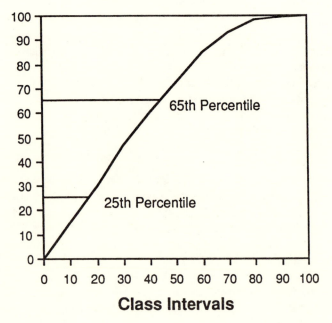

65th Percentile

25th Percentile

Class Intervals

rich and super-rich. The horizontal axis would have to be about two hundred yards long to display the very rich accurately!

Cumulative Frequency Distribution

The cumulative frequency distribution is easily constructed from the frequency distribution. The horizontal axis remains the same. The vertical axis, however, expresses cumulative percentages, zero to one hundred. It gives the percentage of cases below (or above) each class boundary, as figure 1-2 indicates. It permits the frequency distribution to be partitioned at any point, according to the investigator's interests. For example, the lower twenty-five percent can be separated from the upper seventy-five percent of the income recipients. This partitioning represents the first quartile. Centile partitioning divides the total frequency into one hundred equal parts. Figure 1-2 includes designation of the first quartile and the sixty-fifth percentile.

Figure 1-3
Ordinary Lorenz Curve

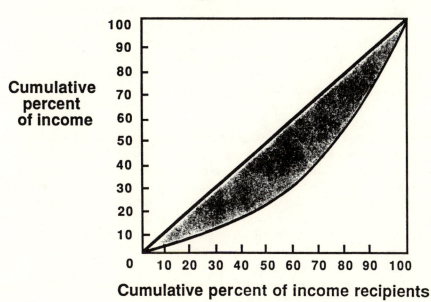

Cumulative percent of income recipients

8   *Distribution in Social Science*

The Lorenz Curve

The American statistician, Max Lorenz (1905), devised the most widely used diagrammatic display of distribution (Pen, 1971). Called the Lorenz curve, it appears in figure 1-3. First, the income-earning units, individuals or families (sometimes classes of individuals or families), must be arrayed in ascending order. The horizontal axis plots the number of income recipients, from lowest to highest income earners, in cumulative percentage terms. As we move along the horizontal axis to point twenty, we have the lowest twenty percent of income earners or income-earning families. At point fifty, we have fifty percent of all families (the fifty percent that earns the least). At one hundred, we have all of them. The vertical axis plots the cumulative percentage share of income going to each percentage share of income earning units (individuals or families). It also starts at zero and goes to one hundred percent.

The Lorenz curve gives the relation between the percentage of income recipients and the percentage of income they earn. The diagonal represents total equality, in other words, one percent of the families receives one percent of the income, five percent receives five percent, ten percent receives ten percent, etc. through all families and all income. The curve traced by a given empirical income distribution, however, will usually sag beneath the diagonal. For example, the bottom thirty percent of the families might earn only eight percent of the income. Similarly, the top ten percent may earn thirty percent of the income. The greater the sag in the curve below the diagonal, the greater the inequality. If all individuals or families had equal income, the curve would coincide with the diagonal. If one individual or family received all the income, the curve would coincide with the vertical and horizontal axes.

Because the Lorenz curve is a particularly useful analytical device, we will return to it often in subsequent discussions. It provides the theoretical basis for several important inequality indexes. It is also used to compare income distributions among two or more countries, in a single country before and after some tax reform, among occupational groups in a single country, etc. If the Lorenz curve of distribution A is everywhere above and no where below the Lorenz curve of distribution B (i. e., A is everywhere northwest of B), then distribution A is said to "Lorenz-dominate" distribution B. Distribution A is more equal or less unequal than distribution B. Two Lorenz curves that intersect, however, cannot be ranked with respect to their inequality. Comparing distributions with intersecting Lorenz curves requires use of other distributional characteristics. Nonetheless, the Lorenz curve conveys a graphically distinct, geometrically-derived impression of a distribution.

THE ORGANIZATION OF THIS BOOK

This chapter introduces inequality as a social science concept and illustrates three key graphical tools in distribution analysis. Chapter two details numerous conceptual and operational criteria that comprise inequality theory. These principles are also helpful in selecting an appropriate statistical index with which to measure distribution, given a substantive or conceptual definition of inequality. In addition, chapter two presents the statistical notation necessary to measuring inequality.

Inequality theory and the statistical notation discussed in chapter two are important and prominently reappear in all of the subsequent chapters. The principles of inequality theory are used to evaluate each of the inequality indexes presented, that is, to describe the way it performs under varying conditions and to explain why. In some cases, satisfying the criteria represents strength. In other instances, it simply represents an alternative. The main point of these criteria is to provide researchers with the tools necessary to conceptualize distribution properly and to make rational measurement choices, given the distributional problem to be analyzed.

The last inequality principle discussed in chapter two is the mathematical model from which a particular inequality index is derived. This criterion is so important that I use it as the organizing principle for the next four chapters that present intragroup inequality measures. Most measures of inequality are derived from one of four mathematical models: deviations, combinatorics, entropy, and the social welfare function. Chapter three presents measures of inequality based on a deviations model. Indexes based on combinatorics receive attention in chapter four. Chapter five examines measures utilizing entropy. Chapter six analyzes distribution indexes based on the social welfare function. Discussion of each measure is designed to highlight both its underlying mathematical logic and its step-by-step computational procedure. The mathematical model provides both the quantitative logic underlying a given equation and a means of interpreting its results.

Chapter seven extends the logic developed in the previous four chapters to examine measurement of intergroup inequality. Intragroup indexes measure inequality between persons or components in a single population. Intergroup indexes measure inequality between people in different groups, for example, occupational status differences between blacks and whites.

Chapter eight deals with inequity. In this case, equality is deemed to be inappropriate, and some other standard must be used. First, the investigator must decide how many units each component should possess—an unequal but "equitable" share of the units. Then, an index of inequity will measure the extent to which the actual distribution conforms to the chosen equity standard or equitable distribution. Inequity indexes are particularly useful in cases in which the investigator can justify some form of inequality among components of a system as appropriate or desirable.

Chapter nine recapitulates the major substantive and technical points contained in the previous chapters and draws some conclusions about the importance of distributional inequality for social science. It also suggests several research avenues that would help to improve the measurement of inequality.

2

INEQUALITY THEORY

Inequality theory provides two types of criteria for evaluating inequality measures, conceptual and technical, discussions of which are widely scattered throughout the social science and statistics literature. The conceptual criteria include a set of essential principles in terms of which one conceptually defines inequality, that is, determines the major properties that one's conception of inequality shall possess. To emphasize the importance of inequality theory, Allison (1978:865) warned that "the choice of an inequality measure is properly regarded as a choice among alternative definitions of inequality rather than as a choice among alternative ways of measuring a single theoretical construct." These conceptual criteria translate into mathematical properties of the indexes. The technical criteria primarily concern index characteristics that affect convenience of computation or interpretation.

In this chapter, I present a non-technical discussion of inequality theory designed to facilitate easier understanding of some of the more technical material presented in subsequent chapters. It should make clear that inequality is a complex concept, that inequality indexes differ in important ways, and that most of these differences impose major theoretical and/or mathematical assumptions (Rae, 1981).

As a means of transition to the technical statistical material in subsequent chapters, I conclude this chapter with a discussion of statistical notation that must be mastered in order to understand inequality measurement. This basically simple notation is essential to understanding the inequality equations that indicate the quantitative procedures to be undertaken and (sometimes) the logic that underlies the procedures.

CONCEPTUAL CRITERIA

Understanding these conceptual criteria will enable the investigator to define an inequality problem, select an appropriate index for a given measurement task, evaluate the index's performance, and compare the performance of several measures applied to the same or different distributions. The conceptual properties of each index make it more or less appropriate for a given measurement task.

Each implicitly assumes a particular conceptualization of inequality and specifies a set of statistical procedures to measure distribution in terms of that conceptualization.

Polarity

Is the phenomenon to be conceptualized equality or inequality? Polarity concerns whether a concept that ranges from minimum to maximum value ranges from equality to inequality or in the opposite direction. Different indexes have different polarities. If a measure is properly bounded, however, subtracting it from unity reverses its polarity. Correct choice of polarity usually depends on the investigator's preference.

Sensitivity to Concentration

Should the conceptualization of distribution include inequality only or also incorporate concentration? Inequality is the generic term. Concentration is a major variant or dimension of inequality; all concentration is inequality, but not all inequality is concentration. Each concept leads to a different, statistically justifiable kind of operational definition. Inequality among components of a system was defined in chapter one as any difference in the size of their shares (Coulter, 1983b; Smithson, 1979). Degree of inequality can, for example, be measured by determining the number of units (and their proportion of the total) that would have to be redistributed in order to achieve perfect equality among all components. If all shares are not equal, some components have a surplus and some have a deficit of the units. Any surplus for one component creates a deficit for one or more other components. For conceptualizing inequality, it does not matter where the surplus is located, for a given deficit. It can be located in one, a few, or many components. Inequality pertains to the number or proportion of units that must be redistributed in order to create uniform shares, not with their location.

Concentration is concerned with the location of surplus units. It is conceptually defined as the extent to which the surplus is clustered in one or a few components or dispersed among numerous components (Coulter, 1983b; Smithson, 1979). Smithson argued that the existing degree of concentration should be measured in relation to the greatest possible amount permissable at a given level of inequality in a system. Not all concentration measures achieve this precision, but most index the clustering of surplus in some fashion.

A brief example will clarify this conceptual distinction. Assume two ten-component systems, each containing one hundred units. Complete equality would occur if each component possessed ten units. Observe the differences in their actual distributions:

| System A | 5 | 5 | 5 | 5 | 5 | 15 | 15 | 15 | 15 | 15 |
| System B | 5 | 5 | 5 | 5 | 5 | 10 | 10 | 10 | 10 | 35 |

Twenty-five units must be relocated in either system in order to achieve equality. In system A, however, the twenty-five units of surplus are evenly spread among five components. In system B, one component possesses all of the surplus units. A pure inequality index does not reflect the difference between these two systems. A concentration measure does.

Concentration indexes can be further subdivided into absolute and relative concentration, based on their sensitivity to the number of shares. Absolute concentration reflects the number of components in the system. Relative concentration is based on comparison of sizes of proportional shares without regard to their number (Ray and Singer, 1973). We return to this point later.

An operational definition of inequality or concentration should reflect the investigator's conceptual definition. The main operational distinction between inequality and concentration indexes is called the "multiplication principle" (Coulter, 1983b). A concentration equation must, by definition, contain at least one of three possible types of multiplication in its summational core. Probably the most widely used type is exponentiation. If each proportional share is compared to (subtracted from) the mean of all proportional shares in a concentration index, the differences may be squared and then summed. Exponentiation is nothing more than multiplying a number by itself one or more times. Second, some concentration indexes require ordering components by their size, for example from largest to smallest, and multiplying each share by its numerical rank. Third, some indexes involve multiplying each share by its logarithm. All three of these operations are forms of multiplication, and all have the same effect, namely to produce sensitivity to concentration. In contrast, an inequality measure contains none of these three in its statistical procedure.

The reason multiplicative inequality indexes reflect concentration of the unequally distributed portion of a distribution is straightforward. For example, squaring the shares, or the differences between each share and the mean share, allots a disproportionately heavy weight to larger shares or larger differences than to smaller ones. Smaller proportional shares, when squared, virtually disappear, whereas large ones remain relatively large. A concentration index score is greatly influenced by the size of the largest shares and basically discounts the smaller ones. This mathematical sensitivity to large shares means that a concentration equation gives most attention to that portion of the unequally distributed resources that is clustered in one or a few components. The typical inequality index gives approximately the same weight to numerous tiny differences as it does to one or two large differences, other things being equal. The key difference between inequality and concentration is location of the surplus (and deficit) created by inequality (Coulter, 1983b; Champernowne, 1974).

Most so-called inequality indexes are also sensitive to concentration, in varying degrees, as well as to inequality. An investigator must decide which concept is appropriate in a given analysis. Many pairs of inequality or concentration indexes will produce different values when applied to the same distribution because they are variably sensitive to one or both dimensions. Inequality and concentration represent an important conceptual and operational choice that the investigator must make.

Comparative Standard

Inequality indexes at least implicitly compare each share in a distribution to some comparative standard. This comparison is explicit in the case of indexes based on the deviations and social welfare models (chapters three and six) and implicit in the case of measures based on other models.

Except in the case of inequity indexes, the comparative standard is some statistical property of the distribution itself. Two measures that use different comparative standards usually produce different inequality values when applied to the same distribution, other things being equal. Other things, including the mathematical model on which the index is based and the index's unique set of statistical procedures for treating the comparisons, however, are almost never equal. Two indexes, for example, might be derived from the same model and use the same comparative standard but treat the comparisons differently. They would produce different index values when applied to the same distribution and might rank several distributions differently, because they treat the comparisons differently. Using different comparative standards is one reason why various indexes behave differently under similar conditions, but only one reason.

Indexes based on the deviations and social welfare models explicitly compare each share of a distribution to some standard. This comparison usually involves subtracting each share from the standard and either disregarding the sign or squaring the difference. Deviations indexes frequently compare each share to the mean of the distribution, the mode or largest share, the next smaller share, each other share, and the next share in terms of occurrence or sequence in time.

The standard used in an inequality index influences its sensitivity to various properties of the distribution, one reason why different measures produce different results when applied to the same distribution. Measures using the mean as the comparative standard are more sensitive to the number and size of extreme shares, both large and small.

Indexes using the largest share as the standard are especially sensitive to the number and size of the smallest components. Naturally, whether an index includes null components in the computation and the number of null components in a particular distribution are important in this regard.

Some measures require arranging components in ascending order for the purpose of comparing each to the next larger category. Nine such comparisons or differences exist, for example, in a system of ten components. Using the next larger share as the standard entails particular sensitivity to large discontinuities in the ordered frequency distribution. Such discontinuities have the opportunity to be largest when there is one relatively large share. Such a measure is insensitive to several or many nearly identical shares because any adjacent pair has no or nearly no difference between them, regardless of whether they are large or small shares. For example, adding one or twenty null categories will produce the same effect on such a measure.

Another comparative standard is every other share. This standard entails evaluating each component with respect to its difference from every other component in the system. Measures employing this standard are especially sensitive to the number and size of extreme shares, but disproportionately sensitive to the single largest share and many small shares, and relatively insensitive to shares nearer the mean of the distribution. Every other share resembles the mean share as a comparative standard. However, comparing the largest share to all other shares (excluding itself, the largest) differs from comparing it to the mean. The mean of all shares will generally be larger than the average of all others (excluding the largest), because the mean is sensitive to extreme (i.e., large) shares. The average difference between the largest and all other shares will be larger than the difference between the largest and the mean. Using all other shares as the standard accords disproportionately more weight to the largest shares, and to a lesser extent the smallest shares, relative to the shares in the middle range of the distribution.

Combinatorics-based indexes (chapter four), entropy-based indexes (chapter five), and intergroup measures (chapter seven) utilize a different type of comparative standard. They use random distribution as the standard with which to compare an actual distribution. This standard usually involves, for example, comparing the probability of selecting a pair of individuals from the same nominal or ordinal category in an actual multicategory distribution to the probability of selecting a similar pair if the individuals were randomly distributed among the same categories. Naturally, combinatorics and entropy treat these implicit comparisons in substantially different ways.

Inequity indexes (chapter eight) employ a more complicated type of comparative standard. They compare each component's share in a distribution to that component's share in an entirely different distribution. This produces discrepancies between actual and standard distributions that the inequity equation then treats according to its own unique set of statistical rules or procedures.

It is conceptually and operationally important to know which comparative standard is appropriate to a given distributional analysis. Choosing an appropriate comparative standard is easier if the investigator has sufficient information about the distribution of interest (e.g., number of components and units, whether it has many or few extreme values or null categories and whether it is unimodal or skewed) and can use that information in combination with a particular conceptualization of inequality. In any case, measures that employ different standards yield different degrees of inequality and often rank-order distributions differently, regardless of their treatment of the comparisons.

Intragroup or Intergroup Inequality

An intragroup measure indexes inequality among persons in a single population, such as the distribution of income among individuals. An intergroup measure indexes inequality between people in two different groups (Agresti and Agresti, 1977; Fossett and South, 1983; Lieberson, 1969), such as the distribution of income among income classes of whites and blacks or the distribution of blacks and whites among urban neighborhoods (segregation). An intragroup measure cannot be used to measure intergroup inequality. Unfortunately, we know less about the properties of intergroup indexes, and fewer of them are available. The nature of the research problem at hand determines which conceptualization is appropriate. An investigator should choose an intragroup index if inequality within one group is to be measured. Selecting an intergroup index is appropriate if the problem calls for measuring inequality between two different groups in a system. Chapter seven details intergroup indexes and presents a special set of principles of intergroup inequality theory for them, because they differ from intragroup indexes.

Inequality or Inequity

One type of inequality is Aristotle's proportionate equality or inequity (Barker, 1958:205; Rae, 1981:59-60). It differs from inequality because it uses as its comparative standard an entirely different distribution, not some quantitative property of the original distribution itself. Each share in a distribution of interest can be compared to the share in another, completely independent distribution (Coulter, 1980 and 1983b; Coulter and Pittman, 1983). The investigator chooses the second distribution, to which the first is compared, because it represents an acceptable normative standard. The comparative distribution is basically what the investigator expects or prefers the first distribution to look like; it does not represent some property of the distribution of interest. Indexes using this comparative standard are sensitive to discrepancies between the shares of the actual distribution and the shares of the standard distribution.

This type of index assumes that all shares should not necessarily be equal in order to achieve equity, but that each should assume some specified value. For example, the equity standard for distributing federal anti-crime dollars to states might be each state's proportion of all reported felonies. A state with five percent of the felonies should receive five percent of the financial aid, and a state with ten percent of the felonies should receive ten percent of the aid, etc. The total amount of discrepancy between the actual aid received and the normative standard is called inequity (Coulter, 1980; Nagel, 1984).

Inequity indexes are conceptually and operationally more complicated than inequality measures. The investigator's conceptualization of the distributional problem will determine whether an inequality index or an inequity index is appropriate. The detailed discussion of inequity measurement in chapter eight also includes its own unique set of principles of inequity theory, because they differ somewhat from those of inequality theory.

Principle of Transfers

The Pigou-Dalton principle of transfers (Pigou, 1920; Dalton, 1920) states that inequality is diminished if units such as income are transferred from a larger share to a smaller share. It is assumed that the transfer is not so large that the recipient becomes richer than the donor. The simplest case is a system of two unequal shareholders. If some income is transferred from the richer to the poorer, inequality declines (Dalton, 1920). An example involving comparison of distributions with the same number of persons and the same mean income will clarify the transfers principle and indicate why it is important. If one distribution A can be made to match another distribution B by transferring some units from a larger to a smaller share in A, then distribution A is by definition less equal than distribution B, according to the Pigou-Dalton principle (Schwartz and Winship, 1979; Champernowne, 1974). The principle of transfers is widely accepted by inequality analysts.

If the principle of transfers is a desirable property, then an inequality measure should be sensitive to transfers at any level in a distribution and regardless of whether the transfer occurs between two shares above or below the mean or between two shares on opposite sides of the mean. An index satisfies only a weak principle of transfers if it fails to reflect a redistribution of income among those above (or below) the mean (Schwartz and Winship, 1979; Cowell, 1977:64-70).

The principle of diminishing transfers (Kolm, 1976a and 1976b) is another variation on the Pigou-Dalton criterion. Kolm's modification of the principle of transfers is concerned with the sensitivity of inequality measures to two factors: (a) the distance of the transfer, measured by the difference between donor and recipient, and (b) the level in the distribution at which the transfer takes place. The principle of diminishing transfers states that the effect of a transfer from a richer donor to a poorer recipient should be greater when the difference between their shares is greater and when the transfer occurs lower down in the distribution. Many analysts accept the principle of diminishing transfers but disagree about how much greater the effects of a transfer should be at different levels in a distribution. Conceptualizing inequality involves deciding if transfers are more important at some levels of the distribution than others, and if so, where they are more important, and how much so (Rae, 1981:110-112).

Some of the more complicated intragroup inequality measures based on the social welfare function (chapter six) allow the investigator to make value judgments about the relative importance of different levels in the distribution and how different types of transfers should affect an index. The investigator implements these value judgments through selecting an appropriate value for a generalized exponent in an inequality equation. We return to this point in chapters six and eight.

Principle of Scale Invariance

The principle of scale invariance or proportionate additions (Dalton, 1920; Champernowne, 1974; Schwartz and Winship, 1979) concerns change in an index when every component's raw share or frequency is multiplied by a positive constant. Different measures behave differently under these conditions, that is, some increase, some decrease, and some remain the same.

Not all social scientists agree that multiplying every share by a constant should leave the degree of inequality unchanged. Consider a three-component system with three hundred units. One component has one hundred fifty units, the second component has ninety, and the third component has sixty, that is, 0.50, 0.30, and 0.20 respectively. If each share is doubled, the first components has three hundred units, the second has one hundred and eighty, and the third has one hundred and twenty. Conceptually, has inequality increased, decreased, or remained unchanged? Different indexes yield different answers to this question. The scale invariance criterion insists that it remains unchanged, because each share retains the same proportion of units when multiplied by two. Relative differences among shares remain identical, although the rich benefit more absolutely than the poor from the change. According to Rae's (1981: 112) least-difference criterion, however, multiplying each share by a positive constant increases inequality, because it increases the absolute difference between the greater and lesser entitlement. We will return to disagreements about this important criterion.

Principle of Constant Additions

What should happen to inequality when a positive constant is added to every share? Allison (1978) argued that it should decline and offered an interesting example, exaggerated to make a point, in support of his argument. Suppose that in a three-person system, the individuals have incomes of $5,000, $15,000, and $25,000. The individuals involved would clearly consider these differences important. If each of them is given a million dollars, however, the remaining differences are trivial, and it is reasonable to assert that inequality has declined.

Many social scientists, especially welfare economists such as Dalton (1920) and Sen (1977), find this axiom acceptable. They agree that equal additions to shares should diminish the score of an inequality index and that equal subtractions should increase it. We should interpret Dalton's argument in terms of his original welfare economic definition of inequality. Welfare economists use inequality to refer to monetary income differences, but they are interested primarily in the distribution of economic welfare, not just the distribution of income or wealth as such. Dalton's arguments make more sense when inequality is defined in terms of economic welfare.

Population Symmetry

If two groups have the same number of components and have identical income distributions, income inequality is identical in each. The population symmetry criterion requires that if the two populations were combined, inequality in the combined population would be the same as that of each of the two separate groups (Sen, 1973). This axiom allows comparison of distributions among two populations of unequal size, but with the same mean. For example, assume two populations with different numbers of people, m and n. Two populations with the same number of people and the same mean income can be obtained by adding the m population n times to itself and adding the n population m times to itself. Then, one population can be compared to the other using the transfers principle (Schwartz and Winship, 1979). If measured inequality is the same for any such replication of a system of components, the inequality measure satisfies the principle of population symmetry.

Cowell (1977:63-64) argued that satisfying this conceptual criterion might not be desirable for all or even most cases of measuring distribution. For example, consider a two-person system in which one person has all the units and the other person has none. Then, replicate the system and combine it with the first. Now we have a four-person system with two totally destitute persons and two persons who share units equally. Are these two systems equally unequal? A measure that satisfies the population criterion says that they are. Other measures do not.

Sensitivity to Number of Components

Sensitivity to number of components in a system, similar to population symmetry, differentiates two important types of inequality—relative and absolute (Waldman, 1977). Indexes whose values are independent of the number of components are relative measures of inequality. Indexes whose values are sensitive to the number of components are absolute measures of inequality.

Conceptualizing inequality as independent of the number of components, for relative inequality measures, means that maximum and minimum inequality do not vary with the number of components on which computations are based.

Conceptualized in this way, inequality is maximum regardless of whether one in three components or one in a hundred components has all the units and is minimum when all shareholders have equal shares, provided the system has at least two components. Absolute inequality measures depend on the number of components in the sense that maximum or minimum equality varies with the number of categories in a distribution (Waldman, 1976).

Waldman (1977) identified three types of relative inequality measures and two types of absolute inequality measures. Relative inequality measures convert the absolute frequency possessed by each share to a percentage or relative size and are, of course, insensitive to number of components. They also differ, however, in the way they treat the number of null components or components that possess no units. First, a "no-null-component" conceptualization of relative inequality excludes null components from the computation and reaches its upper limit when the number of components is one. Second, the "j-null-components" conceptualization includes up to "j" (some specified number) null components and achieves its upper limit when any j components are null. Waldman's third concept of relative inequality is "any-number-of-null-components" (ANONC) inequality. All null components are included in the computation, and this type of inequality reaches its upper limit when one component has all the units.

Both types of absolute inequality measure depend on the number of categories and include all null categories. One of them, type A, is maximum only when one of an infinite number of categories has all the units and minimum when all categories have equal shares. The type B absolute inequality index reaches its maximum only when one of a finite number of components has all the units and reaches its minimum only when the number of components equals the total number of units (i.e., each component possesses one unit).

Whether an index should be sensitive to the number of components depends on the investigator's theoretical assumptions and preferences. An investigator who wants to compare distributions with differing numbers of components (e.g., people or groups) might want to use a measure of relative inequality. If the number of categories is constant across distributions, then an absolute measure might suffice, other things being equal. Naturally, absolute measures are sensitive to the relative sizes of the components as well as to the number of components (Waldman, 1976). Does the distribution of interest contain null components? Does the investigator wish to include null components in the analysis? If so, how many should be included? Which constitutes greater inequality, one component in three with all the units or one component in one hundred with all the units? Answers to these questions help to determine conceptually whether a measure should be dependent or independent of the number of categories and, further, which type of relative or absolute inequality is appropriate.

No-null-component measures do not distinguish among a one-component system, a two-component system in which one component has everything, and a fifty-component system in which one component has everything. The number of null components and whether to include them can be important issues, as Taagepera (1979) pointed out. If a country has only one political party that is entitled to be represented in the national legislature, it is natural to wonder whether other parties are being suppressed by brute force. These other parties represent potential null components.

If nine equally large landowners seized the land of the remaining one hundred very small farm owners and divided it equally among themselves, many inequality measures would indicate a change from gross inequality to virtually perfect equality. If the almost or completely dispossessed (near-null and null components) are excluded from computation, some inequality indexes will decrease just at the time when the outcomes of the grossest forms of inequality (e.g., starvation) are occurring.

The Wilcox (1973) rule states that the investigator should retain a null (or near null) component in the computation whenever it is possible for a case to be placed or to place itself in that component. For example, it is impossible for a voter to place himself or herself in the category of a particular candidate or party in a voting district if that candidate or party is not on the ballot (assuming no write-in ballots). In the parliamentary elections of multi-party political systems, for example, not every party runs a candidate in every election district. Wilcox also offered two practical exceptions to his rule. Null components can be eliminated either (a) to facilitate comparability between distributions or (b) when the investigator deems that they are not "meaningful."

Coulter's rule on how to handle null components differs from Wilcox's rule. The investigator should include all null and near-null components when the primary interest centers on the collective status of components but should exclude them when the interest centers primarily on the location of units. This rule is correctly based on the investigator's conceptualization of inequality, rather than simply on practical or computational criteria.

Some indexes increase in value when the number of categories increases, some decrease, and some are insensitive to changes in the number of components. Which of these is preferable depends on the investigator's conceptualization of inequality. Consider three contrasting examples (Ray and Singer, 1973). If nation A possesses ninety percent of the aircraft within a three-nation subsystem, and the rest of the aircraft are divided evenly between the other two, inequality is certainly high in that subsystem. If two more nations enter the subsystem, however, but nation A manages to retain its ninety percent share through increased production or imports, it would seem that inequality in the subsystem has increased. Originally, nation A constituted one-third of the components and possessed ninety percent of the resources. Then, ninety percent of the resources are possessed by a mere twenty percent of the components (nation A, again). Nation A's share of the aircraft remained the same, as did the shares held by the other subsystem nations. Yet it might be plausible to argue that the increase in number of components should cause an increase in the value of an inequality index (Ray and Singer, 1973).

Industrial concentration provides a different example. Suppose that an industry were formerly concentrated entirely in the hands of three firms. Then two firms are added. One can argue that the concentration of this industry has decreased, even if the largest firm retains a ninety percent share, because the entire industrial sector is now divided among five firms rather than just three. This situation conceptually seems to call for an index that decreases with an increasing number of components.

Based on Hall and Tideman's (1967) "doubling principle," a third example indicates the diversity of opinion about the three types of relationship between measures of inequality and number of components. Consider a five-component system in which each component possesses twenty units (twenty percent), that is, a system of perfect equality. Then divide each component into two equal components, creating a ten-component system in which each component possesses ten units (ten percent). This change reduces the absolute difference between any two components, preserves the relative differences, maintains the same number of units, but doubles the number of components.

Rae (1981:105-128) criticized relative measures of inequality, claiming that they artificially force agreement of four different criteria concerning ranking of distributions. His "maximin" criterion says that any distribution that improves the position of the less advantaged is more equal. The "minimax" criterion states that any distribution that reduces the units of the more advantaged is more equal. The "least-difference" criterion stipulates that any distribution that reduces the size of the difference between the most and least advantaged increases equality. The "ratio" criterion says that any distribution that increases the ratio of least to most advantaged is more equal. Rae argued that any index that forces these criteria always to agree, given some distribution, is fraught with difficulties. The investigator must decide which conceptualization is appropriate.

Ordinary Lorenz Dominance Criterion

The principles of scale invariance, transfers, and population symmetry are all closely related to the ordinary Lorenz dominance criterion and to the comparative rank order that different inequality indexes give to several distributions. Recall from chapter one that the Lorenz curve plots on the vertical axis the cumulative percent of units possessed and on the horizontal axis the cumulative percent of the population that possesses each cumulative percent of units. In a situation of perfect equality, the Lorenz curve is a straight line. The diagonal, designated A in figure 2-1, is the standard against which actual Lorenz curves are assessed. If twenty-five percent of the population has five percent of the units, fifty percent of the population has twenty percent of the units, etc., then the

Lorenz curve will sag below the diagonal, as curve B does in Figure 2-1. Curve C is the Lorenz curve of a distribution characterized by even more inequality than the distribution of curve B.

The Lorenz criterion states that units in distribution B are more equally distributed than units in distribution C if the Lorenz curve for B is nowhere below and somewhere above the Lorenz curve for C (Schwartz and Winship, 1979). In curve B in figure 2-1, the poorest x percent of the population always has an equal if not larger share of the total units than the poorest x percent of the population in curve C for all x between zero and 100 percent.

The Lorenz criterion relates to the transfers, scale invariance, and population symmetry principles in several ways. For two systems with the same number of components and mean units, accepting the Lorenz criterion is the same as accepting the transfers principle. In the case of two systems with different numbers of components but the same mean units, accepting the Lorenz criterion is identical to accepting the transfers and population symmetry principles. When there are two systems with different numbers of components and different mean units, accepting the transfers, proportionate additions, and population symmetry criteria is identical to assuming the Lorenz criterion.

Figure 2-1
Ordinary Lorenz Curve Dominance and Intersection

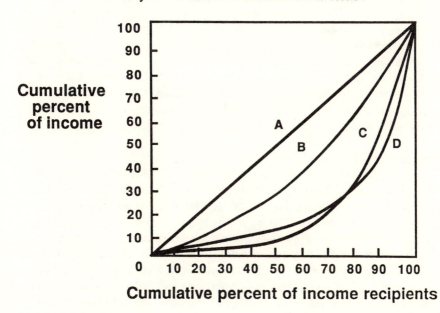

Curve C in figure 2-1, which falls entirely below curve B, corresponds to a larger inequality index value than curve B for any measure that satisfies the principles of scale invariance and transfers. Curve B is said to "Lorenz-dominate" curve C. All scale invariant measures that satisfy the transfers principle will give the same rank ordering of several distributions if their Lorenz curves do not intersect. When two Lorenz curves intersect, such as curves C and D, an index that satisfies the transfers and scale invariance principles might give one ranking, while another similar index might yield a different ranking (Allison, 1978). The point is, however, that when two Lorenz curves do not cross, the ordinary Lorenz criterion is sufficient for determining which distribution is characterized by greater inequality. Based on their criticism of relative measures, both Rae (1981: 123-126) and Sen (1973) argued that inequality's inherent multidimensional complexity makes impossible any such simplistic exercise as unambiguous ranking, except in the case of gross differences. We will return to a more advanced discussion of these three principles and generalized Lorenz dominance in chapter six.

Combining the principles of transfers, scale invariance, and population symmetry in the Lorenz criterion leads to another useful concept - equivalence (Cowell, 1977:69-70). Ordinal equivalence between two indexes means that they rank several distributions in the same order from most to least inequality. Cardinal equivalence means that one index can be obtained from another by multiplying the first by a positive constant and adding a positive or negative constant, for example, $I_1(C_1) + C_2 = I_2$, where I_1 is one index value, C_1 and C_2 are constants, and I_2 is the second, cardinally equivalent index value (Cowell, 1977:10-11). Two or more indexes can be evaluated with respect to whether they are ordinal or cardinal equivalents or neither. Ordinally equivalent measures can be interchanged if only rank-ordering distributions is required. Cardinal equivalence is a more demanding standard, since it requires that the exact values of one index can be derived from the exact values of another index, when applied to each of a series of distributions.

Underlying Mathematical Model

Each inequality index is derived from one of four mathematical models that contains the logic linking the conceptualization of inequality to a particular operational measure and provides the interpretations of a measure's values (Waldman, 1977). The four models—deviations, combinatorics, entropy, and the social welfare function—are so fundamental that I have used them as the organizing principle for discussing the numerous indexes in chapters three through six, and I refer to them where appropriate in chapters seven and eight. Duncan and Duncan (1955:217) argued that "the mathematical analysis of . . . index formulas discloses the areas of redundancy and ambiguity among them, i.e., it permits a conclusion as to the circumstances in which two indexes will give interchangeable results and in which they will give incompatible results. Hence it goes beyond the truism that the empirical results obtained with an index are in part a function of the mathematical form of the index, to indicate what specific property of the index is responsible for the kind of results obtained." Each of the next four chapters begins with a discussion of a mathematical model and then presents the measures that are derived from it. For that reason, I describe the models only briefly at this point.

First, some indexes are explicitly based on the deviation of the components' shares from some norm or standard (Mueller, Scheussler, and Costner, 1970:156-167). The sum of these deviations or differences, either absolute or exponentiated values, specially treated and sometimes bounded, forms the basis for many indexes of distribution. The sum of the deviations of each component's share from the average share of all components is a typical example of an index derived from the deviations model, which is explained fully in chapter three.

Second, combinatorics (Mueller, Scheussler, and Costner, 1970:224-229), deals with the probability that two or more events will occur in combination. If an urn contains fifty red marbles, thirty white marbles, and twenty blue marbles, a random selection of one marble has a fifty percent probability of producing the color red, a thirty percent chance of white, and a twenty percent chance of blue. But what is the chance of selecting two blue marbles in a row? Or a pair composed of one red marble and one blue marble? Or any pair of different-colored marbles? Inequality can be conceptualized in terms of the probability of randomly selecting a combination of two similar units from a group, such as red marbles from a diverse population. Some inequality indexes are based on this principle of the probability of combinations of similar (or different) items. Chapter four presents a lengthy discussion of this mathematical model.

Third, both information theory in communication engineering (Shannon and Weaver, 1949) and thermodynamics in physics (Kittel, 1958) rely on the concept "entropy," which provides the basis of a third mathematical model from which a family of inequality measures is derived. In information theory, entropy refers to a measure of the information content of a message evaluated as to its uncertainty. In thermodynamics, entropy refers to a measure of the degree of disorder in a substance or a system. Both incorporate a concept of the probability of occurrence of one event among several statistically independent, alternative events. The information content of an alternative is its probability of occurring. If it has a high probability of occurrence, being told that it occurred is not very exciting. Consequently, we evaluate it as less valuable information and assign it a low number. Information that an improbable event has occurred is more exciting, and we assign it a relatively high number. Low probabilities mean more uncertainty, less information, more randomness, less organization, less orderliness, in short, more entropy. The mathematical expression of entropy can be used to measure inequality in social systems. Chapter five's introduction explains entropy in detail.

Fourth, the formal theory of social welfare provides the mathematical basis for a small set of inequality measures. Based on the social welfare function, these indexes incorporate the relationship between the geometric mean (Mueller, Scheussler, and Costner, 1970:148-149) and the arithmetic mean. The geometric mean is always equal to or smaller than the arithmetic mean in a distribution of positive units among components in a system. How unequal the components are determines the degree of difference between the two types of average. This simple mathematical fact is used to measure distributional equality, particularly when deployed to elaborate principles of social welfare theory. This model is discussed in chapter six.

TECHNICAL CRITERIA

Definition

A measure should be defined for all possible distributions (Galtung, 1967: 207-208). In other words, for all distributions with the characteristic (m, n, r) there should be one and only one value of the index. A measure using a denominator that can take on the value zero should be avoided. For example, some indexes are computed as the ratio between two percentages. Similarly, indexes that are based on the mode can also cause trouble in bimodal or uniform distributions.

Information Use

Most investigators agree that an index of inequality should use as much information as possible about the distribution it describes, in order to convey as much information as possible about that distribution (Ray and Singer, 1973; Waldman, 1977; Alker and Russett, 1964). Maximum information use means that index values reflect all the shares in the system and are not unduly influenced by one or a small number of those categories, unless such influence is a deliberate part of the measurement strategy. The difference between mean and median averages is analogous. The mean finds the average by summing all values and dividing by the number of values. The median is the midpoint of all values arrayed in ascending order. The smallest value could be halved or the largest value doubled, and the median will not change. The mean will change, of course, to reflect the changing value of one of its extreme components. As we shall see, some indexes do not use all the information in the distribution, for example, when they exclude null components.

Simplicity
        A measure of inequality should be simple to understand and to compute
(Wilcox, 1973; Galtung, 1967:208). In one sense, all computation is simple
with modern computers and powerful pocket calculators. However, when any one
of several indexes meets the investigator's theoretical specifications, the simpler
one is preferable, other things being equal.

Interpretability
        Interpretability concerns the upper and lower limits of an index. Some in-
dexes are "properly" bounded, in other words, they can vary from a minimum
value of zero to a maximum value of unity (Ray and Singer, 1973; Allison,
1978; Hall and Tideman, 1967). Some measures are not bounded; their lower
limits are not zero and/or their upper limits are not unity, in some cases infinity
(Theil, 1969). The mathematical characteristics of a given inequality equation
determine its upper and lower bounds.
        Most authors agree that an inequality index value should be zero under
conditions of perfect equality, when each component has an identical share. They
also tend to agree that deviations from perfect equality should produce positive
index values for an intragroup measure. Further, most agree that an index should
assume its maximum value whenever one component possesses all of the units.
Some social scientists disagree, however, about what the minimum and maximum values should be. Whether a measure's values are bounded from zero to
unity is related to a larger and theoretically more important issue discussed earlier, the relationship of index values to the number of components in the system.
        Properly bounding an index makes it more interpretable in three ways.
First, a bounded measure is easier to interpret when an investigator uses one index to describe inequality in one distribution. In this situation, no standard exists, other than zero to one, by which to appraise the extent of inequality in the
distribution. Second, an analyst might want to use the same index to compare
the inequality of several distributions with different numbers of components and
different amounts of units. The number of components and units affects the values (including upper and lower limits) that an index can assume. Third, an
investigator might want to compare the performance of several indexes when
used to measure the same distribution. Judging their relative sensitivity to the
characteristics of the distribution is difficult or impossible if these indexes have
different upper or lower bounds.
        Most unbounded measures can be standardized, however, usually by a
simple statistical procedure. I present bounded versions of unbounded indexes
throughout chapters three through seven, not necessarily as better than their unbounded versions, but simply as alternatives for an investigator who wants a
bounded version of that particular measure.

Not all social scientists agree that bounding a measure from zero to one is appropriate. For example, Cowell (1977: 70) argued that "standardization of the measure in a given range (such as 0 to 1) has only a superficial attractiveness to recommend it; it may well be worthwhile sacrificing this in order to put the measure in a cardinal form more useful for analysing the composition of, and changes in, inequality."

Lieberson (1969) presented probably the best arguments in favor of using an unbounded index. An investigator, Lieberson reasoned, might want to use an unstandardized measure "for purely descriptive purposes" (1969: 860). Similarly, an investigator making comparisons among populations with the same number of categories or components might not care whether a bounded or unbounded index is used. Suppose, for instance, that an analyst wishes to compare several nations with respect to their occupational diversity and that all occupational categories are at least minimally represented in each nation. An unbounded index and its standardized version would correlate perfectly, since the standardized procedure would divide the unbounded values by the same constant. In fact, Lieberson argued that the unbounded measure has the advantage of indexing the actual level of diversity in each nation.

Further, an unadjusted index might offer an advantage even when comparing diversity among populations that differ in the number of categories. Compare religious diversity between two groups of 30 and 31 people. The first group contains ten Jews and twenty Catholics. The second group includes ten Jews, twenty Catholics, and one Protestant. An unstandardized measure will produce very similar results for the two groups. Many standardized indexes will yield very different values. But the actual levels of diversity within the two groups are very similar. Lieberson concluded: "Whenever the goal is to describe the actual level of diversity, then the unadjusted measures are desirable" (1969:861).

Whether a measure is bounded or unbounded does not determine its inherent goodness or badness. Rather, an investigator should choose a measure because it is appropriate to the analysis task at hand. Most researchers seem to agree, however, that in general, in principle, properly bounded measures provide greater interpretability.

Scale of Measurement

The scale of measurement is important to distribution indexes with regard to the mathematical assumptions that a given index equation makes about the scales on which units and components are measured. First, units can be measured with nominal, ordinal, interval, or ratio scales (Mueller, Scheussler, and Costner, 1970:14-15). An ordinal scale measures a case as ranking higher or lower than another case with respect to the ordinally scaled property, but how much higher or lower is unknown. An interval scale indicates that one case is greater or less than another with respect to some property and by exactly how much. We know the distance between two cases, for example, scores of fifty and seventy five on an occupational prestige rating, but we do not know the ratios between them. A ratio scale has a natural origin or theoretically fixed zero-point, and therefore elements of the scale can be expressed as multiples of one another. Occupational prestige has no natural zero, but age does. Someone who is fifty years old is twice as old as someone who is twenty five years old. Sixty is thirty years greater than thirty and twice as large. Age measures time on a ratio scale.

Because an interval scale has no natural zero, its origin can be changed arbitrarily by adding a constant to every score without changing the interval nature of the scale. An inequality index value based on intervally scaled units is sensitive to such additions, because they change the origin of the series. Allison (1978:870-871) showed that such a measure is inappropriate for characterizing a single distribution if the units are intervally scaled. The same prohibition also holds for comparing the inequality of two distributions, both measured on the same ordinal scale.

Some items are measured on a nominal scale and have no magnitude of difference between them, only qualitative difference. They are either identical or different. In such a case, we count the number of differences rather than measure magnitudes. An example is a social science conference attended by political scientists, economists, sociologists, and geographers. We do not measure the ordinal ranking of each social scientist or the intervals between them, because none exists. Rather, we determine the total number of conferees in each discipline and count the numerical differences among the disciplines. The total number of differences among the disciplines determines the extent to which the meeting is heterogeneous or homogeneous.

The second way in which scale of measurement affects inequality indexes concerns the assumption an index makes about the scale on which components are measured and the combination of units and components. Three such combinations are important: (a) units measured on an interval or ratio scale (e.g., dollars of income) distributed among individuals or groups, presumably with few or no ties; (b) people distributed among ordinally ranked classes or components; or (c) people or other units distributed among nominal components.

In the interval and ratio type of inequality index, individual units are ranked, and each unit has one component (person, place, or group) associated with it. An example is ranking the annual incomes of a sample of individuals. All of the actual incomes in dollars are arrayed from highest to lowest, and one income-earner is associated with each listed income. Ties may occasionally occur. The components themselves, individuals/incomes, have more than an inherent rank-order. This kind of arrangement comprises either a ratio or interval scale. It is a ratio scale if the measured quantity has an absolute zero, for example, income and age. It is an interval scale if no such natural zero exists; neither IQ nor social status has an absolute zero.

In the second combination of units and components, the ordinal type of inequality index assumes ordered classes that serve as components among which individual units are distributed. This type is the traditional frequency distribution with categories that possess an inherent rank order even in the absence of frequencies associated with each class or component. An example is income categories with frequencies of income-earners from a sample survey as units. The ordered categories are the components and contain frequencies of people as units.

Third, the nominal type of index assumes unordered categories as components that contain frequencies of units such as people. The categories have no inherent rank-order, although they can be ordered in terms of their frequencies, once those are known.

Table 2-1 contains hypothetical data on all three combinations: nominal frequencies, ordinal frequencies, and interval magnitudes. The table also points out the difficulties of appropriately matching inequality concept and index. The nominal categories are four colors among which fifty marbles are distributed. In other words, we have frequencies of four colors of marbles that contain no inherent rank-order. The ordinal categories are income classes that contain an inherent rank-order. The same frequencies are associated with these four income classes as are associated with the four colors. They produce the same proportions reported in column five of table 2-1. The interval magnitudes appear in column four of table 2-1 in the form of annual incomes of four individuals. Each individual's proportion of the total income is reported in column five and is, of course, the same as the proportions for the nominal and ordinal categories.

Table 2-1
Hypothetical Data for Combinations of
Components and Units Measured on Different Scales

1 nominal categories	2 ordinal categories	3 N	4 interval magnitudes	5 categories proportions
green	$0-4999	5	$4000	0.10
blue	5,000-9999	10	8000	0.20
red	10,000-14,999	15	12,000	0.30
black	15,000-19,999	<u>20</u>	16,000	<u>0.40</u>
	total	50		1.00

The data in table 2-1 represent three distinct problems in inequality measurement: distribution of a) people among nominal categories, b) people among ordinally-ranked categories, and c) dollars among people. Some indexes assume ordinal components. Some call for arraying the frequencies in ascending order of magnitude and treating them as interval. Others assume using such an array to construct a cumulative frequency distribution. The investigator should first conceptualize the distribution research problem and then choose an index whose assumptions match the characteristics of the problem as conceptualized.

Most inequality indexes categorize individuals into nominal components and then count the members or find the frequencies. Counts are cardinal numbers in the classical sense, and we can do any arithmetic we want. Both counts and proportions can be treated as ratio scales. For example, some indexes treat the four income classes of a sample of income-earners the same as one would treat the total expenditures of each of four political parties in an multiparty election campaign. Income classes comprise a strong, natural, ordinal scale of components containing frequencies of income-earners. But political parties comprise a nominal scale unless they are ordered in terms of their campaign expenditure units in dollars. Both can be plotted as Lorenz curves. The income distribution would be plotted as cumulative proportion of income earners against cumulative proportion of income earned. The campaign expenditure distribution would be plotted as parties' cumulative proportion of campaign expenditure (lowest to highest) against cumulative proportion of political parties in the campaign. The latter represents a weaker form of measurement scale, because only four parties were involved in the campaign and each represented twenty-five percent of the parties. In this case, the frequencies (and proportions) of party expenditure are individually rank-ordered and one component (a political party) associated with each amount of money spent. This involves considering frequencies as intervally-scaled components with one component distributed to each of them.

Most of the equations for measuring inequality will operate on the data and produce an index value equally well in either case. The analyst, however, should carefully match conceptualization with technical measurement assumptions to avoid reaching invalid conclusions.

ESSENTIAL STATISTICAL NOTATION

Understanding inequality requires familiarity with both the statistical procedures that manipulate quantitative information about the distribution and the mathematical logic underlying the procedures. Most of the index equations are based on a small body of elementary statistical notation. They use many of the same symbols in different combinations to inform the investigator of data requirements and the set of sequenced procedures for treating the data. The reader might notice certain differences between the form of an index equation provided in this book and its form in its original source. The equations are mathematically identical, however. Only the symbols expressing the form might be different. I have used standardized statistical notation wherever feasible throughout chapters three through eight for simplicity and consistency of presentation. The list of standardized symbols and their brief definitions follow.

Statistical Symbols

i component (person, place, or group) possessing a share of the units; for indexes involving rank, i indicates rank by increasing component size, from i to K

N total number of units distributed among all components

N_i number of units possessed by the i_{th} component; $\Sigma N_i = N$.

$\overline{N}$ arithmetic mean of N or N/K

P_i proportional share or percentage of total units possessed by the i_{th} component; $P_i = N_i/N$ and $\Sigma P_i = 1.0$.

P_m maximum, modal, or largest share

P_{min} minimum or smallest share

K number of components or shares; $1/K$ = mean proportional share

Σ take the sum of; $\sum_{i=1}^{K}$ indicates take the sum of all i beginning with the first and continuing through K (the last). The double summation sign $\Sigma\Sigma$ means sum the differences or products of various combinations of each i and other j shares as indicated by the subscripts and superscripts attached to the summation signs. Subscripts and superscripts will be omitted when no ambiguity is possible.

$\log_{10}$ logarithm to base ten

$\log_2$ log to base two

antilog$_{10}$ antilogarithm to base ten

antilog$_2$ antilogarithm to base two

α   alpha, a generalized exponent that must be assigned a value by the investigator, based on theoretical grounds

t   point in time in a time series of components

Familiarity with this small body of statistical symbols will enable the reader easily to understand most of the procedures. An example of a simple system will illustrate use of the statistical notation.

i	1	2	3	4	5
N	20	15	10	5	0
P	.40	.30	.20	.10	.00

The system includes five components that possess fifty units, so $K = 5$ and $N = 50$. The mean share size is $N/K = 10$, and the mean proportional share is $1/K = .20$. Component three possesses ten units, so $N_3 = 10$ and $N_3/N = P_3 = .20$. $\Sigma N_i = N_1 + N_2 + N_3 + N_4 + N_5 = 20 + 15 + 10 + 5 + 0 = 50$. ΣP_i produces the same summation but over proportional shares and would equal unity. Also, $P_m = .40$, and $P_{min} = .00$. These are the basics. Other symbols will be explained as they are introduced in a discussion of a particular index equation.

We have reviewed twelve conceptual and six technical criteria for thinking about inequality, evaluating a given distribution measure, and selecting an appropriate index for a given research problem. One of them, the underlying mathematical model, provides a convenient mechanism by which to organize our discussion of most inequality measures.

The introduction in chapter one and the theoretical discussion in this chapter should prepare the reader to master the mathematical logic and specific operations of inequality measurement in the remaining chapters. Chapter three details the logic of the deviations model and examines the specific procedures of inequality measures derived from it.

3

INDEXES BASED ON
THE DEVIATIONS MODEL

The deviations model is the simplest mathematical model from which any inequality measure is derived. This chapter discusses eight different indexes (and five equivalents) based on the deviations model. In all cases, I present an operational definition equation for the measure that expresses the deviations logic directly and clearly. In some instances in which that equation is unduly difficult or time-consuming to calculate, I also present a computational equation, in this and subsequent chapters. This latter equation does not reveal the deviations logic as clearly, but the investigator can use it more easily to measure inequality empirically. I analyze the major parts of each equation and state them in verbal terms. The discussion also refers to the originator's intended purpose of the measure. In addition, I assess each index in terms of the conceptual criteria presented in chapter two.

THE DEVIATIONS LOGIC
    The deviations model assumes that the distributional characteristics of any numerical series are best described in terms of the deviations of each value from some standard (Alker and Russett, 1966) derived from the series itself. To understand the deviations model, two questions must be answered: (a) Deviations from what standard? and (b) How are the deviations to be statistically treated? Deviations of each component's share can be taken from at least five norms of equality: (a) the modal or largest share, (b) the arithmetic mean share, (c) every other share, (d) the next smaller share (when shares are arrayed in descending order of magnitude), and (e) the temporally adjacent share (when shares are arranged in the order of their occurrence).
    Deviations from what? Both the mode and the arithmetic mean are, of course, measures of central tendency of a distribution. They represent an intuitively useful fixed standard in our common social experience. The mode is the actual, largest component of a distribution, the share that contains the largest number of units. The mean is the value from which deviations above and below are in balance. All other components, as a deviational standard, represents all the

variational characteristics of the remainder of the distribution, in raw form. Comparing each share to the next smaller share requires ordering all shares from largest to smallest. The temporally adjacent share is used as a deviational standard to measure inequality as distributional change over time.

How are deviations to be statistically treated? Deviations of each share from the standard are computed either as absolute or as squared deviations. In the case of absolute deviations, minus signs are disregarded, and all deviation values are considered to be positive. Algebraic deviations from the mean, in contrast, must be treated in some fashion, or they will always sum to zero (Mueller, Scheussler, and Costner, 1970:161-162). Squaring the deviations is a mathematically legitimate procedure that "clears" the signs and permits them to sum to a positive number. The sum of squared deviations from the mean is also minimal; that is, the sum of squared deviations from any other value is greater than the sum of squared deviations from the mean.

Squaring, one treatment of deviations, is an exponential computation that has the effect of weighting the deviations disproportionately as they increase in magnitude. This effect partially remains even after taking the square root of the mean of the squared deviations. Larger deviations from the standard are, therefore, disproportionately more important in producing the index value.

Another treatment of the summational core is multiplicative weighting of deviations by their sequence number when arrayed in descending order or by the frequency of units in the component. In sequential weighting, for example, the largest component is given a weight of one, the second largest a weight of two, the third largest a weight of three, and the K_{th} largest a weight of K.

In summary, deviations from the standard are computed either as absolute or squared (and the square root usually taken later), possibly weighted, and summed. This procedure produces the treated summational core, which often comprises a numerator that is standardized and/or bounded by a denominator in order to express it in unit-free terms and constrain its variation between zero and unity. Sometimes the treated summational core is not bounded. The way in which deviations are computed, the treatment of the summational core, and whether it is bounded incorporate the logic of measures derived from the deviations model. Deviation or difference is the conceptual link between the mathematical model and interpretation of its indexes.

Some of the index computations are based on raw frequencies of units possessed by each component; others use proportional shares in the computation. In some instances, several different measures with their own names and reputations are mathematically equivalent to each other. For example, some indexes are complementary; one index measures equality and another measures inequality by subtracting the first from unity. Or one measure of inequality is the square (or square root) of another. In fact, some index equations based on one model (e. g., deviations) are mathematically equivalent to index equations based on another model (e. g., combinatorics) and can be converted into or derived from the other through a series of appropriate algebraic substitutions.

Table 3-1 lists formal names and equations for eight indexes. Names of identical and equivalent indexes are also listed parenthetically. Seeing all of them together facilitates understanding the way in which they use the same deviations logic but incorporate different statistical treatment of deviations in order to capture different aspects of distribution (Yntema, 1933).

Table 3-1

Indexes Based on the Deviations Model

A. Absolute Deviations from Central Tendency

    1. Wilcox's Deviation from the Mode

$$DM = 1 - \frac{\Sigma(P_m - P_i)}{K - 1}$$

    2. Dahl's Index of Polyarchy

$$P = 1 - \frac{\Sigma N_i |P_i - 1/K|}{\Sigma N_i P_i}$$

    3. Schutz's Coefficient of Inequality (also known as Relative Mean Deviation, Wilcox's Average Deviation Analog, and Martin and Gray's Relative Variation)

$$S = 1/2 \Sigma |P_i - 1/K|$$

B. Squared Deviations from Central Tendency

    4. Mayer's Measure of Uniformity

$$M = 1 - \frac{\Sigma(P_i - 1/K)^2}{1/K}$$

5. Nagel's Index of Equality

$$E = 1 - \frac{\Sigma(N_i - N/K)^2}{\Sigma(Z^* - N/K)^2}$$

C. Differences from All Other Components

6. Gini Coefficient of Inequality

$$G = 1/2 \sum_{i=1}^{K} \sum_{j=1}^{K} \left| (1/K)P_i - (1/K)P_j \right|$$

7. Gini's Coefficient of Relative Mean Difference (also known as Kendall's Difference and Wilcox's Mean Deviation Analog)

$$RMD = \frac{\sum_{i=1}^{K-1} \sum_{j=i+1}^{K} |P_i - P_j|}{K}$$

D. Differences from Temporally Adjacent Components

8. Przeworski's Index of Instability

$$D_t = 1/2 \, \Sigma \left| P_i \, (t + 1) - P_i \, (t) \right|$$

---

*For an explanation of Z, see the section on Nagel's Index of Equality.

Table 3-2 summarizes the primary conceptual and technical properties of these eight indexes (and five equivalents or complements) and provides a convenient means for evaluating or selecting an index. The remainder of this chapter explains the measures and describes their statistical properties.

Table 3-2: Primary Properties of Indexes Based on the Deviations Model

	Polarity	Type of index	Concentration	Comparative standard	Constant additions	Transfers	Scale invariance	Population symmetry	Lorenz dominance	Scale	Definition	Information use	Upper and lower limits	Simplicity
Wilcox's deviation from the mode (DM)	equality	relative, ANONC	no	mode	increase	yes	yes	no	no	nominal	yes	good	1, 0	good
Dahl's polyarchy (P)	equality	absolute, type A	yes	mean	increase	yes	yes	yes	yes	interval	yes	good	$1-(1/K), 0$	fair
Schutz's inequality (S)	inequality	absolute, type A	no	mean	decrease	no	yes	yes	no	nominal	yes	poor	$1-(1/K), 0$	good
Mayer's uniformity (M)	equality	absolute, type A	yes	mean	increase	yes	yes	yes	yes	nominal	yes	good	$K-1, 0$	good
Nagel's equality (E)	equality	relative, ANONC	yes	mean	decrease	yes	yes	yes	yes	nominal	yes	good	1, 0	good
Gini's mean relative difference (MRD)	equality	relative, ANONC	yes	all other components	increase	yes	yes	yes	yes	interval	yes	good	1, 0	fair
Gini coefficient (G)	inequality	absolute, type A	yes	all other components	decrease	yes	yes	yes	yes	interval	yes	good	$1-(1/K), 0$	poor
Przeworski's instability (D_t)	inequality	absolute, type A	no	adjacent component	decrease	yes	yes	yes	yes	nominal	yes	good	$t_n-1, 0$	poor

ABSOLUTE DEVIATIONS FROM CENTRAL TENDENCY
    The first set of indexes measures absolute deviations from central ten-
dency. This particular version of the deviations model provides the most intuitively straightforward model for measuring inequality. The three equations
derived from it, however, are distinctively different in terms of their sensitivity
to distribution.

Wilcox's Deviations from the Mode (DM)
    Wilcox's (1973) measure of deviations from the mode is expressed in the
following formula:

$$DM = 1 - \frac{\Sigma(P_m - P_i)}{K - 1}$$

    Wilcox's DM is a measure of equality, rather than inequality, because if
one component possesses all units, DM reaches its minimum value, and if all
components possess the same number of units, DM reaches its maximum value.
It is best understood as a measure of the extent to which the non-modal components resemble the modal component. The ratio is a measure of inequality, but
because it is subtracted from unity, DM's polarity is toward equality. The numerator of the ratio, the summational core of the formula, is the sum of the deviations of each component from the modal or largest share in the distribution.
To insure that its upper limit is unity (complete equality) and its lower limit is
zero (maximum inequality), the denominator bounds the measure. The
denominator is the maximum value that the numerator can attain, given the
number of components, K.
    DM uses all available information when it subtracts each component from
the modal component. Even though it is precisely defined for all possible distributions, however, DM is unable to distinguish between a unimodal and a bimodal distribution. When every component's share is the mode, however, DM =
1.0. It is a relatively simple index to compute.
    This index assumes that the components are nominally scaled and that the
units are distributed among these unordered categories. For example, income is
distributed among provinces in a nation, or votes are distributed among political
parties in a legislature. DM is a measure of relative inequality that includes any
number of null components and reaches its limit only when one category has all
units. It is insensitive to concentration, because its summational core contains
no multiplicative function.
    Although its upper and lower limits do not depend on the number of
components, the values of DM do. Increasing the number of components causes
DM scores to decline. For example, dividing each component of a given

distribution in half doubles the number of components but maintains the same level of relative inequality among components. DM declines substantially under this condition.

DM is scale invariant because its value does not change when each share is multiplied by a positive constant. Adding a positive constant, however, causes the measure to increase, indicating an increase in equality. A transfer from a rich donor to a poorer recipient increases the value of DM, reflecting an increase in measured equality. DM thus satisfies at least a weak principle of transfers. It is not consistent with the principle of population symmetry; if two identical systems are merged, the DM score for either is not replicated in the new, combined system. The reason can be found in the use of K, number of components, in the denominator.

DM therefore fails to comport with the Lorenz dominance principle. Even if distribution A's Lorenz curve lies everywhere above that of distribution B, one still cannot say that distribution A is less unequal.

Dahl's Index of Polyarchy (P)

Dahl (1956:84-87) originally created the polyarchy index to measure the extent to which collective decision-making in a political system or a bureaucracy approximates polyarchy, a condition in which everyone's vote is weighted equally in reaching decisions. Specifically, Dahl's index seems most useful in measuring polyarchy in any large organization in which the members or subdivisions exert different amounts of influence on collective decisions. Dahl's P takes into account both the proportion of votes, or voters weighted excessively, and the comparative weights of votes. The equation for P is:

$$P = 1 - \frac{\sum N_i \left| P_i - 1/K \right|}{\sum N_i P_i}$$

In terms of Dahl's original conceptualization of polyarchy as an example of distributional equality, he let P_i be the relative value of a particular vote, N_i the frequency of individuals with this vote, and $1/K$ the average vote value. Note that the formula uses both proportions (P_i) and raw frequencies (N_i). The summations are over K different voting classes or categories, and each category has a different vote weight. The sum of these deviations is divided by the total number of votes ($\sum N_i P_i$) rather than the total number of voters ($\sum N_i$).

Dahl conceptualized proportionate shares in terms of the relative weights of each of the classes of voters or other participants. For example, consider an organization composed of four management levels in the hierarchy, with one indicating the highest and four the lowest level. Assume that individuals in top management have about four times as much influence on organizational policy making as those at the bottom level, that those at the second level have three times as much influence as those at the bottom, and that those in the third level have about twice as much influence as those in the fourth echelon. This influence hierarchy indicates that an average individual in the first level has four votes in each decision, whereas a person in the second echelon has three, a person in the third echelon has two, and a person at the bottom has one.

This influence hierarchy can also be expressed in terms of the relative contribution of each individual to the final decision, representing all (1.00) of the influence exerted in the process. If one manager from each level participated in a decision about hiring a new chief executive officer, their influence on the final choice would be (in descending order) 0.40, 0.30, 0.20, and 0.10, because the total influence present is unity. But what if all managers participate in the decision and different numbers of managers serve at each level, for example, five, ten, twenty, and thirty from top to bottom? Table 3-3 contains this information and the procedure necessary to compute Dahl's polyarchy index.

Reference to the equation presented earlier indicates that the index of polyarchy equals $1 - 6.5/11 = 1 - .59 = .41$. The computations in table 3-3 help to clarify Dahl's conceptualization of components' proportional shares. The index is quite versatile. For example, it can be used to measure such diverse systems as participation in organizational decision-making or voting of corporate stockholders weighted by the number of shares they own.

Table 3-3
Computation of Dahl's Index of
Polyarchy Based on Hypothetical Data

N_i	P_i	$|P_i - 1/K|$	$N_i |P_i - 1/K|$	N_iP_i
5	.40	.15	.75	2
10	.30	.05	.50	3
20	.20	.05	.75	3
30	.10	.15	4.50	3
	1.00		6.50	11

* $1/K = .25$.

Examining the equation's major elements in terms of the logic of the deviations model reveals its general usefulness as a measure of equality. The equation is unity minus a ratio; the ratio is a measure of the complete absence of polyarchy. Subtracting the ratio from unity gives the index an equality polarity.

The numerator of the ratio is the sum of the absolute differences between each proportional share and the mean of all proportional shares, weighted by the frequency of units in each component. The denominator is the sum of all components' proportional shares weighted by their frequencies or number of units. Its purpose is apparently to bound the index, but it does not, as is explained later.

When all proportional shares are equal, the numerator equals zero, the ratio equals zero, and $P = 1$, perfect polyarchy. When one share possesses all units (i.e., all individuals are in the same share or component), the numerator equals $N - N/K$, the denominator equals N, the ratio equals $1 - 1/K$, and $P = 1/K$, the complete absence or opposite of polyarchy. It is evident that the ratio (and thus P, itself) is not properly bounded. The ratio's lower limit is zero when all components are equal. However, its upper limit is $1 - 1/K$ when one component has all. To bound Dahl's P from zero to unity, simply divide the ratio by the term $1 - 1/K$, which produces the following properly bounded equation:

$$\text{Corrected } P = 1 - \frac{\Sigma N_i \, | \, P_i - 1/K \, |}{\Sigma N_i P_i \, (1 - 1/K)}$$

Dahl's original P is, therefore, a measure of absolute inequality in that its upper limit is a function of the number of components. Inequality is greater in a group of ten components in which one component has all than in a group of five components in which one has all. When Dahl's P is properly bounded, however, it becomes a measure of relative inequality that includes any number of null components and reaches its maximum when any component has all the units.

The polyarchy index is simple to calculate, although it involves weighting the absolute deviations from the mean, the standard with which each share is compared. It makes good use of all information available in the distribution and is defined for all possible distributions. P is sensitive to concentration of surplus units as well as to inequality, because it weights each deviation by the frequency possessed by each component.

A proportionate increase in all shares produces no change in the polyarchy score, indicating that P is scale invariant. Adding a positive constant to each component increases P's score, demonstrating an increase in equality. P also satisfies the principle of population symmetry. And a transfer of units from a richer to a poorer component increases the value of P, indicating an increase in the level of equality. Therefore, P also satisfies the principle of Lorenz dominance. If distribution A has a larger polyarchy value (indicating greater equality) than distribution B, the Lorenz curve of A will dominate the Lorenz curve of distribution B; the curve for A will lie everywhere above the curve for B.

Dahl designed the index for use on intervally-scaled components. Each component has an interval score based on its inherent formal authority or actual influence in organizational decision making. That interval-scale value is then weighted by the frequency of units (people) it possesses. It will also operate on ordinally-scaled components.

Schutz's Coefficient of Inequality (S)

Also based on the sum of absolute deviations of shares around their central tendency is Schutz's (1951) coefficient of inequality. Schutz originally designed the following index to measure inequality:

$$S = \sum_{P_i \geq \overline{P}} (P_i / \overline{P} - 1)$$

The original Schutz formulation is based on deviation of the Lorenz curve from the line of perfect equality. His index cumulates, in either direction (but not both) from the mean or equal share point on the Lorenz curve, the difference between the slope of the cumulative distribution and that of the line of equality. The difference is computed by dividing each actual proportional share above (or below) the mean by the mean of all shares. The equal share point is the point on the Lorenz curve where the slope equals one. The index sums "ratios of advantage," which are comparisons of the shares of the advantaged (above the mean) or disadvantaged (below the mean) to the mean percentage share of all components in the system, by dividing those shares by the mean share. The form of the Schutz equation above assumes that the index sums ratios of advantage, that is, ratios of each component above the equal share point to the mean share for all components. It could easily be rewritten to sum ratios below the mean (Ray and Singer, 1973; Alker and Russett, 1964).

Another form of the Schutz coefficient that produces identical scores also makes clear that it uses the mean as a comparative standard. Its formula requires taking half of the sum of the absolute differences between each proportional share and the mean proportional share:

$$S = 1/2 \sum |P_i - 1/K|$$

The Schutz coefficient suffers from several potential problems that reduce its usefulness. First, S is not properly bounded. Its lower limit is zero when all components are equal, but its upper limit is influenced by the number of components. Its upper bound, when one component possesses all units, is $1 - 1/K$. This is a particularly bothersome problem when one needs to compare inequality among several small systems with a changing number of components, because the upper limit changes with K. For example, in a four-component system, the upper bound is .75; in a five-component system, the upper bound is .80; in a ten-component system, the upper bound is .90. Consequently, unbounded Schutz is a useful index only for systems with a large number of components when the upper bound approximately equals unity. Either of the two Schutz equations presented above can be bounded so that it varies between zero and unity:

$$\text{Corrected } S = \frac{\Sigma(P_i / \overline{P} - 1)}{K - 1} \text{ and}$$

$$\text{Corrected } S = \frac{\Sigma | P_i - 1/K |}{2 (1 - 1/K)}$$

In the case of the first bounded Schutz equation, the numerator still sums the ratios of advantage. The denominator, however, is the number of components minus one, which is the maximum or upper bound of the numerator. In the case of the second corrected Schutz equation, the numerator still sums the absolute differences between the mean proportion and all proportional shares. The denominator standardizes the numerator in two ways. Because the numerator of the second Schutz equation sums deviations both above and below the mean, it must be divided by two or it will count deviations twice. Also, the denominator bounds the numerator by increasing its maximum value to 1.0. When Schutz is properly bounded, it becomes equal or complementary to three other indexes: the relative mean deviation (Schwartz and Winship, 1979; Cowell, 1977:26-29), Wilcox's (1972) average deviation analog, and Martin and Gray's (1971) relative variation. Unbounded, the Schutz coefficient is a type A absolute inequality measure; it reaches its maximum only when one component has all and the number of components is infinite. It achieves its minimum, zero, when all components are equal. Properly bounded Schutz is a measure of relative inequality that includes any number of null components. In any of its forms, Schutz is insensitive to concentration because it involves no multiplicative treatment of the absolute deviations.

A second unattractive feature of S is the fact that it does not take good advantage of all available information (Ray and Singer, 1973). Schutz can be calculated either by summing the ratios of advantage for components above the mean or by summing the ratios of disadvantage of components below the mean. Naturally, the index cannot be sensitive to variations within that part of the distribution that is excluded from the computation. The same holds true for the alternative Schutz equation.

Third, S has a serious problem with respect to the transfers principle. A transfer from a richer to a poorer component, both of which are above (or below) the mean does not change the Schutz index value, provided no share previously below the mean is increased above it, and conversely. Only a transfer across the mean affects the Schutz value, so it conforms only to a weak principle of transfers.

Schutz is scale invariant; when each share is multiplied by a positive constant its value does not change. When a positive constant is added to each share, S declines, indicating a decrease in inequality. S does conform to the population symmetry criterion by remaining constant when two identical systems are merged. Failure to satisfy the transfers criterion means, of course, that S does not comport with the Lorenz dominance principle.

A fourth potential problem with the Schutz coefficient is caused by its dependence on the arithmetic mean. This particular average is strongly affected by extreme values, and it may not be the most representative value in some distributions. In fact, no value in the distribution may equal the mean (Yntema, 1933).

The Schutz coefficient, with its inequality polarity, is defined for all possible distributions and simple to compute. It is appropriate for measuring distribution among nominally scaled components.

The Schutz index or some form of it is known by several different names. The relative mean deviation (RMD) is identical to the bounded form of the Schutz coefficient and of course has the same properties (Allison, 1978; Schwartz and Winship, 1979; Dalton, 1920; Cowell, 1977:27-28). The relative mean deviation is expressed as follows:

$$RMD = \frac{1/K \; \Sigma \, | \, P_i - 1/K \, |}{2/K}$$

The Wilcox (1972) average deviation analog (ADA) is the complement of the bounded Schutz index and assumes the following computational form:

$$ADA = 1 - \frac{K \, \Sigma \, | \, P_i - 1/K \, |}{2 \, (K - 1)}$$

Bounded Schutz is the ratio part of the ADA equation. Therefore, ADA = 1 – S, or S = 1 – ADA, because they are complementary indexes. Schutz is a measure of inequality, and ADA's polarity is equality.

Martin and Gray (1971) computed the mean absolute deviation, normed it by dividing by its mean, and then bounded the resulting measure. When expressed in terms of components' proportional shares, rather than as their raw values, Martin and Gray's index of relative variation, $S(D_x)$, is algebraically identical to bounded Schutz. It looks different, of course, in its raw-value form, but it produces identical scores. Despite its potential problems, researchers still find Schutz's index of inequality useful (cf. Jackman, 1975).

SQUARED DEVIATIONS FROM CENTRAL TENDENCY

Mayer's Index of Uniformity (M)

Mayer (1972:408) devised the index of uniformity to "test the hypothesis that the observations are uniformly distributed among the categories." His measure's formula is:

$$M = 1 - \frac{\Sigma(P_i - 1/K)^2}{1/K}$$

The whole measure, unity minus the ratio, has an equality polarity. The numerator of the ratio sums the squared deviations between each component and the mean of all components. It is squared in order to avoid the differences summing to zero, because signs are taken into account. Squaring also gives disproportionately more weight to larger deviations in the final M value, making M sensitive to concentration as well as to inequality. The denominator is the mean proportional share and is presumably intended to bound the index. The comparative standard used in the numerator is, of course, the mean.

Despite the denominator, 1/K, M is not properly bounded from zero to unity, so interpretation of its scores is difficult. With 1/K as the denominator, the maximum upper limit is K – 1, and the lower limit is zero. In order to create a ratio that can vary from zero to unity, the denominator should be 1 – 1/K, producing the following properly bounded equation:

$$\text{Corrected } M = 1 - \frac{\Sigma(P_i - 1/K)^2}{1 - 1/K}$$

When Mayer's M is properly bounded, it is mathematically identical to the complement of an index constructed by Amemiya (1962) a decade before Mayer published the first article on his measure of uniformity. The ratios in the two formulae may not at first glance appear identical, although they both involve summing the squared differences of each proportional share from the mean share. Amemiya's original index of economic differentiation assumes the following form:

$$\text{IED} = \sum \frac{K}{K-1} (P_i - 1/K)^2$$

Corrected Mayer's M = 1 – Amemiya's IED because $1 - 1/K = (K-1)/K$. Each of the two terms in the equation is simply a different way to express the upper bound of the summational core. Multiplying the summational core by Amemiya's quotient is the same as dividing it by Mayer's denominator. The properties of properly bounded M also apply to IED.

Another interpretation problem remains even with a properly bounded M or 1 – IED. The measures' summational cores are squared but their square roots are not subsequently taken. This means that the approximate magnitudes of the deviations are never even partially restored. Therefore, the effects of larger deviations are especially heavily weighted in comparison to smaller deviations. For example, the ratio of a small and large deviation is exaggerated when squared. Assume two deviations, 0.20 and 0.10. The ratio is two to one. If they are squared, they become 0.04 and 0.01, respectively, and their ratio becomes four to one. M truly inflates the importance of larger components compared to smaller ones. For this reason, it approaches its upper limit quickly as components approach equality and does not distinguish well among different degrees of substantial inequality.

Uncorrected Mayer's uniformity, with 1/K as its denominator, is a type A absolute inequality measure. Its value is influenced by the number of components, it reaches its lower bound only when one of an infinite number of components has all the units, and it is maximum when all components are equal. Properly bounded, uniformity is a relative measure that includes all null components, reaches zero only when one component possesses all units, and reaches unity when all shares are identical. The scores of neither bounded and unbounded M are influenced by the number of components. For example, if each share is split in half, doubling the number of shares while maintaining the relative size of each, the M score remains unchanged.

Transfers from a richer donor to a poorer recipient increase the value of M, indicating greater equality, so it conforms to the transfers principle. Adding a positive constant to each share increases the value of M. Multiplying each component by a positive constant does not change the index's value, so it is scale invariant. Moreover, M complies with the population symmetry criterion. It also, therefore, conforms to the Lorenz dominance principle.

Mayer's uniformity formula uses all available information in the distribution and is simple to compute. It is defined for all possible distributions and appropriate for application to nominally scaled distributions, for example, the distribution of votes among parties in a multiparty system. Amemiya used his IED to index distribution of people among industrial job categories.

Nagel's Index of Equality (E)

Nagel's (1984:81-85) equation for his index of equality is:

$$E = 1 - \frac{\Sigma(N_i - N/K)^2}{\Sigma(Z - N/K)^2}$$

Notice that Nagel's equality formula uses component frequencies rather than proportions. The numerator sums the squared differences between each numerical share and the mean numerical share. The denominator sums the squared differences between the worst possible numerical allocation (Z) to each component and the mean numerical share. Z stands for the worst possible allocation, "which is giving one person everything and everybody else nothing" (Nagel, 1984:81). The denominator is, therefore, the maximum possible inequality or worst allocation. Dividing the numerator by this worst possible distribution produces a percentage of the maximum possible inequality achieved by the actual inequality. Because the ratio is an inequality measure, subtracting it from unity yields the index E with equality polarity.

Using the Z distribution makes Nagel's equality measure conceptually and operationally different from even the other inequality measures that square deviations from central tendency. A simple example will clarify the logic underlying Z and its use in the denominator of this equation. Assume five people among whom ten units are distributed as follows: four, three, two, one, and zero. Subtracting each from the mean of two, and squaring and summing the differences yields ten, the numerator of the E equation.

Z in the denominator symbolizes the hypothetical distribution of all ten units to one person and nothing to each of the other four people. From that maximally unequal distribution, we then subtract the mean, square the differences, and sum as follows: $(10 - 2)^2 + (0 - 2)^2 + (0 - 2)^2 + (0 - 2)^2 + (0 - 2)^2 = 64 + 4 + 4 + 4 + 4 = 80$, the denominator. Thus $E = 1 - 10/80 = 1 - .125 = .875$.

E is sensitive to concentration as well as to inequality, because it squares the differences between actual and mean shares and never takes the square root. It performs according to Lorenz dominance expectations with regard to all relevant criteria. Equality scores increase with a transfer from a richer donor to poorer recipient, remain the same when each share is multiplied by a positive constant, and remain unchanged when two identical systems are merged. They also increase when a positive constant is added to each score. Therefore, if the E score for distribution A is smaller than the E score for distribution B, then the Lorenz curve of distribution A will lie everywhere above and nowhere below that of distribution B.

Values of Nagel's E are sensitive to the number of components in the system. For example, splitting each component in half, which doubles the number of components but maintains the relative size of each, increases measured equality. But the upper and lower limits of Nagel's equality are not sensitive to number of components. E achieves its maximum of unity under conditions of complete equality among all components and its minimum of zero when one component possesses all units and all other components possess nothing. E is defined for all distributions, makes good use of information, and is easy to compute and interpret. It assumes that components are nominally scaled.

Four other measures based on squared differences deserve mention. The standard deviation and coefficient of relative variation can be viewed as forms of inequality measurement. Most introductory statistics textbooks explain these two measures. In addition, variance of the logarithms and standard deviation of logarithms can be used as inequality indexes (Sen, 1977; Sawyer, 1976; Champernowne, 1974; Schwartz and Winship, 1979; Schwartz, 1978; Cowell, 1977:30-31). Because these measures possess several peculiar statistical properties, they should usually be avoided.

DIFFERENCES FROM ALL OTHER COMPONENTS

At least two important indexes use all other components as the standard with which to compare each proportional share. Most scholars attribute both to Corrado Gini (1912), although astronomer F. R. Helmert (1876) discussed one of them thirty-six years before Gini's work first appeared (Cowell, 1977:170; David, 1968). Gini strongly preferred using differences among all components rather than deviations of each from the mean as the comparative standard (Yntema, 1933).

Gini's Mean Relative Difference (MRD)

Many authors cite this index as relative mean difference and use the letters RMD as its acronym. However, the name Gini's mean relative difference and the acronym MRD will be used in order to avoid confusing it with relative mean deviation (RMD), discussed earlier in this chapter. Gini's MRD is also known as Kendall's (1952:42) coefficient of mean difference and Wilcox's (1973) mean difference analog. Its formula is:

$$MRD = 1 - \frac{\sum\limits_{i=1}^{K-1} \sum\limits_{j=i+1}^{K} |P_i - P_j|}{K-1}$$

The numerator in the ratio sums the absolute differences between all pairs of components, without repetitions. In other words, the double summation sign ($\Sigma\Sigma$) means take the difference between each proportional share only once. For example, take the difference $P_1 - P_2$, but do not also take the difference $P_2 - P_1$, etc. The denominator is the upper bound of the numerator and constrains its variance from zero to unity. Subtracting the ratio from unity provides an index with equality polarity, because an MRD of zero indicates total inequality and a value of unity is total equality.

The definitional formula given above clearly reveals the deviation (difference) logic underlying Gini's MRD. The computational formula is simpler, although its logic is less apparent. It also requires arraying all proportions in descending order of magnitude (i. e., P_1, P_2, P_3 ... P_K). The computational formula, which retains the equality polarity, is:

$$MRD = \frac{2(\Sigma_i P_i - 1)}{K - 1}$$

A hypothetical example will clarify this procedure. Assume four proportional shares in descending order: 0.40, 0.30, 0.20, and 0.10. Multiply each proportional share by its sequence number and sum as follows: $\Sigma_i P_i = 1(0.40) + 2(0.30) + 3(0.20) + 4(0.10) = 2.0$. Insert this sum into the equation, and MRD = $2(2 - 1)/(4 - 1) = 2/3 = .667$.

This computational equation reveals two interesting characteristics of MRD. First, it is closely related to Gini's coefficient of inequality through the Lorenz curve, a point to which we will return later. Second, it incorporates sensitivity to location of surplus units, or concentration, not just to inequality. The summational core is not exponentiated, but each proportional share in the descending array is weighted (multiplied) by its sequence number. The size of the weight is smallest for the largest component and largest for the smallest component. Nevertheless, such a weighting scheme makes the index sensitive to concentration as well as to inequality (Coulter, 1983b).

Because Gini's MRD is bounded from zero to unity, it is easily interpretable. It is a relative measure that includes any number of null components and reaches its lower limit (zero) when one component possesses all units (complete inequality), regardless of the number of components, and reaches its upper limit (unity) when all components are uniform (complete equality). Although its upper and lower limits are not sensitive to the number of components, RMD's scores are. Cutting each share into two equal shares, thereby doubling K and maintaining relative sizes of shares, causes RMD to increase, indicating greater equality.

MRD makes use of all information in the distribution (including shares' sequential order) and is defined for all distributions. Once the concept of differences between each share and all other shares is understood, the index is simple.

The measure certainly has intuitive appeal and, as mentioned earlier, Gini preferred using every other share as the comparative standard rather than the average share, differences rather than deviations. Economists also praise MRD primarily for three reasons: (a) it avoids exclusive use of the mean to compute deviations, (b) it avoids squaring the summational core, and (c) it is a more direct measure because it is based on differences between every pair of components (Yntema, 1933; Sen, 1973:31).

Gini's MRD remains unchanged when the distribution is multiplied by a positive constant and decreases with addition of a positive constant. It is also consistent with the population symmetry principle. The MRD is "perfectly sensitive to transfers" from a richer to a poorer component (Dalton: 1933:353). Therefore, it adheres to all three of the requirements of the Lorenz dominance criterion.

The MRD procedure converts nominal categories to interval values, based on the categories' frequencies, orders the components' proportional shares from largest to smallest, and then weights the shares by their sequence numbers. For example, it views a committee composed of five whites, three Hispanics, and two blacks as if it were three interval values expressed as proportions: 0.50, 0.30, and 0.20. It does not consider qualitative differences among the three nominally-scaled ethnic groups.

Gini Coefficient of Inequality (G)

The Gini (1912, 1936) coefficient, with its inequality polarity, is the oldest and most widely used measure of inequality in the social sciences. Social statisticians have developed several formally-equivalent equations to represent the Gini logic and procedure for discrete distributions, and I present some of these later. G is based on the Lorenz curve, which gives its logic a special visual effect because of the Lorenz graph. It has been used to measure the distribution of all kinds of units among all kinds of components, although Gini designed it to measure income distribution. It has several definite strengths and weaknesses and several other properties that make it distinctive.

Explication of at least two separate Gini formulae and one graphical technique (Lorenz curve) is required to clarify three important definitional characteristics of its underlying quantitative logic. First, the following equation (Allison, 1978; Kendall and Stewart, 1977:48), which operates on raw frequencies, indicates that Gini is a measure of difference, specifically the Gini coefficient of mean relative difference (MRD), normed by twice its mean.

$$G = \frac{1/N^2 \sum\limits_{i=1}^{K} \sum\limits_{j=1}^{K} |N_i - N_j|}{2N/K}$$

Thus G is the average absolute difference between all pairs of components, divided by twice its mean to avoid double counting differences and to norm it. Reference to the previous section on the relative mean difference will confirm the similarity of the two measures. For the investigator who wants an equation that clearly defines Gini as a normed measure of absolute differences but that uses proportional shares rather than raw frequencies, Theil (1972) recommended the following formula:

$$G = 1/2 \sum\limits_{i=1}^{K} \sum\limits_{j=1}^{K} |(1/K)P_i - (1/K)P_j|$$

A second major definitional characteristic of Gini is the fact that its summational core weights each of the components by their rank order in a descending array. The weight attached to the largest component is unity, to the second largest component is two, third largest component three, and so on through the K_{th} component. In this way, larger components are more lightly weighted and smaller components are more heavily weighted. Since the weighting scheme is multiplicative (i.e., the component is multiplied times its rank), components in or near the modal category yield the largest products and are, for this reason, disproportionately more influential in a value of G. We return to this point in detail later. An equation that highlights Gini's rank-weighting characteristic and operates on raw frequencies is (Sen: 1973:31):

$$G = 1 + (1/K) - (2/K^2) (N/K) [1N_1 + 2N_2 + \dots KN_k]$$

The right-hand side of this formula contains three main parts. The first is simply unity plus an average share. The second, a negative element, is the product of the two parenthetical expressions. This product is multiplied times the third part, which is each component weighted by its rank. Then the sum is taken.

Taagepera and Ray (1977) devised an equivalent formula using proportional shares rather than raw frequencies:

$$G = 1 + 1/K \ (2/K) \ \Sigma i P_i$$

The third definitional aspect of Gini requiring emphasis is its relationship to the Lorenz curve. Recalling the general explanation of the Lorenz curve from chapter two should help to clarify the present discussion. Figure 3-1 presents a typical Lorenz curve describing an income distribution among ordinal classes, although the curve could just as well describe distribution of any units among any appropriate components. The diagonal line of perfect equality connects the lower left corner of the square with the upper right. The Lorenz curve sags noticeably below the diagonal, indicating substantial income inequality.

Figure 3-1
Ordinary Lorenz Curve

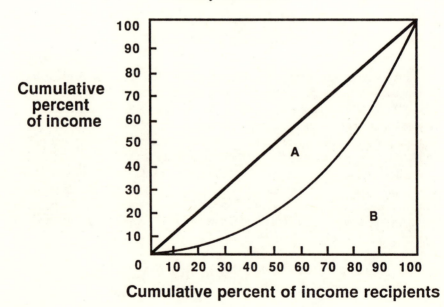

Cumulative percent of income recipients

The Lorenz curve measures inequality graphically and areally. The area enclosed within the diagonal and the Lorenz curve (area A) represents the actual amount (per cent) of distributional inequality. The maximum amount of inequality that could possibly exist is the total area below the diagonal (area A + area B). Area A is a proportion of areas A + B. The Gini coefficient is a quantitative expression of the ratio of area A to areas A + B. It is a statistical expression of Lorenz's graphical method.

One criticism of the Gini coefficient is that it is relatively complicated to understand and to compute (Allison, 1978). It does make use of all information about the distribution and is defined for all distributions. However, its interpretability is problematic, because any of its discrete data equations can reach its upper bound only in an infinite distribution. Gini is sensitive to the number of components (K) in that the actual maximum inequality score of any distribution is not unity, but $1 - 1/K$. The reason for this characteristic is that Gini originally devised his index to measure inequality in continuous rather than discrete distributions (Ray and Singer, 1973). In systems with a large number of components, this characteristic does not represent a serious problem, because unity and $1 - 1/K$ are approximately equal. In small, finite systems, however, the sensitivity of its upper limit to K is serious. But the Gini value of a small system can be bounded simply by dividing it by its upper bound, $1 - 1/K$. In that way, it varies from zero to unity. One Gini formula that corrects for this peculiarity is (Ray and Singer, 1973):

$$\text{Corrected } G = \frac{1 + 1/K - (2/K) \sum P_i}{1 - 1/K}$$

A critical property of Gini is that its sensitivity to inequality depends on the shape of the frequency distribution. It is more sensitive to differences in the middle range of a unimodal distribution than among the larger or smaller components (Allison, 1978; Champernowne, 1974). Gini is also sensitive to concentration as well as to inequality (Coulter, 1983b). An example will demonstrate the simple statistical principle underlying these two properties. Consider two adjacent columns of numbers; column a's values are one through ten, and column b's values are ten through one. If a product is formed from each of the pairs in the rows, the largest products are at the middle where the average numbers appear in each column, not at either extreme where the largest and smallest numbers are.

(col. a)	(col. b)	row product
1	10	10
2	9	18
3	8	24
4	7	28
5	6	30
6	5	30
7	4	28
8	3	24
9	2	18
10	1	10

The same relationship holds in the Gini procedure. When rank (ascending order) is multiplied times components (largest through smallest), the products form a decidedly unimodal and perhaps roughly normal distribution, with the largest numbers in the middle range. Multiplying each component by its rank is a weaker transformation than exponentiation, but it does give disproportionately heavy weight to middle-sized components in determining the Gini score. The investigator using Gini should note this relatively unrecognized characteristic. As is evident in the Gini coefficient's close relationship to Gini's mean relative difference (MRD), G uses all other components as the standard to which each component is compared.

Gini is scale invariant, because its score remains unchanged when each component is multiplied by a positive constant (Allison, 1978). Nor does it change when one system is combined with an identical system: consequently, it obeys the principle of population symmetry. And, when a positive constant is added to each component, the Gini score declines.

The Gini coefficient's behavior under conditions of a transfer from a richer to a poorer component is appropriate, according to the Pigou-Dalton criterion, in the sense that it declines (Allison, 1978; Ray and Singer, 1973). However, it declines in an unusual way, and this behavior is related to the weighting scheme that exaggerates the influence of components near the mean on the size of a Gini value.

Gini's sensitivity to transfers depends on the size of the transfer, of course, but also on the donor's and recipient's ranks rather than on the sizes of their frequencies or proportional shares. A change in the value of G due to a transfer depends on the number of components with shares lower than the recipient and higher than the donor. Gini's transfer sensitivity is a linear function of the number of components between donor and recipient. For a typically shaped U.S. income distribution, for example, unimodal with a large middle class, G tends to be most sensitive to transfers around the mean and least sensitive to transfers among the rich or the poor (Allison, 1978; Champernowne, 1974; Schwartz and Winship, 1979). Cowell (1977:28) commented: "It is not evident that this is a desirable property for an inequality index to possess."

Specifically, a transfer of ten units from component a to component j will change the Gini coefficient by $(a - j) (2/K)(10)$. In other words, Gini's change will equal the numerical difference in ordinal ranks between donor and recipient multiplied times $2/K$ multiplied times the size of the transfer. This mathematical property of Gini's transfer behavior leads to several peculiarities. For example, a transfer of a given amount from the very largest component equally to every other component has the same impact as a transfer of an equal amount from every other component to the smallest, even though the change in units will add proportionately more to the smallest than it subtracts from the largest (Sawyer, 1976). Gini stresses absolute differences in components' shares rather than proportionate differences.

Under Atkinson's (1970:249) more rigorous interpretation of the principle of transfers (chapter six), Gini simply fails. He argued that "a necessary and sufficient condition for us to be able to rank two distributions independently of the utility function (other than it be increasing and concave) is that one can be obtained from the other by redistributing income from the richer to the poorer." But the ranking of distributions that Gini provides is not an unambiguous ranking (Dasgupta, Sen, and Starrett, 1973; Newberry, 1970; Rothschild and Stiglitz, 1973). Nonetheless, under more relaxed conditions, Gini satisfies the Lorenz dominance criterion, because it is scale-invariant, handles transfers well enough, and obeys the population symmetry requirement (Allison, 1978).

The Gini coefficient is an absolute inequality measure, given that its maximal inequality depends on the number of categories (Waldman, 1977). Its value is maximal (total inequality) only when one component has all units among an infinite number of components and minimal (complete equality) only with a uniform distribution. If the index is properly bounded, however, it becomes an any-number-of-null-components measure of relative inequality, and its scores as well as its upper and lower limits are insensitive to number of components. For example, bounded G remains unchanged when each component is split in half, doubling the number of components but preserving relative inequality (Coulter, 1984; Ray and Singer, 1973).

G is an interval-scale index, because it arrays even nominally-scaled components in terms of their sizes and weights them by their sequence numbers. Allison (1978) argued that the Gini index is inappropriate for use on interval-level units that lack a theoretically fixed zero point and is best used for numerous components that comprise a reasonably strong ordinal scale among which people as units are distributed.

Numerous peculiarities in the Gini coefficient have been mentioned: sensitivity of upper and lower bounds to system size, especially in small systems, causing incomparability among systems of changing size; dependence of its transfer sensitivity on ranks of donor and recipient; and exaggerated sensitivity to dispersion near the mean of the distribution. Two final potential weaknesses should be added to the list. First, Gini attaches equal importance to equal absolute differences in shares even though one of the differences is taken between two small components and the other is taken between two large components (Kravis, 1962). Second, very different distributions can generate Lorenz curves that deviate to the same extent from the line of perfect equality (Jasso, 1981). G will yield the same value for both of them. For example, a distribution in which one component has a near monopoly can generate the same G as another distribution that has several severely deprived components (Ray and Singer, 1973).

DIFFERENCES FROM TEMPORALLY ADJACENT COMPONENTS
All of the indexes discussed so far are cross-sectional; they reflect distributional differences among several components in a system at a given point in time. However, a system can experience distributional change over an extended period of time, with respect to some variable characteristic of interest. It then becomes useful to measure the distribution of some units across periods of time or between events, a temporal rather than cross-sectional index of distribution. A time-serial index measures changes in components' possession of units through time rather than deviations and differences in possession of units among a cross-section of numerous components at one point in time. The final index considered in this chapter measures temporal instability.

Przeworski's Index of Instability (D_t)
Przeworski (1975) called his index a measure of "deinstitutionalization," defined as political decay or the opposite of political development, reflecting the specific purpose for which he devised it. In fact, the measure is more generally an index of temporal instability that Przeworski devised to use as an independent variable to explain deinstitutionalization (Laakso and Taagepera, 1979). The equation for this instability index is:

$$D(t) = 1/2 \sum | P_i(t + 1) - P_i(t) |$$

where t = time point or event

The formula simply takes one-half the sum of the absolute differences between the shares of all components at time $(t + 1)$ and time t. The comparative standard for each proportional share is its proportion at the next time point. D(t) assumes that shares are expressed as proportions (rather than raw frequencies) and that the several components at any time point collectively possess 100% of the units.

Przeworski originally devised D(t) to measure changes in the distribution of votes cast for political parties in a multiparty system across several elections, which serve as the points in time. He used the index to test the theory that large-scale increases ("massive waves of mobilization") or decreases ("intense demobilization") in voter participation tend to weaken the institutional stability of a political system (Przeworski, 1975:49). The index shows the minimal proportion of an electorate that must have shifted its vote, given the observed aggregate change, and is, therefore, an index with inequality polarity. Differences between time-sequential shares can be positive (increase) or negative (decrease) for any given party, but they are computed without regard to sign.

The formula takes one-half the summational core to correct for the fact that electoral shifts are counted twice—once as a gain for one party and once as a loss for another party. The number of parties can change from one election to another, so K includes all parties that received any votes in either of two consecutive elections. In addition, the procedure controls for variation in turnout or size of the electorate by using parties' proportionate shares of the total vote.

A hypothetical example will help to clarify this operational definition of inequality over time. Assume a three-party system over six elections. Table 3-4 provides the necessary information.

The equation for D(t) computes differences between electoral support in successive elections for each party separately. To illustrate, party number one experienced a shift of 0.05 between the first election (t) and the second election (t + 1) and a shift of 0.10 between the fourth and fifth elections. Party number one experienced a total absolute shift of 0.30 across the six elections. Party number three experienced a total absolute shift of 0.50. Computing such gains and losses, disregarding signs, for all three parties yields a total of fifteen changes to sum: (K) $(t_N - 1) = (3)(5) = 15$. In the present hypothetical example, the fifteen changes sum to 1.10. Multiplying this sum by one-half produces D(t) = .55, the instability score for six elections in a hypothetical nation with a three-party system.

Przeworski's D(t) is neither easy to understand nor simple to compute. It involves changes in K components' shares over t_N points in time. The investigator must not only conceptualize distribution among several components, but must think of that distribution in terms of changes over several points in time. Both conceptualization and operationalization are complicated. The index does use all information available in the distribution and is defined for all distributions.

Indexes Based On the Deviations Model

Table 3-4
Hypothetical Data on Electoral Support
in a Three-Party System Across Six Elections

components of	% of vote across time (elections)					
party system (P_i)	t	t+1	t+2	t+3	t+4	t+5
party # 1 (P_1)	.20	.25	.25	.20	.30	.40
party # 2 (P_2)	.30	.35	.40	.60	.60	.60
party # 3 (P_3)	.50	.40	.35	.20	.10	.00

D(t) is not easily interpretable because it varies from zero (complete stability) to $t_N - 1$ (maximum instability), or from zero to five in the case of our hypothetical example in table 3-4. Because the upper bound is finite at $t_N - 1$ (number of time points or elections minus one), it is possible to bound the measure from zero to unity. A properly bounded index of instability looks like this:

$$\text{Corrected } D(t) = \frac{1}{2(t_N - 1)} \; \Sigma \left| \, P_i(t + 1) - P_i(t) \, \right|$$

This bounded index produces a score of D(t) = .11 for our hypothetical example. The equation is clearly a measure of inequality rather than concentration because it requires no multiplicative transformation of the summational core. Three shifts of .05 each count the same as one shift of .15 in computing the index value. D(t) compares each component with the temporally adjacent component. Using this comparative standard makes the index time-serial as well as cross-sectional.

The index is scale invariant with respect to proportionate increases of all shares. However, when a positive constant is added to each component the index declines, indicating greater stability. D(t) also performs well in terms of the principle of transfers. A transfer from a richer to a poorer component at each time point reduces the size of the index score, reflecting a decrease in instability (or increased stability). Przeworski's index also satisfies the principle of population symmetry. Of course, it satisfies the Lorenz dominance criterion.

The upper limit of this time-serial index of instability, as originally devised by Przeworski, is a function of the number of components and, therefore, $D(t)$ is a measure of absolute inequality. Its minimal value is zero when all components have equal shares at all time points. It achieves its maximal when one component, of an infinite number of components, has all. When $D(t)$ is bounded, on the other hand, it is a measure of relative inequality that includes any number of null components. Values of $D(t)$, whether unbounded or bounded, are sensitive only to relative inequality, not to the number of components. Splitting each share in half does not change the value of either $D(t)$ value. It is naturally a nominal scale index, because it assumes unordered categories that possess units.

Laakso and Taagepera's (1979) fluctuation index also measures distributional change over time, but it is not presented in this chapter for two reasons. It is based on combinatorics rather than deviations, and its equation includes a somewhat more complicated element called "effective number of components." Laakso and Taagepera's f is considered in chapter four, which presents measures based on combinatorics and discusses effective number of components.

CONCLUSIONS

A researcher should choose an index based on the deviations model only if a deviations interpretation is preferred. These indexes measure inequality in terms of statistically treated deviations or differences of each share from central tendency or an adjacent share, and that is the interpretation the deviations model provides for a computed index value. Of substantial importance in this consideration are which central tendency measure to use and whether the problem calls for defining components' adjacency in terms of their ordered sequence in size or their occurrence in time. The eight equations exhibit considerable variety in their treatment of deviations, and that also might influence an investigator's choice. If the deviations interpretation is not preferred, an index based on some other mathematical model should be selected.

4

INDEXES BASED ON THE COMBINATORICS MODEL

More inequality indexes are based on combinatorial analysis than on any other mathematical model. This chapter presents twenty-one such measures, each bearing the name of its originator, although when duplicates, equivalents, and complements are eliminated, fourteen unique measures remain. I begin the chapter with a brief discussion of the elementary principles of combinatorics, its application to the multinomial expansion, and its use in constructing inequality measures. Next, a list of the measures by name and equation precedes an extended discussion of each in terms of the conceptual and operational criteria presented in chapter two.

THE LOGIC OF COMBINATORICS

Probability is a branch of statistics that deals with the chance that some specific event will occur. A simple event is, for example, getting a five with one roll of a fair die. The statistical rule governing simple events states that the probability of a simple event is the ratio of the frequency of the event to the total frequency of all possible events in the set. When all the frequencies of events in a set are identical, as they are in the case of a fair die, the rule reduces to the following statement: the probability of a given set of equally likely events is unity divided by the total number of possibilities. The probability of rolling a five is 1/6, because six events are equally likely possibilities.

A compound event is the occurrence of two or more distinguishable events together, for example, getting two fives when rolling a pair of dice. The rule for compound events, called the product theorem, states that the probability of two or more independent events occurring together is the product of the probabilities of the individual events. The probability of rolling two fives is (1/6)(1/6) = 1/36 (Mueller, Scheuller, and Costner, 1970:217-223).

But what if all possible events are not equally likely? What if, for example, event r has a fifty per cent chance of occurring, event w a thirty per cent chance, and event b a twenty per cent chance? An urn containing fifty red marbles, thirty white marbles, and twenty blue marbles (for a total of one hundred) would present such a situation in terms of the probability of selecting a marble of a particular color. The three events, randomly selecting a red or white or blue marble, are not equally likely; rather their probabilities are .50, .30, and .20, respectively. Since the urn contains no other marbles, the probability of selecting a marble of any color equals unity, the sum of the three separate probabilities.

This discussion assumes that random selection for pairing two objects is accomplished with replacement or from an infinitely large population. In other words, it assumes either that whenever one marble is selected from the urn, it is replaced before the second marble is selected, or that the urn contains a very large number of marbles in the specified proportions. In fact, some conditions exist under which neither of these assumptions is valid. These conditions and the indexes they require are discussed later in the chapter.

Combinations and Permutations

Crucial to understanding probability in this context is combinatorial analysis, the mathematics that deals with a subset of objects considered without regard to their order. In order to understand combinatorics, however, it is essential to grasp the elements of permutations, a related area of mathematics that deals with a subset of objects in particular sequential ordering (Mosteller, Rourke, and Thomas, 1961:19-48; and Hammond, Householder, and Castellan, 1971:227-231).

Permutation of the letters a, b, and c in all possible ways produces a total of six ordered arrangements: abc, acb, bac, bca, cab, and cba. The problem involved in permutations is determining efficiently the number of ways in which a given set of objects may be permuted. This is especially important when dealing with a large number of objects. Specifically, how many permutations exist of n objects taken r at a time. If a, b, and c are conceived as a set of books to be placed on a shelf, in how many different ways can this be done? We already know that the answer is six, but can we use this problem and solution to generate a simple formula that will permute a large number of objects? Fortunately, such a formula exists.

In placing the books on the shelf, we can fill the first space in any of three ways: book a, book b, or book c. After we have filled the first space, we have either of two remaining books with which to fill the second space. When we fill the second space, we have only one way in which to fill the last space. We can fill the first two spaces in 3 X 2 , or 6, ways. We can fill the three spaces in 3 X 2 X 1, or 6, ways. Multiplication provides the way we can find the total number of arrangements.

The multiplication principle of permutation states that if an operation can be performed in n1 ways and, after it is performed in any one of these ways, a second operation can be performed in n2 ways and, after it is performed in any of these ways, a third operation can be performed in n3 ways, and so on for j operations, then the j operations can be performed together in (n1)(n2)(n3) ... (nj) ways. The special notation devised to indicate a product whose factors run consecutively downward to 1 (as in 4 X 3 X 2 X 1) is !. It is written n! and called "n factorial."

In how many ways can eight objects be permuted eight at a time (in abstract terms, N objects N at a time)? The answer is 8! = 8 X 7 X 6 X 5 X 4 X 3 X 2 X 1 = 40,320. Permuting eight objects four at a time (i. e., N objects r at a time), however, presents a different problem, called partial permutation. The formula is a directive to carry out the permutation only through r stages, instead of through the total N: $_NP_r = N(N - 1)(N - 2) ... (N - r + 1)$. This formula takes another convenient form if we multiply by $(N - r)!/(N - r)!$, which produces $_NP_r = N!/(N - r)!$. To permute eight objects four at a time, $_8P_4 = 8$ X 7 X 6 X 5 = 1,680.

Similarly, combinations can be calculated for N objects taken N at a time. In such a case, only one combination exists, because combinations are (sub)sets without consideration of order or sequence. But what about a combination of N objects taken r at a time? Two simple steps are involved. First, compute the number of permutations of N objects taken r at a time. Second, clear the result of these permutations by dividing by r!, which is the number of ways in which each combination can be permuted. Each combination can have r! permutations, of course, so that we obtain the number of combinations by dividing the number of permutations by r!. The appropriate formula expressing these two steps is as follows: $_NC_r = N!/[r!(N - r)!]$. Combining eight objects four at a time yields $_8C_4 = 8!/[4!(8 - 4)!] = 8!/4!(4)! = 40,320/576 = 70$. According to this formula, we could select four items from a pool of eight in seventy different ways.

Multinomial Probabilities

Combinatorics is important in calculating multinomial probabilities (Spiegel, 1961:122-141; Hammond, Householder, and Castellan, 1970: 231-243). Consider the binomial expansion as a special case of the multinomial expansion. Every possibility set can be reduced to two mutually exclusive possibilities and the resulting outcomes labeled "success" and "failure." An outcome termed success may be an event, such as rolling a five with a die, or one of a group of events, such as selecting an ace from a deck of cards. The probabilities would be 1/6 and 4/52, respectively, in these two instances.

Combinatorial methods are used in calculating the binomial expansion. The point is to illustrate the meaning of an expanded binomial or multinomial. For example, the binomial expansion $(a + b)^2 = a^2 + 2ab + b^2 = 1.0$ gives the proportion of pairs with each possible letter combination. The odds of choosing two letter a's in a row is a^2. The probability of choosing an a and a b in two random selections is 2ab. If a = 0.6 and b = 0.40, these probabilities would be

0.36 and 0.48, respectively. The probability of choosing two b's is 0.16, for a total of 1.00.

Consider the multinomial, $(a + b + c + d)^2$, in which $a = 0.40$, $b = 0.30$, $c = 0.20$, and $d = 0.10$ (totaling 1.00). For the purpose of illustration, assume that the letter terms represent the four ethnic groups in a community. Squaring the multinomial produces $(a + b + c + d)^2 = a^2 + b^2 + c^2 + d^2 + 2[(ab) + (ac) + (ad) + (bc) + (bd) + (cd)] = 1.0$. This multinomial expansion gives the proportion of randomly selected pairs with each possible ethnic combination. The proportion of pairs with a common ethnicity, U, is simply the sum of squares for all ethnic groups, the first four terms in the expansion: $U = (0.40)^2 + (0.30)^2 + (0.20)^2 + (0.10)^2 = 0.30$. U stands for ethnic uniformity in this case, because we have a 0.30 probability of randomly choosing two people with identical ethnicity.

Because the total probabilities sum to 1.00, all the other, non-U terms in the multinomial expansion can be expressed as $1.00 - U = D = 0.70$. In this case, D (the sum of all the terms except the first four) stands for ethnic diversity, because it indicates the probability that two randomly selected persons in the community will be ethnically different. If every resident had a different ethnicity, D would equal 1.00 and U (uniformity) would equal 0.00.

This introduction to probability theory, combinatorics, and the multinomial expansion presents the basics of the mathematical model on which several important inequality indexes are based. Essentially, it is concerned with the probability of selecting a subset of two identical (or different) objects from a set of objects as a way of determining the uniformity or diversity of the set with respect to some characteristic of interest. Components' shares serve as the counterpart to probabilities.

Table 4-1 lists fourteen inequality equations based on combinatorics and seven identical or complementary indexes. Several of the fourteen featured indexes, especially those near the top of the list, simply excerpt the sum of squares from a multinomial expansion and clearly illustrate the combinatorics logic. Other equations are computational and conceal their reliance on this logic.

Table 4-1
Indexes Based on the Combinatorics Model

1. Herfindahl-Hirschman Index of Industrial Concentration (complement of Blau's heterogeneity, Greenberg's diversity, Rae's fractionalization, Gini-Simpson diversity; Michaely's concentration is 100 $\sqrt{HH}$)

$$HH = \Sigma P_i^2$$

2. Lieberson's Index of Population Diversity (Labovitz and Gibbs' division of labor)

$$D = \frac{1 - \Sigma P_i^2}{1 - 1/K}$$

3. Horvath's Comprehensive Concentration Index

$$CCI = P_m + \sum_{i=2}^{K} P_i^2 \, [1 + (1 - P_i)]$$

4. Hall and Tideman's Index of Industry Concentration

$$TH = \frac{1}{(2\Sigma_i P_i) - 1}$$

5. Taagepera's Index of Imbalance

$$T = \frac{\displaystyle\sum_i \frac{(P_i - P_i + 1)}{i} - (\Sigma P_i^2)^2}{\sqrt{\Sigma P_i^2 - (\Sigma P_i^2)^2}}$$

6. Rae and Taylor's Fragmentation (complement of Coleman's unanimity)

$$RT = 1 - \frac{\Sigma N_i(N_i - 1)}{N(N - 1)}$$

7. Mueller, Scheussler, and Costner's Index of Qualitative Variation

$$IQV = \frac{\Sigma N_i N_j}{\frac{K(K - 1)}{2}(N/K)^2}$$

8. Hammond's, Householder, and Castellan's Index of Dispersion

$$D_h = \frac{K (N^2 - \Sigma N_i^2)}{N^2 (K - 1)}$$

9. Leik's Measure of Ordinal Consensus

$$C = \frac{2\Sigma d_i}{K - 1}$$

10. Ray, Taagepera, and Singer's Generalized Index of Concentration

$$C_\alpha = \left[\frac{\Sigma P_i^\alpha - K^{1 - \alpha}}{1 - K^{1 - \alpha}} \right]^{1/\alpha}$$

11. Taagepera and Ray's Equivalent Two-Component System (ETS)

$$2P_m = 1 + \left[\frac{\Sigma P_i^2 - 1/K}{1 - 1/K} \right]^{1/2}$$

12. Laakso and Taagepera's Effective Number of Components (ENC_1 = Thiel's entropy)

$$ENC_\alpha = \left[\Sigma P^\alpha\right]^{1/(1-\alpha)}$$

13. Taagepera and Grofman's Effective Size

$$ES_\alpha = \frac{\Sigma (N_i)^\alpha}{\Sigma (N_i)^{\alpha-1}}$$

14. Laakso and Taagepera's Index of Fluctuation

$$f = \left[\frac{1}{ENC/K}\right]\left[\left(\frac{1}{K-1}\right)\Sigma\left(E_t - E_{t-1}\right)^2\right]^{1/2}$$

For a convenient, synopotic view of the primary properties of all of these combinatorics-based indexes, see table 4-2.

HERFINDAHL AND HIRSCHMAN'S INDEX OF CONCENTRATION (HH)
    Herfindahl (1950) and Hirschman's (1945) index of industrial concentration, one of the simplest inequality measures, is especially popular among researchers in marketing, banking, and finance. Its equation is:

$$HH = \Sigma P_i^2$$

This equation calls simply for summing the squares of all proportional shares. It is based on the results of the multinomial expansion discussed earlier, except that it requires the sum of only the single squared terms produced by the expansion, not the mixed terms. HH in effect omits null components completely. It practically omits all very small components, because the square of a very small proportion is virtually null [e. g., $(0.05)^2 = 0.0025$].

Table 4-2: Primary Properties of Indexes Based on the Combinatorics Model

	Polarity	Type of index	Concentration	Comparative standard	Constant additions	Transfers	Scale invariance	Population symmetry	Lorenz dominance	Scale	Definition	Information use	Upper and lower limits	Simplicity
Herfindahl and Hirschman's concentration (HH)	inequality	relative, no null components	yes	all pairs	decrease	yes	yes	no	no	nominal	yes	fair	1, 1/K	good
Lieberson's diversity (D)	equality	relative, ANONC	yes	all pairs	increase	yes	yes	no	no	nominal	yes	good	1, 0	good
Taagepera's imbalance (T)	inequality	relative, no null components	yes	all pairs	decrease	yes	yes	no	no	ordinal	yes	fair	*	poor
Horvath's concentration (CCI)	inequality	hybrid	yes	all pairs	decrease	yes	yes	no	no	nominal	yes	fair	$a, >P_{max}$	poor
Hall and Tideman's concentration (TH)	inequality	absolute, type A	yes	all pairs	decrease	yes	yes	no	no	nominal	yes	good	1, 0	fair
Rae and Taylor's fragmentation (RT)	equality	absolute, type B	yes	all pairs	increase	yes	no	no	no	nominal	yes	good	?,0	good
Mueller's index of qualitative variation (IQV)	equality	relative, ANONC	yes	all pairs	increase	yes	yes	no	no	nominal	yes	good	1, 0	poor
Hammond's dispersion (D_h)	equality	relative, ANONC	yes	all pairs	increase	yes	yes	no	no	nominal	yes	good	1, 0	fair
Leik's ordinal dispersion (OD)	equality	relative, ANONC	no	cumulative ogive	increase	no	yes	yes	no	ordinal	yes	good	1, 0	fair
Ray's et al generalized concentration (C_k)	inequality	relative, ANONC	yes	all pairs	decrease	yes	yes	no	no	nominal	yes	good	1, 0	good
Equivalent two - component system (ETS)	inequality	relative, ANONC	yes	all pairs	decrease	yes	yes	no	no	nominal	yes	good	1, 0.5	fair
Effective number of components (ENC)	equality	relative no-null components	yes	all pairs	increase	yes	yes	no	no	nominal	yes	fair	K, 1	good
Effective size (ES)	N/A	N/A	yes	all pairs	increase	yes	no	no	N/A	nominal	yes	good	>0, ∞	good
Laakso and Taagepera's fluctuation (f)	inequality	relative no-null components	yes	all pairs; temp. adj. components	decrease	N/A	yes	no	no	nominal	yes	fair	>1, 0	poor

$$^* \;\; 1, \; 1 - \frac{(1/K)^2}{\sqrt{K} - (1/K)^2}$$

The combinatorial procedure on which HH is based implicitly compares every randomly selected pair of units to every other possible randomly selected pair, while taking into account the component in which a unit is located. This means that it implicitly compares random selection probabilities in terms of existing component frequencies. HH specifically compares all pairs in order to arrive at the probability of randomly selecting a homogeneous pair.

The HH lower limit is sensitive to the number of components. It varies in value from a minimum of 1/K, when all components are equal, to unity, when the one component (in a one-component system) possesses all units. Bounding HH from zero to unity requires three steps: (a) subtract the HH value from unity, (b) divide that result by 1 − 1/K (which produces Lieberson's index of diversity, an index discussed later in this chapter), and (c) subtract the ratio from unity to reestablish a concentration polarity. This operation produces the following equation:

$$\text{Corrected HH} = 1 - \frac{1 - \text{HH}}{1 - 1/K}$$

Uncorrected HH yields a score of 0.33 for a uniform distribution among three components. Corrected HH yields a score of zero for such a distribution. Note also that corrected HH takes into account all null components when it employs the mean proportional share (1/K) in the denominator of the ratio. When one or more null components are involved in a problem, uncorrected and corrected HH operate on systems of different sizes.

The HH exponentiation procedure strenuously emphasizes concentration rather than just inequality. This makes it disproportionately more sensitive to larger shares and, of course, relatively insensitive to smaller shares (Ray and Singer, 1973).

Interpreting the HH treatment of null categories is tricky. One view is that the index excludes them from the computation entirely, because K does not appear in the equation in any form, and zero units squared will equal zero and count for absolutely nothing in the HH score. In other words, this view defines a component in a system as an entity that possesses one or more units. An entity with no units is either not a component or a component not in the system. In this view, HH is a no-null-category measure of relative equality that reaches its maximum only when K = 1.

The second view assumes that each component (including null components) is weighted by its proportional share of the units, meaning that all components are, in fact, considered, but that the null weighting of components with no units has the quantitative effect of excluding them (Hall and Tideman, 1967). However, their values are incorporated in the final HH score. This interpretation means that HH is an any-number-of-null-categories measure of relative inequality that reaches its maximum when any one category has all units. This interpretation is rejected in favor of HH as an absolute measure that excludes null components.

Because of its exponentiation and exclusion of null components, HH is an almost pure measure of concentration. Perhaps its most important property is its exclusive concern with the location of the units rather than with how much each component has. Adding one or twenty null components to a system does not affect the value of HH. Components that are totally deprived are totally excluded. Remember, however, that Herfindahl and Hirschman intended HH as a measure of concentration, not inequality. A component without any units is a component without any concentration of units, so HH is operationally true to its originators' conceptualization.

HH represents the concept of economic market concentration rather well. For example, how concentrated is the microcomputer sales market among the firms that sell microcomputers in Tuscaloosa? A microcomputer firm that has not yet sold a microcomputer (a unit) will not be included in the answer. When that firm makes a sale (possesses a unit), it will break into the market and become a deconcentrating force, even if it captures only a tiny share.

A proportionate increase of each share has no effect on the value of HH, so HH is scale invariant. Adding a positive constant to each share reduces the value of HH, a deconcentrating effect. A transfer of units from a richer donor to a poorer recipient also has a deconcentrating effect; it reduces the HH score by an amount dependent on the difference between donor and recipient (Cowell, 1977:65-66). However, HH violates the population symmetry principle; if two identical systems are combined, the HH score for the merged system is only one-half its value for either of the two identical systems. Therefore, HH is not consistent with the Lorenz dominance criterion.

HH assumes distribution of units among nominally scaled components. It is a simple index that is defined for all distributions and makes use of all information in the distribution (unless exclusion of null components represents failure to make use of information). HH is a no-null-components index of absolute inequality, because it excludes null components and reaches its maximum only when K equals unity. Because the original HH is unbounded, its interpretability is problematic. It is easy to bound, however.

Four measures are the complement of HH and reverse its polarity: Blau's (1977:78) heterogeneity, Greenberg's (1956) diversity (A), Rae's (1967:55-58; 1968) fractionalization (F), and Gini and Simpson's (1949) diversity (D_{gs}). For example, Rae's $F = 1 - \sum P_i^2$. The larger the number of components and the more uniformly distributed the units over the components, the larger these index values tend to be (Agresti and Agresti, 1977). Diversity, heterogeneity, and fractionalization are the conceptual and operational opposites of concentration. If HH

= .75, then F = .25, indicating a situation of considerable concentration and a little fractionalization.

These complements of HH have been used to index religious heterogeneity, racial segregation, political party system fractionalization, and differentiation of social status. They assume that distribution is conceptualized in terms of equality, rather than inequality, in contrast to the Herfindahl-Hirschman index. Otherwise, they have the same conceptual and operational properties as HH. It is important to remember that their polarity differs from that of HH. They are based on the probability that any two randomly chosen units will belong to different components (Wildgen, 1971).

The lower limit of these four measures is zero, indicating that one component has all the units. The upper limit, $1 - 1/K$, is reached when all components are equal. Under conditions of equality or maximum fractionalization, number of components and index value do not have a linear relationship. In fact, once above five components (an index value of 0.80), these indexes do not differentiate well (Wildgen, 1971). Doubling the size of the system only increases the index value by 0.10. However, Rae (1971) argued that linearity between number of components and index value lacks intuitive appeal.

Finally, Michaely (1962) devised a measure of geographic concentration that simply takes the square root of HH and multiplies it by one hundred.

$$M = 100 \sqrt{(\Sigma P_i^2)}$$

Michaely's M shares the properties of the Herfindahl-Hirschman measure. Extracting the square root partially restores the squared shares to their original sizes. This means that M does not weight the largest shares quite as disproportionately heavily as does HH. Multiplication by one hundred simply converts a decimal fraction to a percentage. Resembling HH, the Michaely measure conceptualizes inequality, rather than equality. Not properly bounded, M's upper limit is unity, when one component possesses all units, but its lower limit is $1/K$. When M is properly bounded, as in the following formula, it becomes one hundred times the square root of Lieberson's D:

$$\text{Corrected M} = 100 \sqrt{\frac{1 - \Sigma P_i^2}{1 - 1/K}}$$

LIEBERSON'S INDEX OF DIVERSITY (D)

Lieberson (1969) designed diversity with the same polarity as the complements of the Herfindahl-Hirschman index of concentration, in other words, to measure inequality in terms of the absence of concentration. The formula for Lieberson's index is:

$$D = \frac{1 - \Sigma P_i^2}{1 - 1/K}$$

D is bounded from zero to unity. Recall from the discussion of inter-pretability in chapter two Lieberson's argument that an unbounded index is often preferable to a bounded one. In his original discussion of D (Lieberson, 1967:851), the equation appeared simply as a complement of the Herfindahl-Hirschman index. However, Lieberson reported the upper limit of D, given a fi-nite number of components, as $1 - 1/K$, for readers whose research problem and conceptualization require a bounded index (Lieberson, 1976:860). That theoretical upper bound is included in the equation above. Lieberson's diversity uses the same comparative standard as the Herfindahl-Hirschman index.

Independent of the number of components, Lieberson's D is an index of relative inequality that includes any number of null components. Properly bounded, it varies from zero or maximum concentration, to unity or maximum diversity. D does not conform to the population symmetry criterion, because splitting each share in half increases the D score, indicating increased diversity or equality.

Multiplying each component by a positive constant produces no change in the value of D; it is scale invariant. In contrast, adding a positive constant in-creases the value of D, indicating that diversity has increased. A transfer from richer to poorer component produces an increase in the index value, again indicating an increase in diversity. D does not comport with the Lorenz domi-nance principle.

Lieberson's D, which assumes that components are nominally scaled, is defined for all distributions and uses information from the entire distribution. Because it is bounded, it is easily interpretable as a relative measure that includes any number of null components. As Lieberson emphasized, it can be used with-out its denominator, in which case it becomes one of the complements of the Herfindahl-Hirschman index of concentration. It is a simple measure to use.

Labovitz and Gibbs (1964) earlier designed an index of the division of la-bor that is algebraically identical to the bounded Lieberson index of diversity. Because it uses frequencies rather than proportions, the Labovitz and Gibbs measure appears different at first glance. Close examination, however, reveals that it is just an alternative algebraic expression of Lieberson's D. The Labovitz and Gibbs measure is:

$$DL = \frac{1 - (\Sigma N_i^2)/N^2}{1 - 1/K}$$

Labovitz and Gibbs' DL equals Lieberson's D because $\Sigma N_i^2/N^2 = \Sigma P_i^2$. The only difference is that DL is expressed in frequencies, and D is expressed in proportions.

Labovitz and Gibbs conceptualized their index as measuring inequality, which they equated with division of labor. They insisted on including the number of occupations (components) in a population and the distribution of individuals (units) among occupations in their operational definition of inequality. They argued that "as the number (of occupations) increases, the maximum possible amount of differences among individuals also increases" (Labovitz and Gibbs, 1964:5), but also that the distribution of individuals among occupations is important because, "given an equal number of occupations, the more even the distribution among them, the greater the division of labor" (1964:6). In this conceptualization, the maximum division of labor (equality) occurs when no two persons have the same occupation.

HORVATH'S COMPREHENSIVE CONCENTRATION INDEX (CCI)

Horvath (1970:446) devised his comprehensive concentration index because he perceived "a disparity between the concern about economic concentration and the analytical refinement necessary to measure it." In economics, a monopolist is one who has the power to increase profit by restricting output. But in politics, most Americans believe that democracy cannot survive under concentrated economic power. The courts, reasoned Horvath, usually end up making decisions that permit or terminate monopolistic practices, but "government measures to check monopoly could undoubtedly be more intelligent and more effective if the measurement of monopoly power were practicable" (Machlup, 1952:470). So, for these policy-related reasons, Horvath developed the following index:

$$CCI = P_m + \sum_{i=2}^{K} P_i^2 \, [1 + (1 - P_i)]$$

This measure, "which owes its intellectual parentage to the Herfindahl Summary Index" (Horvath, 1970:448), requires adding the modal share to the summation of the square of the proportional shares of each other firm, reinforced by a multiplier reflecting the proportional size of the rest of the system. The modal component has a prime role in this equation; it is included in the summation untransformed in any way. The smaller components play a lesser role. Each is squared and multiplied times unity plus the proportion of the units that it does not have. They are added to the modal share. Horvath conceptualized the power of business firms in the economy as diminishing more rapidly than their material position (i.e., their assets, sales, employment, profits, value added, etc.). His CCI is "a modulated geometric function (that) approximates the process (of increasing or decreasing power)" (Horvath, 1970:447).

The Herfindahl-Hirschman index reflects the degree of concentration among the largest firms, but Horvath's measure heightens that sensitivity to concentration by reflecting absolute and relative concentration simultaneously, a novel feature (Horvath, 1970:448-449; Ray and Singer, 1973). The equation reflects absolute magnitude by separately including the untreated proportional share of the largest component in the CCI value. This CCI feature makes it resemble the concentration ratio (Adelman, 1951), which is simply the proportion of total units held by the first four, eight, or twenty firms. The formula captures relative dispersion in the sum of squared proportional shares, beginning with the second largest, times the multiplier $[1 + (1 - P_i)]$. It compares the sizes of firms in the industry in terms of the probability of randomly selecting two units (e.g., employees) from the same firm, regardless of the number of firms that exist.

Consistent with Horvath's conceptualization of concentration, CCI stresses the divergence between the largest component and the rest of the components and exaggerates the largest in contrast to the others. Horvath dismissed this potential weakness by pointing out that this exaggeration "occurs in a consistent pattern, so that inter-industry or inter-temporal comparisons should not suffer" (Horvath, 1970:449-450). Indeed, CCI seems to be most effective when used to differentiate monopolistic distributions and to compare changes in them over time. Analyzing changes in the level of concentration of the American tobacco, aluminum, and automobile industries, Horvath showed that "CCI gives both the direction of changes and a clearer representation of absolute magnitudes" (Horvath, 1970:452) than does the Herfindahl-Hirschman index.

CCI's polarity is toward inequality in the form of sensitivity to pure concentration. In terms of its status as an index of either relative or absolute inequality, it is a confusing hybrid. Because its lower limit is not constant, it qualifies as neither an index of relative inequality nor a type B absolute inequality measure. Nor is it a type A absolute inequality measure, because its upper limit is constant (Horvath, 1970:448; Waldman, 1977). It treats null categories in the same fashion as HH; it omits them.

It is a scale invariant index, since multiplication of each component by a positive constant produces no change in the CCI score. When a positive constant is added to each component, the index value declines. It also behaves in the preferred manner when an amount is transferred from a richer to poorer component; it declines, indicating deconcentration. But the amount of the decrease depends on the weight (rank) of donor and recipient, on whether the donor is the largest category, and on the size of the transfer. CCI emphasizes transfers from a richer donor, not to a poorer recipient. Transfers from the largest component to any other component have the largest impact, because P_m is untransformed in the

summational core. Horvath originated CCI to analyze distributions measured
with a ratio scale, dollars and people, although it is actually designed to operate
on nominally-scaled components.

Regarding population symmetry, instead of remaining constant when two
identical systems are combined, Horvath's index registers a decline in measured
concentration. Because of this property, sensitivity to number of components, it
does not satisfy the Lorenz dominance criterion.

CCI is defined for all distributions, although it is potentially weak in
measuring bimodal distributions. It uses all information, with the potential
weakness just mentioned. Interpretability is a problem. CCI's upper limit is
unity, in the case of complete monopoly, but its lower limit is not constant. It
is always greater than the size of the largest component's proportional share, assuming a system with two or more components. The index is not simple, because it blends relative and absolute inequality measurement and weights the
squared shares with a somewhat complicated multiplier term.

HALL AND TIDEMAN'S INDEX OF INDUSTRY CONCENTRATION (TH)

Hall and Tideman (1967:162) devised their index of industry concentration
because "a measure that is well-grounded in economic theory has eluded the
(monopoly and industrial concentration) researchers," and because "traditional
economic theory does not yield operational insights as to how to measure concentration." Their computational equation is as follows:

$$Th = \frac{1}{2\sum_i P_i - 1}$$

Although this formula contains familiar elements, the logic underlying its
procedure is by no means immediately apparent. However, its operational definition becomes simple once Hall and Tideman's weighting scheme and method of
bounding the measure are understood.

Notice that the summational core is not exponentiated. Hall and Tideman
wanted an index that takes two factors into account: (a) the only guidance they
felt economic theory provided about measuring economic concentration, which is
that "many sellers mean low concentration and few sellers mean high
concentration;" and (b) the relative size of each component (Hall and Tideman,
1970:163; see also Väyrynen, 1972:141-142). These two factors refer to absolute
and relative inequality, respectively. Hall and Tideman's TH, using the
probability of randomly selecting a homogeneous pair as the comparative standard, weights each component by its proportional size (null components are
weighted with zero). It also weights (rather than squares) each share by its rank,

in descending order. This weighting is required, Hall and Tideman argued, because many firms means easy entry into a market and few firms means entry is blockaded.

In operational terms, this double weighting scheme in the summational core yields $\sum_i P_i$, which emphasizes both the absolute number of components (i) and their relative size (P_i). If a business firm's sales are an appropriate measure of its size, P_i may be considered as the probability that a firm of rank i will obtain a random dollar of sales, and $\sum_i P_i$ is the expected value of that rank. This term varies from unity to infinity, but because Hall and Tideman wanted a properly bounded index, they transformed it to its reciprocal, $1/\sum_i P_i$, which varies from zero to unity.

However, $1/\sum_i P_i$ fails to conform to another principle that Hall and Tideman considered essential in an index. This principle states that if each component in a system is divided into two components of equal size, thus doubling the number of components but preserving their relative sizes, a measure of concentration should be reduced by one half (Hall and Tideman, 1970). They designed their final index equation, therefore, to conform to their "doubling principle," which requires the opposite of the principle of population symmetry. Consequently, if two identical systems are merged, the value of TH will double. Because of its other properties, TH also satisfies the Lorenz dominance criterion.

The polarity of TH is from equality to inequality, as TH varies from low to high, and it is definitely sensitive to concentration as well as inequality. It is a type A measure of absolute inequality, in that it is sensitive to the number of components, maximum only when one of an infinite number of components has all units, and minimum only when all components are equal. Recall that it also takes relative size of components into account.

TH is scale invariant; a constant proportionate increase of all components does not change its value. Adding a positive constant to each share decreases TH. Its value declines with a transfer of units from a richer to a poorer component, indicating deconcentration. This index was designed to operate on units distributed among nominally scaled components, but its weighting scheme imposes ordinality among the components.

Hall and Tideman's measure is defined for all distributions and makes good use of all information in a distribution. Its interpretability is convenient, because it is bounded from zero for total equality to unity for maximum concentration. It is not a simple measure to understand, but it is simple to compute.

TAAGEPERA'S INDEX OF IMBALANCE (T)

Taagepera (1979:282) argued that "there is one aspect of the size distribution of components that does not seem to be expressed by any of the existing indices," and he defined that aspect, imbalance, as the "size of the largest components compared to the size of the next largest ones." The problem that led him to devise his index is an interesting one. Consider two distributions, each with forty components, that Taagepera (1979:283) offered as an example.

System A			System B	
size	number		size	number
.30	2		.40	1
.03	1		.10	2
.01	<u>37</u>		.04	1
	total 40		.01	<u>36</u>
				total 40

Systems A and B are identical in two respects. They are characterized by a fairly low level of concentration (HH = .185 for both distributions) and moderately high inequality (Gini = .57 for both distributions). Yet these two distributions are quite different in an important respect. System A is bipolar and system B is unipolar. Think of system A as a nation in which two linguistic groups, political parties, or cultural regions balance each other and perhaps compete for the support of the smaller components. In contrast, system B represents a nation dominated by one group. Although the dominant group is less than a majority, it is in a position to exert almost complete control through economic or military means, or politically through being an essential majority coalition partner.

The distributional characteristic that differentiates these two systems is imbalance. To capture that characteristic, Taagepera devised the following index:

$$T = \frac{\sum_i \frac{(P_i - P_{i+1})}{i} - (\Sigma P_i^2)^2}{\sqrt{\Sigma P_i^2 - (\Sigma P_i^2)^2}}$$

where i = rank in decreasing order.

Many conventional inequality and concentration indexes are insensitive to imbalance primarily because they sum some transform of relative component sizes. Imbalance, however, is concerned with the differences between component sizes, especially the difference between the largest components. To insure this sensitivity, Taagepera's T requires arranging components in descending order and summing the weighted differences between each component and the next smaller one in the core expression (the ratio in the numerator). The weighting scheme divides each difference by the rank of the first component in the subtraction. The differences must be weighted; if they were not, their sum would always equal the value of the largest component, so that no index of imbalance would result. Several different weighting schemes could be used (e.g., i^2 or $\sqrt{i}$), but dividing by rank, a gradually increasing factor, emphasizes the differences between the largest components.

The weighted summational core can assume values from a minimum of $(\sum P_i^2)^2$ to a maximum of $\sum P_i^2$. The remaining operations required in the equation, subtracting $(\sum P_i^2)^2$ from the core expression and dividing that result by $[\sqrt{\sum P_i^2} - (\sum P_i^2)^2]$, simply eliminate the residual correlation of the core expression with $\sum P_i^2$. This transformation assures that the resulting index value can vary from near zero to unity for any degree of system concentration, assuming at least two components. Taagepera (1979) showed that nearly any combination of T and the Gini index can occur and that nearly any combination of T and HH can be obtained at low values of HH. For example, in a system with $P_1 = 0.1$ and 900 other $P_i = 0.001$, Gini = 0.10, HH = 0.01, and T = 0.95. Taagepera's T clearly reflects the extent of imbalance in this distribution, whereas Gini and HH do not.

Keep in mind that this index is primarily sensitive to the size difference (imbalance) between the two largest components. The greater the difference between them, the larger the T value, indicating greater imbalance. The closer in size they are, the smaller the T value, indicating less imbalance. T's polarity is not straightforward, because it is designed to measure imbalance rather than inequality or concentration. However, it assumes a distributional conceptualization from less to more imbalance (suggesting less to more inequality). It is based on the same comparative standard as Herfindahl and Hirschman's index.

Taagepera's imbalance is a relative measure of inequality that effectively eliminates null components, based on the same logic that similarly classifies HH. Because T weights each component by its proportional share, it assigns a weight of zero to null components. Therefore, T's consideration of the total number of components is problematic. For example, it does not distinguish among a one-component system (K = 1; $P_1 = 1.0$), a two-component system with a null component (K = 2; $P_1 = 1.0$, $P_2 = 0.0$), and a ten-component system in which one component has all (K = 10; $P_1 = 1.0$, $P_2 = P_3 = ... = P_{10} = 0$). T provides the same index values for all three cases, as does HH. The investigator should take note that Taagepera's imbalance, like Herfindahl and Hirschman's concentration, focuses on location of units, not on collective condition of components.

Taagepera's T is scale invariant; a proportionate increase in all components produces no change in its value. Adding a positive constant to each component causes T to decline, indicating a reduction in imbalance and concentration. T also behaves properly in regard to the principle of transfers. A shift of units from a richer to a poorer component produces a decline in the value of T. However, the size of change in the value of T depends partly on the rank of donor and recipient, because of the rank-weighting scheme employed in the summational core. A T value declines when two identical systems are combined, or when each component of a system is divided into equal parts, indicating that imbalance fails to conform to the population symmetry criterion. Imbalance, therefore, does not obey the Lorenz dominance principle. The imbalance index assumes nominally scaled components, but imposes ordinality on them in terms of their rank based on size.

This measure shares several operational properties with HH. It is defined for all distributions and makes good use of distributional information, except possibly for null components. It is not properly bounded. It has a maximum value of unity, when one component possesses all the resources, and a minimum value of less than zero for systems in which all shares are uniform, which can be interpreted as a form of perfect balance. T's improperly bounded lower limit reflects its dependence on the Herfindahl-Hirschman index, which has a lower bound of $1/K$ for totally equal distributions. In fact, for a uniform distribution, T's lower bound is

$$\frac{(1/K)^2}{\sqrt{(1/K) - (1/K)^2}}$$

rather than zero. T's interpretability, under such conditions, is a problem. Taagepera's T is neither simple to understand nor to compute.

RAE AND TAYLOR'S INDEX OF FRAGMENTATION (RT)

Rae and Taylor (1970) designed their index of fragmentation primarily to measure the distribution of parliamentary seats among political parties in a multiparty system. Its formula, expressed in terms of frequencies, is:

$$RT = 1 - \frac{\sum N_i (N_i - 1)}{N (N - 1)}$$

The numerator in the ratio represents the total number of pairs of units possessed by the same component. The denominator represents the total number of pairs in the system. The ratio, therefore, expresses the proportion of all pairs containing units that come from the same component, essentially a measure of concentration. Subtracting the proportion from unity converts it to a measure of fragmentation. RT compares the probability of randomly selecting two units from the same component with all possible selections by using every other unit as the comparative standard.

Ray and Singer (1973) first pointed out that a slight rearrangement of
RT's equation converts it to an approximate complement of the Herfindahl-
Hirschman index of concentration (i.e., Rae and Taylor's RT $\approx 1 - \sum P_i^2$). The
above equation for RT can also be expressed as follows:

$$RT = 1 - \sum \frac{(N_i)}{(N)} \frac{(N_i - 1)}{(N - 1)}$$

The term N_i/N equals P_i and represents the proportion of the whole made
up by the ith component. The term $(N_i - 1)/(N - 1)$ is only a slight modification of P_i. The larger the number of units in each component and in the system,
the more closely the latter term approximates N_i/N. In systems with a smaller
number of units, such as a legislature or a committee, the two terms will diverge
significantly. For example, if RT is used to measure partisan fragmentation in a
legislature with one hundred members, a party of twenty five would contribute
$(25/100)(24/99) = 0.0606$ to the fragmentation score. Using HH, that party's
contribution to the fragmentation value would be .0625. When summed over
several components in a system, such differences can produce a noticeable difference between RT and HH.

These differences make conceptual sense, especially for systems with a
relatively small number of components. Recall that indexes based on combinatorics conceptualize concentration (or fragmentation) as the sum of the
probabilities that two units randomly selected from the system will belong to
the same component (or different components). It is strictly correct to compute
those probabilities simply by squaring the N_i/N of a system with a smaller
number of units only under the assumption of replacing each unit after it is randomly chosen. Because that is, in fact, virtually never the case, N_i/N should be
multiplied by $(N_i - 1)/(N - 1)$, rather than squared, in order to obtain the required
probabilities.

James S. Coleman's index of unanimity (I), first used by Pinard
(1971:206) to analyze the vote distribution among candidates in Canadian federal
elections at the community level, is the complement of Rae and Taylor's fragmentation index. RT = 1 - I; fragmentation and unanimity are complements of
each other.

RT's polarity is equality, and it is sensitive to concentration. It is a measure of absolute inequality because of its sensitivity to the number of components. This index of fragmentation is maximal when all units, regardless of how
many, belong to one component and minimal when each unit, regardless of the
number of units, belongs to a different component. Naturally, RT excludes null
components.

With respect to both scale invariance and population symmetry, the Rae-Taylor index behaves in an odd fashion. A proportionate increase in each component's number of units produces an decrease in the value of RT, indicating that the distribution has become less fragmented or more concentrated, contrary to the requirements of scale invariance. Adding a positive constant (e.g., giving each component five additional units) causes RT to increase, signalling more fragmentation (less concentration). Thus it violates the Lorenz dominance criterion. A transfer of units from a larger to a smaller component yields an increase in measured fragmentation, consistent with the transfers principle.

RT violates the principle of population symmetry. Combining two systems produces a new system with greater measured fragmentation than either of its parts. Similarly, dividing each component of a system into two equal parts increases measured fragmentation. Rae and Taylor originated RT to analyze variables measured on a nominal scale, such as political parties.

RT is defined for all distributions and uses distributional information well. The upper limit of RT is unity, when all units are in one component, but the lower limit is not zero. This operational feature affects interpretability in two contradictory ways. In conventional terms, it weakens interpretability because the lower limit is unknown. On the other hand, it strengthens interpretability because of the way it relates to probability theory, that is, randomly chosen pairs of units without replacement from a finite set of units. RT's operational definition of fragmentation, based on combinatorics, is both realistic and accurate for smaller systems. Rae and Taylor's index is simple to compute and is a straightforward operationalization of the combinatorics logic.

MUELLER, SCHEUSSLER, AND COSTNER'S INDEX OF QUALITATIVE VARIATION (IQV)

The index of qualitative variation (Mueller, Scheussler, and Costner, 1970:174-178), which operates on raw frequencies, is expressed by the following equation:

$$IQV = \frac{\Sigma\Sigma N_i N_j}{\dfrac{K(K-1)}{2}(N/K)^2}, \qquad i \neq j$$

The greater the number of differences among a set of items, the more heterogeneous the set. The smaller the number of differences, the more homogeneous the set of items. IQV's numerator computes the total number of qualitative differences among the items in a system by counting the number of differences between each item and every other item and summing them. An example might be ten red marbles, five white marbles, and two blue marbles in a box. Marbles (units) are distributed among nominally scaled colors (components). As the earlier discussion of combinatorics indicated, this counting is accomplished operationally through multiplication. The double summation sign in the equation means sum the product of each component multiplied by every other component. The inequality, $i \neq j$, directs the investigator not to use any component multiplied by itself.

The denominator bounds the index. It is the hypothetical maximum number of differences given K. That maximum occurs when all components are equal, so the theoretical upper bound involves squaring the mean component size (N/K) and taking that square as many times as there are possible pairs of components, which is $K(K - 1)/2$.

Because this formula is somewhat more involved than most in this chapter, a computational illustration is offered. Assume that the four parties represented in a legislative body have forty, thirty, twenty, and ten members, respectively. The numerator for IQV is $\sum N_i N_j = (40)(30) + (40)(20) + (40)(10) + (30)(20) + (30)(10) + (20)(10) = 3500$. In the denominator, mean component size is $(N/K)^2 = (100/4)^2 = (25)^2 = 625$. The number of possible component pairs is $K(K - 1)/2 = 4(4 - 1)/2 = 6$. Thus, IQV = 3500/(6)(625) = .933. This score indicates a high degree of heterogeneity, or, in terms of IQV's polarity, a high degree of inequality among the components. Political party diversity in the legislative body is 93.3% of the maximum possible, given four party groups. Nachmias and Rosenbloom's (1973) use of IQV to compare the degree of social integration in selected federal government agencies provides an important application of the measure.

Mueller, Scheussler, and Costner (1970:176-177) also devised an alternative denominator with which to norm the index: $N(N - 1)/2$. This denominator norms the resulting index on the number of all possible pairs that might be formed from all units in all components. It does not norm the index on the number of components. They recommended its use when the research problem involves comparing the heterogeneity of two systems with different numbers of components. Norming in this way permits the index to reflect the larger number of components in one system than in the other. In the above example of the legislative body, using the alternative denominator produces IQV = .707.

IQV is sensitive to concentration because the numerator multiplies each frequency by every other frequency in the numerator's summational core. This treatment also indicates IQV's comparative standard: every other component. Using the regular denominator (as included in the full equation above) bounds the index between zero and unity and makes IQV's range independent of the number of components. It includes any number of null components, reaches its maximum when all components are equal, and reaches a minimum when one component possesses all. If the alternative norming denominator is used, IQV's lower limit is still zero (all cases in a single category), but the upper limit approaches unity as the number of components increases; the greater the number of categories, the higher the theoretical upper limit, until it reaches unity when each unit belongs to a different component.

In terms of scale invariance, the index experiences no change in value when the frequencies of each component are multiplied by a positive constant. Adding a positive constant to each share, however, decreases IQV, marking a decrease in heterogeneity. A transfer of some amount from a richer donor to poorer recipient decreases the index to indicate greater homogeneity or equality. Combining two systems also causes measured heterogeneity to be greater for the combination than for either of the two parts that went into it. Population symmetry is thus violated. Naturally, IQV does not conform to Lorenz dominance.

Mueller, Scheussler, and Costner devised the index to measure qualitative variation among nominally scaled groups. IQV is defined for all distributions and makes good use of information provided in a distribution. It is easily interpreted from zero to unity as 0 to 100 percent of the maximum possible heterogeneity among the components. Interpretation is trickier if the alternative denominator is used. This index is not simple to compute.

HAMMOND, HOUSEHOLDER, AND CASTELLAN'S INDEX OF DISPERSION (D_h)

Hammond, Householder, and Castellan (1970) operationalized their conception of dispersion in the following equation:

$$D_h = \frac{K(N^2 - \Sigma N_i^2)}{N^2 (K - 1)}$$

The Hammond-Householder-Castellan index symbol (D_h) includes the subscript, h, in order to differentiate it from Lieberson's index of diversity, D. D_h is, of course, also based on the number of pairs of units the members of which are in different components. The originators called such combinations "distinguishable pairs" and a combination of two units from the same component an "indistinguishable pair". They designed D_h to be a bounded index of total number of pairs minus the ratio of indistinguishable pairs to total pairs. Deriving each of these parts of the formula and bounding it are procedurally rather complicated, but if one understands the underlying mathematical logic of this family of indexes, derivation should provide no trouble.

The first task is to determine the number of two-unit combinations the units of which are distinguishable, in other words, heterogeneous pairs. The term, $N(N - 1)/2$, yields the number of ways that N units can be taken two at a time. If N units are classified in two components, N_1 and N_2, then $N_1 + N_2 = N$. Any pair of units in the same component are to be rejected as not containing members that are distinguishable. In the first component $N_1(N_1 - 1)/2$ such members exist and $N_2(N_2 - 1)/2$ in the second. These must be deleted from all possible pairs, in order to obtain the distinguishable pairs, in the following way:

$$\frac{N(N-1)}{2} - \frac{N_i\,(N_i-1)}{2} - \frac{N_2\,(N_2-1)}{2}$$

If K components are used, instead of two,

$$\frac{N(N-1)}{2} - \sum\frac{N_i\,(N_i-1)}{2} = \frac{N(N-1)}{2} - 1/2\ \Sigma(N_i^2 - N_i)$$

$$= N^2/2 - N/2 - 1/2(\Sigma N_i^2) + 1/2(\Sigma N_i)$$

$$= N^2/2 - 1/2\ \Sigma N_i^2$$

The right side of the last equation represents the number of distinguishable pairs. We now divide distinguishable pairs by total pairs, as follows:

$$\frac{N^2/2 - 1/2\ \Sigma N_i^2}{N(N-1)/2} = \frac{N^2 - \Sigma N_i^2}{N(N-1)}$$

The higher the ratio, the greater the dispersion. The smaller the number of distinguishable pairs, the lower the ratio and the less the dispersion. The ratio reaches its maximum when each component contains an equal number of units. It attains its minimum value, zero, when all units are in one component. Bounding the ratio, so that it varies from zero to unity, involves norming it on its maximum value. When each $N_i = N/K$, the ratio is:

$$\frac{N^2 - \Sigma(N/K)^2}{N(N-1)} = \frac{N^2 - K(N/K)^2}{N(N-1)} = \frac{N(K-1)}{K(N-1)}$$

This maximum value of the ratio corresponds to maximum dispersion. If the ratio used to obtain this result is multiplied by $K(N-1)/N(K-1)$, the maximum will be unity. This final operation controls for the number of components and produces a properly bounded index, D_h, defined as follows:

$$D_h = \left[\frac{K(N-1)}{N(K-1)} \right] \left[\frac{N^2 - \Sigma N_i^2}{N(N-1)} \right]$$

$$D_h = \frac{K(N^2 - \Sigma N_i^2)}{N^2 (K-1)}$$

D_h's polarity is equality or dispersion, it is sensitive to concentration, and it uses every pair as the comparative standard for every homogeneous pair. Because it is independent of the number of components, it is a measure of relative inequality, and it includes any number of null components. Multiplying each share by a positive constant produces no change in the value of D_h. Adding a positive constant to each share increases the index value, indicating greater dispersion or equality. Transferring some units from a richer to poorer component also increases D_h. If two identical systems are combined, the measured dispersion of the combination is greater than either of its identical parts. D_h, therefore, violates the population symmetry criterion. Thus it also fails to satisfy the Lorenz dominance criterion.

Hammond, Householder, and Castellan (1970:111) claimed that D_h is "a measure of variability for ordinal or nominal data." In fact, its procedure disregards ordinal ranking, if it actually exists in the components. It will work on ordinally ranked components, but it treats them as nominal. In contrast, Leik's (1966) measure of ordinal dispersion (discussed below) does assume ordinally ranked components.

D_h is defined for all distributions and makes good use of information. It rates well on interpretability, because it is bounded from zero to unity. Understanding its operational derivation from combinatorics is complicated, but performing the required computations is simple.

LEIK'S MEASURE OF ORDINAL CONSENSUS (C)

Leik's (1966) measure of ordinal consensus is expressed in the following formula:

$$C = 1 - \frac{2\Sigma d_i}{K-1}$$

Leik labeled his index D, but I call it C, for consensus, to differentiate it from other measures symbolized by D. Both the definition of d_i, a term not included in chapter two's discussion of statistical notation, and the manner in which C's numerator is derived require explanation. Leik created his index to measure distribution of items among rank-ordered components without requiring equal intervals between categories. Consider, for illustration, a sample survey question that asks the respondent if he/she strongly agrees, agrees, doesn't know, disagrees, or strongly disagrees with a statement, in other words, a typical Likert-scale item. Let the distribution of answers to this question be a weak ordinal scale indicated by N_1 ... N_5, and of course $\Sigma N_i = N$. Conversion to a relative frequency distribution yields the set $[N_i/N]$, $i = 1$ ... 5 and $\Sigma N_i/N = \Sigma P_i = 1.00$. Cumulation up to a given component produces a cumulative relative frequency distribution, designated F; $i = 1$ ... 5 where $F_i = (1/K) \Sigma N_j, i, j = 1$ ... 5. Such a distribution might take the hypothetical form expressed in table 4-3:

Table 4-3
Hypothetical Frequency Distribution
and Computations for Leik's C

Opinion	N_i	P_i	F_i	d_i
Strongly agree	45	.15	.15	.15
Agree	85	.28	.43	.43
Don't know	95	.32	.75	.25
Disagree	40	.13	.88	.12
Strongly disagree	35	.12	1.00	0
total	300	1.00		0.95

The cumulative relative frequency distribution, F, is centrally important to deriving the numerator of Leik's index, because it incorporates rank-order among the categories. If no dispersion obtained, all units would be in one category, and all cumulative relative frequencies prior to that category would be zero. Beginning with that chosen category, all entries would be 1.00. For example, if all respondents choose category four (disagree), the cumulative relative frequencies would be 0, 0, 0, 1.00, 1.00. Any departure from one hundred percent choice of one component would cause F entries to be greater than zero but less than unity.

The term d_i stands for difference and is defined as follows:

$$d_i = \left\{ \begin{array}{l} F_i \text{ if } F_i \leq .50, \text{ or} \\ 1 - F_i \text{ otherwise} \end{array} \right.$$

In the case of no dispersion, in other words one component has all, all d_i equal zero. If all respondents choose category four, as in the above example, $d_i = 0, 0, 0, 0, 0$. The first three are zero because they equal F_i and the last two equal zero because they equal $1 - F_i$. The expression $\sum d_i$ equals zero in the special case of unanimity. In the case of the hypothetical distribution in table 4-3, the numerator, $\sum d_i$, equals 0.95.

Leik designed the denominator to be the maximum upper limit of the numerator, given the number of components K. Using cumulative relative frequencies already controls for the number of units. The formula for the maximum $\sum d_i$, the denominator of the ratio, is based on the case in which each of the two extreme categories contains half of the units, in other words, maximal dispersion (i. e., $N_1 = N_K = N/2$). For a system of five components, d_i will equal .50. .50, .50, .50, and 0, and $\sum d_i = 2.00$. For K ordered components, d_i will always equal .50 for d_1 through d_{K-1}, but d_K will always equal zero, under conditions of maximum dispersion. This sum must therefore be maximum $\sum d_i = 1/2(K - 1)$.

The ratio of the index, a measure of diversity, is created by dividing $\sum d_i$ by maximum $\sum d_i$. The term 1/2 in the denominator becomes 2 in the numerator for convenience, and the ratio is subtracted from unity. Leik's consensus uses the cumulative relative frequency distribution as a comparative standard against which to assess the ordinal distribution. The resulting operational definition is the equation presented at the beginning of this section. Leik's C is insensitive to number of units, number of components, mean component size, and assumptions about the size of intervals between components. For the distribution in table 4-3, Leik's C = $1 - .475 = .525$. In other words, that distribution contains 52.5% of the consensus that is possible, controlling for numbers of units and categories, and average.

The polarity of the ratio in Leik's C is more complicated than that of most indexes. Its conceptual continuum runs from (low to high) dissensus to consensus. But what concepts are at the extremes and in the middle? Three possible distributions are particularly puzzling: (a) one component has all, (b) all components are equal, and (c) each of the two extreme components contains one-half of the units. Consider the distribution in which all components are equal, that is, N/K units in each component. Such a rectangular distribution would seem intuitively to be half way between maximum concentration and maximum dispersion (at both ends), yet it does not produce a ratio of .50.

To clarify the puzzle, consider a hypothetical two-component system in which each component possesses N/K units, and, therefore, each extreme component possesses N/2 units. This contradictory situation represents both equality and maximum dispersion. The ratio equals 1.00 under these conditions (and C = 0). As K increases, the value of the ratio associated with N/K units per component approaches 0.5 but reaches that value only for K = infinity. The important point for polarity is that a distribution equally divided between two very opposing alternatives is, for the ratio in this index, more widely divergent than a distribution equally divided among many components, because of the equation's ordinality assumption. Recall that K has no meaning in terms of the distance between the extreme categories. The proper conceptualization is that when K is small, a situation of N/K units per component represents opposing factions. When K is large, a situation of N/K units per component has the character of many small subgroups that are not much different from adjacent groups. The latter situation represents a random distribution, assuming no ordered substantive meaning of the components, rather than factional rivalry. Therefore, as K increases from two to infinity, the ratio goes from maximum dispersion to half of maximum dispersion.

Leik (1966) admitted that "the conception of consensus . . . is simply a lack of dispersion." Therefore, minimal consensus, the bipolar split, occurs in a maximally dispersed distribution. It might be argued that the bifactional split actually represents two highly consensual components in the system and is more consensual than K equally divided components. That argument is invalid, Leik reasoned, because the average distance between randomly chosen pairs is at a maximum for the bifactional split, not for the uniform distribution. Recall that C assumes ordinally ranked components; distance between components is crucial.

Leik did not design his measure of consensus to be sensitive to concentration as such. The clustering of surplus units is not so important to the value of C; rather, the distance between the units in any pair, randomly chosen from the ordinally ranked components, is the important sensitivity of this index. Remember that the ordinal ranking and the frequencies in each component are theoretically unrelated. The components exist in their proper rank order independent of and prior to categorization of units in them. The frequency of the ordinally ranked first component can be smallest, largest, null, or something else, and so on throughout the distribution. Component order and component size measured by frequency of items are theoretically unrelated. Disproportionately greater weight is attached to clustered surplus units when they are farther apart in the ordinal ranking. Such greater clustering at greater distance, approaching a bipolar distribution, approximates concentration.

As a properly bounded index, C is insensitive to the number of components. It is a measure of relative inequality that includes any number of null components. Multiplying each component by a positive constant leaves the value of C unchanged, so it is scale invariant. Adding a positive constant to each share decreases C, indicating diminished consensus. Leik's C conforms to the population symmetry axiom. Combining two identical systems yields the same C value as one of the systems alone.

The effect of a transfer of units depends on the direction of the transfer. If units are shifted from the middle toward either extreme (or both extremes), the value of C declines, indicating diminished consensus. If the transfer occurs from a component near one extreme toward the middle of the distribution (but not past it toward the other extreme), then C increases, signalling greater consensus. It does not matter whether donor and recipient are richer or poorer, only whether a transfer enhances the middle (consensus increases) or either of the ends (consensus diminishes). Because it fails to satisfy the transfers axiom, Leik's C is not a Lorenz-dominant measure. However, ordinal consensus is not fairly comparable to other indexes with respect to ranking distributions.

Leik's consensus is a measure of distribution among rank-ordered components. It will operate on intervally scaled components, but it does not assume equal intervals between classes. It cannot legitimately be used to measure distribution among nominally scaled components, because they have no inherent rank order.

It is defined for all distributions and uses information well, including the rank-order of the components. Even though it is bounded from zero to unity, it is not easily interpretable. In interpreting C, it is important to remember that zero represents a situation in which one component possesses all and that unity represents a situation in which all units are equally divided between the two extreme categories. Equality among components is represented by scores varying from 0.33 to 0.50. The actual score depends on the number of components. For example, C = .33 for three equal components and C = .50 for an infinite number of equal components. C is not simple to understand, but it is easy to compute, even though its formula takes component rank into account.

RAY, TAAGEPERA, AND SINGER'S GENERALIZED INDEX OF CONCENTRATION (C_α)

Ray and Singer (1973) devised an index of concentration called CON, which Taagepera and Ray (1977) generalized (C_α). The equation for the generalized concentration index is as follows:

$$C_\alpha = \left[\frac{\Sigma P_i^\alpha - K^{1-\alpha}}{1 - K^{1-\alpha}} \right]^{1/\alpha}$$

For $\alpha = 2$, we obtain Ray and Singer's index of concentration, CON:

$$C_2 = CON = \sqrt{ \frac{\Sigma P_i^2 - 1/K}{1 - 1/K} }$$

CON is the best place to begin, because its formula contains familiar terms and serves as both a definitional and computational equation. It is a bounded coefficient of relative variation or a normalized, bounded standard deviation (Mueller, Scheussler, and Costner, 1970: 165-66). The standard deviation of percentage shares divided by the maximum possible standard deviation in a system of size K simplifies to CON. The numerator is simply the Herfindahl-Hirschman index of industrial concentration minus the mean proportional share. The denominator, $1 - 1/K$, is the upper limit of $1 - \Sigma P_i^2$. Because all the percentage shares are squared in the numerator, the final step requires extracting the square root of the ratio, in order partially to return it to its original units.

Squaring the shares is a conventional exponentiation, but the shares could be raised to other powers, such as 1.5 or 3, requiring different standardizing terms (Taagepera and Ray, 1977). The summational core can be generalized, that is, ΣP_i^α, where α is any positive number. Under conditions of complete concentration, when one component controls all the units, the value of the summational core is unity. When all components possess an equal number of units, the summational core reaches its minimum value of $[K(1/K)^\alpha] = K^{1-\alpha}$. Therefore, in order for the equation to yield zero for complete equality, $K^{1-\alpha}$ must be subtracted from the core expression. In order to achieve a value of unity for maximum concentration, the core must be divided by $(1 - K^{1-\alpha})$ (Taagepera and Ray, 1977). The result is:

$$B_\alpha = \frac{\Sigma P_i^\alpha - K^{1-\alpha}}{1 - K^{1-\alpha}}$$

Because each P_i is raised to the αth power, carrying out the inverse operation (taking the αth root) preserves the symmetry of the procedure and results in the generalized αth degree concentration index, C_α, presented at the beginning of this section.

When $\alpha = 0$, $C_\alpha = 0$. When α tends to infinity, C_α tends to the value P_m (largest proportional share). When $\alpha = 1$, C_1 equals relative redundancy, an entropy index (chapter five). C_2 is always larger than C_1. The maximum value of any C_α almost always depends on the value of the largest share (Taagepera and Ray, 1977:375-380).

The polarity of the generalized index is inequality, and C_α's sensitivity to concentration increases as the size of its exponent increases. In fact, the investigator should select an exponent on the basis of the desired degree of sensitivity to concentration. C_α uses random selection of pairs as its comparative standard, because it is based on a combinatorics model. C_2 can also be interpreted in terms of the deviations model, and C_1 can also be derived from and interpreted in terms of the entropy model.

The value of C_α is independent of the number of components, reaching its maximum when one component has all units and its minimum when all shares are equal. Thus it is a type A measure of relative inequality. The range of the index is constant, but the values of the index rise and fall with system size, even when all else is constant. Applying Hall and Tideman's (1967) "doubling principle" indicates that the behavior of C_α is about midway between the Gini index and the Herfindahl-Hirschman index (Ray and Singer, 1973). For example, consider a four-component system with proportional shares divided as follows: 0.40, 0.30, 0.20, 0.10. Then assume that each share is split into two equal shares, and K rises to eight. Gini = .25 for both distributions. HH = .30 for the first and .15 for the second, a ratio of two to one. C_2 drops from .26 to .17, a ratio of 1.53 to 1, indicating that it violates the principle of population symmetry. This change in the concentration score also indicates that C_α is less sensitive to concentration than HH.

It is scale invariant, because proportionate increases in all shares produce no change in the value of C_α. Constant additions to all shares, however, reduce the index value, indicating diminished concentration. A transfer from a richer to a poorer component produces the same effect. C_α cannot comply with the Lorenz dominance criterion, because it violates the population symmetry axiom. The Ray-Taagepera-Singer index assumes no inherent ordering of the components, and is, therefore, appropriate for use on nominally scaled components.

The index is defined for all distributions and reflects the share of every component in the system, including all null components. It is easily interpretable, since it is bounded from zero, for equality or maximum dispersion given K, to unity, for total concentration or all units in a single component. C_2 or CON is simple to compute, although the generalized index appears complicated. CON has many equivalents [e.g., Amemiya's index of economic differentiation, IED, equals $(CON)^2$], as Ray and Singer (1973) demonstrated.

TAAGEPERA AND RAY'S EQUIVALENT TWO-COMPONENT SYSTEM (ETS)

One of the more practical features of CON is its use in computing the "equivalent two-component system" (ETS). If a distribution with three or more components has the same C_2 value as a two-component system, these two systems are equivalent on the level of $K = 2$. Although C_1 and C_2 will usually yield different levels of concentration for a given distribution, the ETS values of both indexes are more or less the same over a wide range of K. This property means "that ETS might represent a stable basis for comparing system concentrations" (Taagepera and Ray, 1977:381). The relationship between ETS and C_2 is as follows:

$$2P_m = C_2 + 1 = \left[\frac{\Sigma P_i^2 - 1/K}{1 - 1/K} \right]^{1/2} + 1$$

To illustrate use of this ETS formula, consider an eight-component system with the following proportional distribution: .20, .20, .15, .15, .10, .10, .05, and .05. For this distribution, $C_2 = .41$. Using the equation, ETS $= 2P_m = 0.41 + 1$, and $P_m = 0.705$. This indicates that the eight-component system is the equivalent of a two-component system in which the larger component is 0.705. ETS has an inequality polarity and achieves its maximum value, unity, when one component possesses all units. It reaches its minimum, 0.5, when all components are equal. It is a measure of relative inequality that includes any number of null components, as does C_2. ETS makes good use of information and is defined for all distributions. It represents a simple and efficient way to compare concentration among distributions with different numbers of components, by reducing each distribution to its two-component equivalent.

LAAKSO AND TAAGEPERA'S EFFECTIVE NUMBER OF COMPONENTS (ENC$_\alpha$)

Effective number of components stands as an alternative to the equivalent two-component system. ENC is defined as "the number of hypothetical equal-size . . . (components) that would have the same total effect on fractionalization of the system as have actual . . . (components) of unequal size" (Laakso and Taagepera, 1979:4). Laakso (1977) developed the following equation as an operational definition of effective number of components:

$$ENC_2 = \frac{1}{\Sigma P_i^2} = [\Sigma P_i^2]^{-1}$$

ENC$_2$, or effective number of components, is the reciprocal of Herfindahl and Hirschman's concentration (HH) and is related to Rae and Taylor's fractionalization (F) (Laakso and Taagepera, 1979). Specifically,

$$\text{ENC}_2 = 1/\text{HH} = 1/(1 - \text{F}), \text{ and}$$
$$\text{F} = 1 - \text{HH} = 1 - 1/\text{ENC}_2$$

If all shares are equal, the effective number of components equals the actual number of components. If one component possesses virtually all of the units, ENC$_2$ is slightly larger than unity. ENC$_2$ equals unity when one components has all. One use of the effective number of components that illustrates its interpretation is computing the effective number of parties in a multiparty electoral system. If the parties' proportional shares of the votes in the most recent election are 0.45, 0.20, 0.15, 0.10, 0.05, and 0.05, ENC$_2$ = 1/.28 = 3.57. This political system has the equivalent of three to four equal-size parties in its electoral system. In other words, 3.57 equal-size parties would yield the same concentration (or fractionalization) index value as the existing party shares. The effective number of components is always smaller than the actual number, unless all shares are equal (Taagepera and Grofman, 1981).

Laakso and Taagepera (1979) created a generalized expression for effective number of components, ENC$_\alpha$, that satisfies six conditions. First, when all components are equal, ENC$_\alpha$ = K. Second, when one component has all, ENC$_\alpha$ = unity. Third, null components can be added to the system without changing the value of ENC$_\alpha$. This condition prevents distortion in the index that could result from an arbitrary decision to include or exclude very small components. The effect of near-null components will be virtually nothing, except when small changes in P$_i$ create large changes in K. Fourth, small changes in shares must lead to small changes in ENC$_\alpha$. Fifth, all shares must be treated in the same way and cumulate additively. Sixth, the sum thus obtained must be the same for the actual system and for the equivalent system with K equal components [each share = (1/K): f(P$_i$) = f(1/K)].

One family of functions that satisfies these criteria is $f(P_i) = P_i^\alpha$ in which the exponent α can be any positive number. The equation listed in condition number six above then becomes:

$$\Sigma P_i^\alpha = \Sigma (1/K)^\alpha = K^{1 - \alpha}$$

Consequently,

$$\text{ENC}_\alpha = [\Sigma P_i^\alpha]^{1/(1 - \alpha)}$$

ENC$_2$ results when $\alpha = 2$ in this generalized expression. Another equation for effective number of components (E$_1$), based on the concept of entropy (chapter five), results when α tends toward unity. E$_1$ yields somewhat higher values than E$_2$ when applied to the same distribution. Setting $\alpha = 2$ emphasizes large components; setting $\alpha = 1$ emphasizes many small components (Laakso and Taagepera, 1979).

TAAGEPERA AND GROFMAN'S EFFECTIVE SIZE (ES)

Taagepera and Grofman (1981:65) conceptualized a related property of a distribution, effective size of a system, as "the average size effectively seen by participants (units in the system), as opposed to . . . (that) which may be the average as seen by outsiders." ES is usually larger than the traditional arithmetic mean because "members of a system experience, on the average, larger components than are seen by outsiders, because larger components are experienced by more members" (1981:64). They operationally defined effective size as follows:

$$ES_2 = \Sigma N_i^2 / N$$

To illustrate this "grass-roots" average, consider three college classes (Feld and Grofman, 1977) with 10, 10, and 100 students, respectively. The traditional arithmetic mean class size is N/K = $(10 + 10 + 100)/3 = 40$. The mean probably represents the school administration's view of average class size. Effective class size, however, is ES$_2$ = $[(10)^2 + (10)^2 + (100)^2]/(10 + 10 + 100)$ = 10,200/120 = 85, which probably more accurately represents the students' view of class size. This larger number is closer to the average size that most students experience, because by far most students attend the largest class.

Taagepera and Grofman (1981) demonstrated that effective size and effective number of components are related. For example, dividing total size N by Laakso and Taagepera's effective number of components (ENC$_2$) yields the corresponding size of the effective components:

$$N/ENC_2 = (N)(HH) = N\Sigma N_i^2 / N^2 = \Sigma N_i^2 / N = \text{mean ES}_2$$

This expression is identical to that obtained by Feld and Grofman (1977). Consequently, N = ENC$_2$(mean ES$_2$). Thus, given any two of total size, effective size, and effective number of components, the third can be calculated, as well as several other inequality indexes, such as Herfindahl-Hirschman's concentration and Lieberson's diversity (Taagepera and Grofman, 1981). Effective number of components and effective size can be applied to a variety of social data. For example, effective number of components could be used to compare political party fractionalization in a multiparty system or ethnic diversity in any geographical area. Effective size can be applied to many types of population groupings such as classrooms, cities, and countries.

LAAKSO AND TAAGEPERA'S INDEX OF FLUCTUATION (f)

Laakso and Taagepera's (1979) fluctuation index includes effective number of components (ENC) and is based on a combinatorics model, although it also incorporates the structure of the deviations model. The fluctuation formula is as follows:

$$f = \left[\frac{1}{ENC/K}\right] [(1/T)\Sigma(ENC_t - ENC_{t-1})^2]^{1/2}$$

where ENC = effective number of components with $\alpha = 2$,
     ENC_t = effective number of components at time t,
             starting with t = 0, and
     T = K – 1 or number of time events minus unity.

Several of the elements in this equation require explanation. The summational core gives the f formula the look of a deviations model index. It sums the squares of the differences between successive components over time. In this case, however, the "components" are expressed neither as frequencies nor as proportions but as effective numbers of components (ENC). The ENC terms are based on setting alpha equal to two. ENC/K represents the mean of the effective number of components of a single system over several points in time, for example, the mean effective number of political parties in a multiparty electoral system over a series of elections. The subscript t attached to ENC represents successive elections, starting with the first. Laakso and Tagepera's f is a temporal index. The term K represents total number of elections, so T represents the number of elections minus one.

The formula for f resembles that of the standard error, except that in the summational core, the mean of ENC is replaced by the preceding term (E_{t-1}) and the first term (t_0) is not summed for lack of such a preceding term. The major conceptual difference between standard error and f is that the latter is a time serial index. Fluctuation considers the time sequence of components; standard error does not (Laakso and Taagepera, 1979). For example, two series with the same average and standard error, but one of which increases smoothly and the other of which oscillates appreciably, will yield substantially different fluctuation index values. The latter series will have a much higher f. In terms of the purpose for which Laakso and Taagepera devised the index, f would be most sensitive to the sudden appearance or disappearance of a party with considerable electoral or parliamentary support, the fusion of two or more parties or separation of two factions into parties, by minor parties losing out to major parties, and by drastic changes in electoral laws.

A hypothetical example will illustrate the procedure of this index. Assume a series of five Democratic party gubernatorial primaries in the state of Alabama over a period of five elections. Assume further that the effective number of candidates in each election is 3, 6, 2, 4, 3, respectively, for an average of ENC/5 = 3.6. Five elections means $K = 5$ and $T = K - 1 = 4$. The difference between the effective number of candidates at the first election, $t_0 = 3$, and the number of candidates at the previous election does not exist and is disregarded, because the prior election is not considered in the series. The difference between second and first election is $t_1 - t_0 = 6 - 3 = 3$. The difference between third and second is $t_2 - t_1 = 2 - 6 = -4$. The sum of the four differences squared equals ($9 + 16 + 4 + 1$) = 30. The fluctuation equation for this series reads:

$$f = 1/3.6 \, [1/4 \, (30)]^{1/2}$$

$$f = .76$$

The polarity of f is toward inequality. It is sensitive to concentration, both because it relies on the effective number of components (the reciprocal of the Herfindahl-Hirschman index of concentration) and because it squares the differences between successive effective numbers of components. For the same reasons, fluctuation incorporates elements of both the combinatorics and deviations models.

The fluctuation index is a relative, no-null-components measure, because ENC values on which it is based are themselves based on the reciprocal of the Herfindahl-Hirschman measure. Fluctuation takes the number of time periods into account, however, through use of the term, $1/T$ (recall that $T = K - 1$), which in effect divides the sum of the squared differences by the number of differences taken. This step assures that the index scores do not depend on the number of time periods included in the analysis. This would give f some of the character of a relative inequality measure. It cannot include null components, however, because zero as the effective number of components for a given time period indicates that no distribution occurred. Recall also that the denominator of ENC (Herfindahl and Hirschman's HH) excludes null components in its computation, because it is a pure measure of concentration, concerned only with location of units and not with condition of components.

The effective number of components by definition must equal or exceed unity. The measure f achieves its minimal value, zero, when all effective numbers of components are equal, designating no fluctuation or total equality. It achieves its maximal value when the ENC values alternate between unity and the largest value attainable given the relevant constraints (see the earlier section in this chapter on ENC for a discussion of constraints).

The fluctuation index is not constructed in such a way as to be evaluable in terms of the effects of proportionate increases, constant additions, or transfers. It is applicable to nominally scaled components, in the same way as the Herfindahl-Hirschman index.

It is defined for all distributions and makes excellent use of information. Interpretability presents a problem, however, because f is not bounded between zero and unity. It reaches zero when all effective numbers of components are equal. However, f's maximum value is less than unity, indicating massive fluctuation. Laakso and Taagepera (1979) computed the f values for each of fifteen western European countries for all of its parliamentary elections during the period 1945-1976. Fluctuation index values for these nations varied between 0.05 (Sweden) and 0.67 (Greece). Swedish elections experienced virtually no fluctuation during this period, while Greek elections demonstrated considerable fluctuation. The index of fluctuation is not simple, largely because it is based on two different mathematical models, uses index values from another equation in its own equation, and measures inequality among components across time.

CONCLUSIONS

A combinatorics-based index value reflects the probability of randomly selecting a pair of identical units (for equality polarity) or different units (for inequality polarity) from a pool of units divided among two or more components. If an investigator prefers this particular type of probability interpretation, selecting one of the indexes discussed in this chapter makes good sense.

5

INDEXES BASED ON
THE ENTROPY MODEL

Entropy is an important concept in both physics (thermodynamics) (Carnap, 1977; Denbigh and Denbigh, 1985; Kittel, 1956 and 1958) and information engineering (Shannon and Weaver, 1949; Coleman, 1975; Theil, 1972). In physics, entropy refers to the degree of disorder, randomness, or unpredictability in a substance or physical system. In information theory, it measures the information content of a message, evaluated as to its uncertainty. Entropy in these two fields provides the mathematical model from which a family of six inequality measures is derived as well as the rationale for interpreting those measures.

THE ENTROPY LOGIC

Statisticians frequently use the "checkerboard problem" to explain entropy (Theil, 1972:1-3; Attneave; 1959:1-11). Suppose that a friend challenges you to guess which square of a checkerboard he/she has in mind. To get clues, you are allowed to ask your friend no more than twenty questions that can be answered by "yes" or "no." Table 5-1 presents a checkerboard with its sixty-four squares and the correct answer to the question. That is, your friend is thinking of square number twenty-three.

Six questions, properly asked, are always necessary and sufficient to identify the correct square in the case of a set of sixty-four such squares (assuming probability rather than luck as the controlling force). How does this work? Each question must reduce the alternatives that remain by half. The six correct questions, referring to the checkerboard in table 5-1, are:

1. Is it one of the 32 squares on the left half of the board (i. e., squares 1 - 32)? (Yes)

2. Is it one of the 16 squares in the upper half of the 32 remaining? (No)

3. Is it one of the 8 in the left half of the 16 remaining? (No)

4. Is it one of the 4 in the upper half of the 8 remaining? (No)

5. Is it one of the 2 in the left half of the 4 remaining? (Yes)

6. Is it the upper one of the 2 remaining? (Yes)

Table 5-1
The Checkerboard Game

1	9	17	25	33	41	49	57
2	10	18	26	34	42	50	58
3	11	19	27	35	43	51	59
4	12	20	28	36	44	52	60
5	13	21	29	37	45	53	61
6	14	22	30	38	46	54	62
7	15	*23	31	39	47	55	63
8	16	24	32	40	48	56	64

*chosen square

The parenthetical answers, referring to table 5-1, demonstrate the way progressively to reduce the area of uncertainty until the correct square is identified. Each question reduced the remaining alternatives by half. If the questions are always asked in the same way, any series of six yes and no answers will lead to a unique square on the board. If 1 indicates yes and 0 means no, 100011 represents the answers to the six questions that identified square twenty-three in table 5-1. Six binary digits, called bits, are needed to locate or represent one unique cell out of sixty-four.

The binary number system has many of the same general properties as the decimal system, with which we are more familiar, but it uses only two symbols, 0 and 1, instead of ten. In the decimal system, one digit is needed to specify one alternative out of 10^1 or 10, two to specify one alternative out of 10^2 or 100, three to specify one alternative out of 10^3 or 1000, and so forth. Similarly, in binary numbers a single digit specifies a choice out of two alternatives, two digits specify one of 2^2 or 4 alternatives, and six digits specify one of 2^6 or 64 alternatives, as in the checkerboard game (Attneave, 1959:2-4).

The bit is the unit most frequently used in measuring average information, uncertainty, and entropy, all of which have the same meaning. The uncertainty involved in identifying the correct square on the checkerboard is six bits; that is, six bits of information are necessary to select a particular square. The number of bits, in this case, is the power to which 2 must be raised to equal the number of alternatives; in other words, $m = 2^H$, where m is the number of equiprobable alternatives from which to make a choice, and H is the amount of uncertainty or information required, expressed in binary digits. In the case of our checkerboard, $64 = 2^6$. This is identical to specifying that the number of bits equals the logarithm, to base 2, of the number of alternatives. Therefore, $H = \log_2 m$. Because it is consistent with binary choice, log to base 2, rather than the natural log, is conventionally used in information theory (Attneave, 1959; Väyrynen, 1972; Galtung, 1967:214; Coleman, 1975:25).

Two examples will help to clarify this principle. Recall that $2^6 = 64$ and that $6 = H$ is the amount of uncertainty or entropy associated with 64 equally likely alternatives. For rolling a fair die, $H = \log_2 6 = 2.58$. For drawing a card from a full deck, $H = \log_2 52 = 5.70$. This means that two or three questions will determine which of six die faces has been rolled and that five or six questions will identify the card that has been selected. This is true, provided that the questions are asked in such a way as to reduce the remaining possibilities by fifty percent, so that "yes" and "no" are equally likely answers (Attneave, 1959:4).

The problem, however, is to measure uncertainty or entropy when the alternatives are not equally probable. Recall the equation for m equally likely alternatives: $H = \log_2 m$. Because all alternatives are equally likely, the probability p of any one of them equals 1/m, and conversely, m = 1/p. Therefore, $H = \log_2(1/p)$. This measure may be generalized to cases in which the alternatives are unequal. Let h_i stand for the information involved in the occurrence of a particular alternative i. Then we may write the analogous expression, $h_i = \log_2(1/p_i)$. Assume, for the sake of illustration, that a "trick" coin lands heads ninety percent of the time and tails the other ten percent. That is, p(heads) = .90, and p(tails) = .10. Using the equation, $h_i = \log_2(1/p_i)$, the entropy involved with flipping a head is h (heads) = $\log_2(1/.90) = \log_2 (1.11) = 0.15$ bits, and the entropy associated with getting a tail is h (tails) = $\log_2(1/.10) = \log_2 (10) = 3.32$ bits.

These results confirm our intuitive notions of information. Knowing that heads occurs nine times out of ten when we flip our trick coin, we are not surprised that a given flip lands heads. The information value of being told that the flip produced a head is not very interesting nor surprising. The information value of being informed that we flipped a tail with our trick coin is unusual, interesting, surprising. The occurrence of improbable events contains more information value than the occurrence of expected events.

To arrive at H, the entropy or uncertainty associated with a given flip, we take the average of all the h's that would occur over a large number of flips of the trick coin. Whenever heads is flipped, 0.15 will be added to the average; whenever a tail occurs, we add 3.32 to the average. Because we know that heads results ninety percent of the time and tails ten percent of the time, the average should be weighted accordingly. The average of the two alternatives is weighted with its probability of occurrence as follows:

$$H = 0.90 \ (0.15) + 0.10 \ (3.32) = 0.47 \text{ bits}$$

The result indicates that 0.47 bits of information is required to identify which side of the coin is flipped. It is no surprise, at this point, to realize that one bit is required correctly to identify which side of the coin lands up when an unbiased coin is flipped. Less uncertainty or entropy is associated with the flip of our biased coin than with an unbiased one.

This procedure can now be formalized and expressed in terms that apply to any number of unequally probable alternatives. For m alternatives each with its own p (probability weighting) and h (information value in bits), the appropriate weighted average results from the following expression:

$$H = p_1 h_1 + p_2 h_2 \ ... \ + p_i h_i \ ... \ + p_k h_k$$

$$H = \Sigma p_i h_i$$

The entropy of a system, in other words, equals the sum of the information values of all the individual alternatives, each weighted by its own probability of occurrence. Because $h = \log_2(1/p)$, we may restate the equation completely in terms of p:

$$H = \Sigma p_i \log_2(1/p_i)$$

In information engineering, this equation is called the Shannon-Weiner measure of information (Attneave, 1959:8). It is often written as $H = - \Sigma P_i \log_2 P_i$ because one rule for manipulating logarithms states that $\log_2(1/p) = - \log_2(p)$. Recall that the formula for H produces a weighted average of the information value associated with each of the alternatives. It is not actually a total, as the summation sign suggests. The H we have derived is actually Theil's (1967) index of absolute entropy and refers to the uncertainty, randomness, unpredictability, or average information of a set of alternatives. In this context, entropy translates into inequality or concentration.

The mathematical properties of entropy (Shannon and Weaver, 1949:48-53; Cowell, 1977: 55-56; Coleman, 1960:65-66 and 113-116; Hexter and Snow, 1970; Coleman, 1975; Kinchin, 1957) conform well to the assumptions of both information theory and inequality measurement:

1. As the probability increases, its weight, $h(P_i)$, must decrease, because events or alternatives of high probability are not especially interesting. Logarithms (especially to base 2) are particularly well adapted to this assumption.

2. If all the probabilities are equal, $P_i = 1/K$, then H is a monotonic increasing function of K. With equally likely events, greater choice or uncertainty exists with more alternatives.

3. The alternatives are statistically independent. The probability that alternative 1 occurs does not depend on whether or not alternative 2 occurs, and vice versa. So the probability that both alternative 1 and alternative 2 occur together is P_1P_2. Since it is necessary to sum the information values of messages concerning independent events, h must have the property $H(P_1P_2) = h(P_1) + h(P_2)$. The mathematical function that satisfies this assumption is $h = -\log_2 P$.

4. For a given number of alternatives K, the measure reaches a maximum ($\log_2 K$) when all alternatives are equally likely, in other words, all $P_i = 1/K$. The maximum increases by one bit with each doubling of K. The maximum value intuitively represents the most uncertain situation. When H reaches its maximum, concentration is at a minimum.

5. H equals zero, its minimum value, if and only if all the P_i but one are zero, and this one has the value of unity. In this situation, the outcome is absolutely certain, and concentration is at a maximum.

6. The uncertainty associated with a set of alternatives does not increase if impossible alternatives ($P_i = 0$) are added to the original set of alternatives.

H appears as the first of six entropy-based measures of inequality in table 5-2, all of which use average information value as the implicit comparative standard. In addition, table 5-3 contains a convenient summary of the relevant properties of all six entropy measures.

Table 5-2
Indexes Based on the Entropy Model

---

1. Theil's Entropy

$$H = -\sum P_i \log_2 P_i$$

2. Theil's Relative Entropy

$$H_{rel} = \frac{-\sum P_i \log_2 P_i}{\log_2 K}$$

3. Theil's Redundancy (also known as Ray, Taagepera, and Singer's concentration when $\alpha = 1$)

$$R = \log_2 K - (-\Sigma P_i \log_2 P_i)$$

4. Theil's Relative Redundancy

$$RR = \frac{\log_2 K - (-\Sigma P_i \log_2 P_2)}{\log_2 K}$$

5. MacRae's Negative Entropy (also known as Laakso and Taagepera's effective number of components)

$$NE = \text{antilog}_{10}(-\Sigma P_i \log_{10} P_i)$$

6. MacRae's Relative Negative Entropy

$$RNE = \frac{\text{antilog}_{10} (-\Sigma P_i \log_{10} P_i)}{K}$$

THEIL'S INDEX OF ENTROPY (H)

Theil's (1967 and 1969) index of entropy (H), as a measure of equality, is derived directly from the logic underlying entropy in statistical thermodynamics and information engineering, as discussed earlier in this chapter. The final product in that discussion of entropy logic was, in fact, Theil's H, so no further need exists to discuss the derivation of absolute entropy. The equation for Theil's H, a major component in each of the other five entropy-based measures, is:

$$H = -\Sigma P_i \log_2 P_i$$

The polarity of Theil's H is toward equality; a larger H value means greater equality. In other words, it is a measure of equality or an inverse measure of concentration. Because of its multiplicative summational core, it is sensitive to concentration; each proportional share is multiplied times a transform (log to base 2) of itself (Coulter, 1983b). However, all of the entropy indexes are less sensitive to concentration than the squared measures derived from the deviations model.

H is a measure of absolute inequality that reaches its maximum ($\log_2 K$) only when one of an infinite number of components possesses all units and attains its minimum (zero) when all are equal. It excludes all null components. Proportionate increases in each component do not affect the value of H. Adding a positive constant to each component raises the value of H, indicating increased entropy, that is, increased equality or decreased concentration. Transferring units from a larger to a smaller component is a change toward equalization of probabilities and produces an increase in the value of H (Shannon and Weaver, 1949:51-52). H violates the population symmetry axiom, because if two identical systems are combined, the H score for the combined system is larger than that of either of the two separate parts. Consequently, Theil's entropy does not conform to Lorenz dominance.

Theil's entropy assumes no order among components and is, therefore, a nominal-scale index. H is defined for all distributions and makes good use of information about the distribution. Interpretability can be a problem, because H's upper limit is $\log_2 K$, rather than unity. None of the entropy-based indexes can be considered simple to understand, because of the complexity of the underlying mathematical logic. Sen (1973:36), for example, complained that "the average of the logarithms of the reciprocals of income shares weighted by income shares is not a measure that is exactly overflowing with intuitive sense." However, the entropy model provides a direct means of interpreting an entropy-based index of inequality. The procedure is easy, provided the investigator has a calculator that computes logarithms to the base 2.

THEIL'S INDEX OF RELATIVE ENTROPY (H_{rel})

Theil's (1967) index of relative entropy or relative uncertainty (Wilcox, 1973) is expressed in the following formula:

$$H_{rel} = \frac{-\Sigma P_i \log_2 P_i}{\log_2 K}$$

The index of relative entropy is simply Theil's absolute entropy bounded by its maximum value for any given number of components, K (Bailey, 1985). Relative entropy "accepts as a datum the existence of those . . . (components) already in the system, and then reflects the extent to which the actual degree of concentration as measured by entropy deviates from the maximum attainable

Table 5-3: Primary Properties of Indexes Based on the Entropy Model

	Polarity	Type of index	Concentration	Comparative standard	Constant additions	Transfers	Scale invariance	Population symmetry	Lorenz dominance	Scale	Definition	Information use	Upper and lower limits	Simplicity
Theil's entropy (H)	equality	absolute, type A	yes	mean	increase	yes	yes	no	no	nominal	yes	fair	log K, 0	poor
Theil's relative entropy (H_{rel})	equality	relative, ANONC	yes	mean	increase	yes	yes	no	no	nominal	yes	fair	1, 0	poor
Theil's redundancy (R)	inequality	absolute, type A	yes	mean	decrease	yes	yes	no	no	nominal	yes	fair	log K, 0	poor
Theil's relative redundancy (RR)	inequality	relative, ANONC	yes	mean	decrease	yes	yes	no	no	nominal	yes	fair	1, 0	poor
MacRae's negative entropy (NE)	equality	absolute, type A	yes	mean	increase	yes	yes	no	no	nominal	yes	fair	K, 1	poor
MacRae's relative negative entropy (RNE)	equality	relative, ANONC	yes	mean	increase	yes	yes	no	no	nominal	yes	fair	1, 1/K	poor

given the number of . . . (components)" (Horowitz, 1970:469). The numerator excludes all null components, but the denominator takes them into account.

H_{rel} has an equality polarity and is sensitive to concentration. It is a measure of relative equality, because its upper and lower limits are insensitive to the number of components. It reaches its maximum, unity, when all components are equal and its minimum, zero, when one component has all. These limits indicate complete uncertainty and total certainty, respectively. H_{rel} includes any number of null components. It is scale invariant, but it violates the population symmetry criterion. Constant additions to all shares increase the score, indicating increased equality. Transfers from a larger to a smaller component yield larger values of H. Relative entropy does not conform to the Lorenz dominance principle.

Both this index and its absolute counterpart are designed to operate on nominally scaled components. It is defined for all distributions, makes good use of information, is easily interpretable, but is not simple to understand, although it is simple to compute.

THEIL'S INDEX OF REDUNDANCY (R)
The equation for Theil's (1967) redundancy is:

$$R = \log_2 K - (-\Sigma P_i \log_2 P_i)$$

It should be evident that the redundancy equation (a) subtracts absolute entropy from its own maximum value, and, therefore, (b) reverses its polarity to become a measure of inequality or concentration, rather than equality. Shannon and Weaver (1949:13) defined redundancy as the amount "of the message which is determined not by the free choice of the sender but rather by the accepted statistical rules governing the use of the symbols in question." It is the part of the communication that is unnecessary, because if it were missing, the message would still be basically complete or could be completed.

Consider a four-component system with the following proportional distribution: 0.40, 0.30, 0.20, and 0.10. For this system, H = 1.85, meaning that we require 1.85 (realistically one or two) bits of information to identify a given unit in its proper component. The largest number of proper guesses (that split the remaining alternatives by half) that we could possibly require for any distribution among four components is two. If we subtract the number of bits actually required for this particular distribution from the number required for the most unpredictable or random distribution among four components, we get R = 2 – 1.85 = .15. This represents the amount of information not necessary in order to locate a particular unit in its correct component in a four component system, because of the unequal nature of the distribution of units among components.

Because its upper and lower limits depend on the number of components, redundancy is a type B measure of absolute inequality or concentration (Taagepera and Ray, 1977). It reaches its maximum, $\log_2 K$, when one component has all, indicating complete concentration. It reaches its minimum, zero, when all shares are equal, indicating complete uniformity in the distribution. It excludes all null components. Proportionate increases of shares do not affect R. Constant additions, however, diminish the value of R, indicating more equality. Transferring units from a larger to smaller component produces the same effect. Redundancy assumes no order among components and is a nominal-scale index.

R is defined for all distributions and makes good use of information contained in the distribution. Because it varies from zero to $\log_2 K$, however, it is difficult to interpret.

THEIL'S INDEX OF RELATIVE REDUNDANCY (RR)

Theil's (1967) relative redundancy can be expressed in either of the following equations:

$$RR = \frac{\log_2 K - (-\sum P_i \log_2 P_i)}{\log_2 K}$$

$$RR = 1 - H_{rel}$$

Relative redundancy is simply redundancy divided by its maximum ($\log_2 K$). Bounding it in this way makes it easily interpretable as a percentage of the message or information that is unnecessary. Alternatively, it is the complement of relative entropy. It is a relative inequality index that is sensitive to concentration. RR's limits are insensitive to the number of components in the system. It achieves its maximum value of unity, indicating complete concentration, when one component possesses all units and its minimum value of zero, indicating complete equality, when all shares are equal. It includes any number of null components, in both numerator and denominator. RR is scale invariant. Both constant additions to components and a transfer from richer to poorer share reduce the value of RR, indicating increased equality. It assumes that components are nominally scaled.

Relative redundancy's purely technical properties are identical to those of redundancy, except that it is easier to interpret as a properly bounded measure, assuming that its mathematical model is understood.

MacRAE'S INDEX OF NEGATIVE ENTROPY (NE)

MacRae's index of negative entropy (Kesselman, 1966) is expressed in the following form:

$$NE = antilog_{10} (-\Sigma P_i log_{10} P_i)$$

Most researchers cite Kesselman (1966) as the originator of this index, although in his own work he claimed that MacRae suggested NE to him as an index of "multipartyism." He also cited work in the Spanish language by Soares and Noronha (1960) that used the index.

NE is the antilog of entropy and uses logarithms to base 10 rather than logarithms to base 2. Recall from chapter three that the antilog of a log is the original value from which the log was derived. Another way to express negative entropy is $NE = 10^H$, where H is entropy, the parenthetical element in the formula for NE. To illustrate, $log25 = 1.4$, because $10^{1.4} = 25$. Therefore, antilog1.4 = 25. Väyrynen (1972) criticized both Kesselman's and Coleman's (1960) use of natural logs, because their results cannot strictly be interpreted in terms of the logic of information theory. Log and antilog terms to base two, however, could just as easily be used.

MacRae (Kesselman, 1966:968) devised NE as "an index of multipartyism . . . to measure competition in national and local elections." But Kesselman (1966:969) pointed out that "the index does not measure conflict or competition but rather the convergence (or divergence) of votes among competing parties" or "the closeness of the electoral outcome in multiparty systems." MacRae's NE measures "how disagreement converges upon political parties or how equally disagreement is distributed" (Wildgen, 1971).

A hypothetical example will illustrate operation of this index equation. Assume a four-component system with the following distribution: 0.70, 0.10, 0.10, and 0.10. Using logs to base ten, this system's entropy is H = 0.4058. $Antilog_{10}(0.4058) = 2.56$. Or, $10^{0.4058} = 2.56$. In an empirical example, Kesselman (1966) found that negative entropy for French parliamentary and local elections in the late 1950s varied from 1.00 to 5.53. Similarly, Wildgen (1971) found that NE varied from 1.95 to 6.9 in fifteen European parliamentary elections during the early 1960s.

MacRae's NE has an equality polarity; the higher the value of NE, the greater the equality. It is moderately sensitive to concentration. Negative entropy is a measure of absolute equality; NE's scores depend on both the number and relative sizes of the shares. It reaches its upper limit, K, when all shares are tied. In a K-component system, when all components are tied, NE = K. Doubling the number of components among which units are equally distributed doubles the value of NE. In fact, when all $P_i = 1/K$, NE's maximum values are linearly related to K (Wildgen, 1971). It assumes its lower limit, zero, when one component has all units. It excludes consideration of null components because the $\log_{10}$ of zero is undefined. This index's characteristics contrast importantly and controversially with those of Rae's fractionalization (Rae and Taylor, 1970; Wildgen, 1971; Rae, 1971).

Negative entropy excludes null components but is especially sensitive to many small shares. This characteristic led Wildgen (1971) to call NE an "index of hyperfractionalization." NE's distinctive sensitivity makes it particularly useful for measuring inequality in highly fractionalized systems, especially when it is necessary to differentiate among hyperfractionalized systems.

NE is scale invariant and increases with both an addition of a constant to each share and a transfer from a larger to a poorer component. Such an increase stands for greater equality or uniformity. It assumes that components are nominal categories. Interpretability and simplicity are problems with this index. It does not make good use of all information, because it excludes null components, but it is defined for all distributions.

As indicated in table 5-2, negative entropy is identical to Laakso and Taagepera's (1979) effective number of components (chapter four), which is the hypothetical number of equal-size components that would produce the same amount of fractionalization of the system as have the actual components of unequal size. Laakso and Taagepera derived NE from their generalized expression for the effective number of components as follows:

$$ENC_\alpha = [\Sigma P_i{}^\alpha]^{1/(1-\alpha)}$$

As α tends toward unity, this equation yields negative entropy. NE has all the properties of the generalized expression discussed in chapter four. This identity between ENC_1 and NE allows an even more sophisticated interpretation of the NE values found for various multiparty systems by Kesselman and Wildgen, as reported earlier.

MacRAE'S INDEX OF RELATIVE NEGATIVE ENTROPY (RNE)
The formula for this index is:

$$RNE = \frac{antilog_{10} \ (-\Sigma P_i log_{10} P_i)}{K}$$

RNE is simply a standardized (but not properly bounded) version of negative entropy. Relative negative entropy does reach an upper limit of unity for complete concentration, but it reaches only 1/K for complete equality. Its values are independent of the number of components; it is a relative measure that includes any number of null components. Otherwise, relative negative entropy's conceptual and operational properties are identical to those of absolute negative entropy.

CONCLUSIONS

The interpretation that entropy provides to inequality indexes derived from it depends on whether the index in question is entropy, negative entropy, or redundancy, and whether it is absolute or relative. In any case, all of them are generally based on an interpretation involving the number of bits of information that is necessary to identify the location of any unit in its component. Sometimes the interpretation is straightforward, as with H and H_{rel}. Sometimes the interpretation refers to the total or average amount of information that is unnecessary, as in the case of R and RR. For NE, the interpretation reverts to the number of equal-sized components that would produce the same amount of uncertainty or fractionalization of the system; RNE simply standardizes that interpretation. If the analyst has reason to prefer this information/uncertainty interpretation in a specific inequality measurement problem, one or more of these six indexes would suffice, other things being equal.

6

INDEXES BASED ON THE SOCIAL WELFARE MODEL

Several of the most sophisticated, versatile, and complicated measures of inequality are based on the social welfare function. Because this model is heavily influenced by economic theory, inequality measures derived from it have special appeal to economists. Appropriately applied, however, these indexes offer excellent measurement opportunities to other social scientists, especially when the unit of distribution is income. This chapter presents a brief version of social welfare theory in order to elucidate the conceptual and mathematical bases of this family of indexes. The reader should consult appropriate sources (e.g., Boadway and Bruce, 1984; Sen, 1972) for more detail.

THE SOCIAL WELFARE MODEL
Welfare economics generally concerns "methods of obtaining a *social ordering* over alternative possible *states of the world*" (Boadway and Bruce, 1984:1). Social ordering permits comparison of alternatives and ranks each one as better than, worse than, or equally as good as every other. The ranking should be complete (all states ranked) and transitive (if A is better than B, and B is better than C, then A is better than C). The abstract term, "state of the world," usually refers to the state of the economic system, but could be applied to other social systems as well. Welfare economists are predominantly concerned with ranking alternative distributions of resources such as income.
Ranking alternative economic distributions according to their social welfare is a decidedly normative procedure, but economists generally limit their assumed value judgments to only two, both of which are based on the concept of economic efficiency. The first assumption, individualism, judges that the social ordering should be based on individual orderings of alternative social states. Second, the Pareto principle (Pareto, 1972) assumes that if state A is ranked higher than state B for one individual, and all other individuals rank A at least as high as B, then A should be ranked higher than B in the social ordering (Boadway and Bruce, 1984:2-3).

Welfare economists use these two essentially ethical principles in their utility-maximizing theory of consumer choice, which explains how the state of the world determines an individual's utility or welfare. This theory stipulates that individuals (or households) rank alternative states according to a set of preference orderings. Welfare economists then aggregate the preferences of different households using some form of the Pareto principle (Boadway and Bruce, 1984: 3-5).

Several important characteristics of the welfare model should be kept in mind. Dalton (1920:348) originally articulated the four important points, for any social scientist, that precede the theoretical and mathematical development of this model. Indexes derived from this model are designed to measure inequality in the distribution of income, not inequality in the distribution of any other units such as international power potential, linguistic ability, industrial concentration, or attitude consensus (Atkinson, 1970).

Welfare economists are not so much interested in the distribution of income per se, but rather in the distribution of social welfare, although they generally agree that income or wealth is the best surrogate for welfare. In other words, social welfare is a function of income. Both the total amount and distribution of income among individuals or households affects the total amount of welfare in the system. We return to this last point in more detail later.

RESTATEMENT OF BASIC THEORY

Explanation in social science is almost always based on comparison. In this case, ranking distributions, as a form of comparison, is the predominant reason for inequality measurement. Which of two income distributions is more unequal? Is the income distribution in a given jurisdiction more or less unequal after government implements a new tax policy? Introducing the concept of aggregate welfare and stressing ranking of systems enhance the importance of several axioms in inequality theory discussed in chapter two: transfers, population symmetry, proportionate increases, and Lorenz dominance. Elaboration and reinterpretation of these criteria are necessary.

Remember that we are now developing the conceptual and mathematical models from which measures of social welfare are derived. Social welfare is determined by the total amount of income, distribution of income, and number of people among which the income is distributed. Total income and number of income earners combine in the form of mean income. Thus distribution and mean income are the critical variables (Rae, 1981:112-121).

Transferring an amount from a richer to a poorer person should cause inequality to decline. If distribution A can be made to match distribution B through a series of transfers from rich to poor in A, then we can assume that distribution A was more unequal than distribution B. Social welfare cannot necessarily be assumed to be less in A than in B, however, because both aggregate income and number of people receiving income are important. Thus we cannot necessarily say that A was more unequal than B unless the population symmetry and scale invariance axioms are satisfied.

Sen's (1973:59) symmetry axiom for population states that "if r countries with the same population and identical income distributions are considered together, then the mean welfare of the whole must be equal to the mean welfare of each part." But if two countries have different populations (m and n), adding the first population n times to itself and the second population m times to itself produces two populations with identical populations and mean incomes. They can then be compared simply by using the transfers principle. This axiom allows ranking of populations of different sizes.

Often populations have different mean incomes. This situation is managed in social welfare theory by requiring that inequality indexes be scale invariant, that is, increasing everyone's income by the same proportion leaves measured inequality unchanged. In other words, the size of the pie to be divided has nothing to do with the degree of inequality. Inequality is determined by relative income shares, which remain unchanged when every share is multiplied by a positive constant. Dalton (1920), however, argued that proportionate increases should increase inequality.

Finally, the Lorenz dominance criterion states that any number of distributions whose Lorenz curves do not cross can be unambiguously ranked. If the Lorenz curve of distribution A lies everywhere to the northwest of the Lorenz curve of distribution B, then distribution A is less unequal than distribution B. Curve A is said to "dominate" curve B. The Lorenz curve is closely related to all three axioms. Accepting the Lorenz dominance criterion for two distributions with identical populations and means is the same as accepting the transfers principle. Accepting the Lorenz criterion for distributions with different populations and identical means is the same as accepting the population symmetry criterion. For distributions with different populations and means, accepting all three axioms is identical to assuming the Lorenz dominance criterion (Schwartz and Winship, 1979).

Satisfying the Lorenz criterion is sufficient for unambiguously ranking distributions whose Lorenz curves do not cross. When two distributions' Lorenz curves cross, which is frequently the case, the three axioms and the Lorenz dominance criterion provide only a partial ranking at best. Techniques to "uncross" Lorenz curves and provide a more complete ranking are discussed later in this chapter.

SPECIFIC ASSUMPTIONS ABOUT INDIVIDUAL AND SOCIAL WELFARE

The three key axioms and the Lorenz criterion form the basic theory of inequality. Economists have further developed social welfare theory with a series of definitions and assumptions about individual and social welfare. Schwartz and Winship (1979:16-18) and Cowell (1977:40-45) summarized these points succinctly, and this discussion closely follows their work. Individual welfare is defined as "one's sense of well-being, one's happiness or satisfaction with life, or one's potential (given one's resources) for obtaining these things" (Schwartz and Winship, 1979:16).

Social welfare theorists assume that income is an appropriate measure of individual welfare. Further, they assume that the relationship between income and welfare (the social welfare function) is the same for everyone, that is, all persons have the same utility functions (Boadway and Bruce, 1985: 282). They assume that increased income means increased welfare and that the effect of income on an individual's welfare is independent of other resources the person might possess. Finally, income determines an individual's welfare independent of the amount of income possessed by other individuals.

Similar definitions and assumptions exist for the concept social welfare, defined as society's view of the fairness or desirability of a given distribution. This view is usually based on individuals' income alone or the individuals' social welfare due to income alone. Social welfare increases as a function of increased income. If everyone's income increases, social welfare is increased. If we increase the income of one person, social welfare is increased. The social welfare function ranks distributions in the order of their means when all the persons in each system have equal income. Further, because individual welfare is additive, social welfare is the sum of individual welfares. The welfare gained by society (social welfare) from any person's increased welfare is independent of the welfare of all other individuals.

Preference of one distribution over another, when measured by an additive welfare function, has nothing to do with fairness. Preference is always defined in terms of maximizing the sum of individual welfare. Whatever raises the mean of a distribution (including doubling the income of the richest as well as doubling the income of the poorest) raises the mean of social welfare, but it may not increase fairness or serve justice. Greater social welfare is provided by equally dividing a million dollars among ten people than by equally dividing ten dollars among the same ten individuals.

Finally, social welfare theory assumes that the curve describing the relationship between individual income and individual welfare is strictly quasi-concave, that is, the social welfare function is characterized by diminishing marginal value of additions to income at higher income levels. Concavity involves weighting each person's income in such a way that the weight always decreases as income increases. Technically, a curve is concave if the line segment joining any two points on the curve lies entirely below the curve (and nowhere on it). A function is said to be quasi-concave if all points on an arc MN of the curve other than M and N are higher than or equal in height to the lower of the two points. A function that is concave toward the origin is one whose second derivative is negative. (Chiang, 1984:241-244, 387-391). Concavity resembles the rising contour of the left side of the Liberty Bell.

Generally, welfare economists prefer what is called a strict quasi-concavity assumption; that is, as the income level of one individual increases, given the income levels of the others, less and less relative importance is attributed to the income level of the individual who experiences the increase (Sen, 1972:53; Rae, 1981:82-103). A $1000 increase in income means less to a person who earns $75,000 per year than it does to someone who earns $20,000 per year. The concavity assumption means that, for a given aggregate income, greater equality of income distribution produces more social welfare than less equality of distribution. Welfare economists disagree, however, over how "equality preferring" or "inequality aversive" a social welfare function should be. We will return to this point later in the chapter.

THE SOCIAL WELFARE FUNCTION

Assume a fixed total income to be distributed among K persons. For any possible distribution, a number W indicates the desirability of or societal preference for that distribution. W is called the social welfare function and is expressed in the following notation:

$$W = W(x_1, x_2, ..., x_n) = W(X)$$

Atkinson (1970) used this simple social welfare function to develop measures of inequality and to prove the important Lorenz dominance theorem involving the relationships among W, the Lorenz curve, and the principle of transfers. Atkinson's theorem, of course, assumes that total social welfare is the sum of individual utilities, as expressed in the following conventional social welfare function:

$$W = \sum U_i(x_i)$$

where $U_i(x_i)$ represents the utility of income x for individual i. Because Atkinson also assumed symmetry and concavity for a fixed total income, W (social welfare) is maximized when all individual incomes are equal. Specifically, for two distributions, X and Y, with equal means, if the Lorenz curve of X is everywhere northwest of the Lorenz curve for Y, then W(X) > W(Y). Or if distribution X can be obtained from distribution Y by a series of transfers from richer to poorer individuals in Y, then W(X) > W(Y) (Atkinson, 1970).

Dasgupta, Sen, and Starrett (1973) subsequently developed the following Lorenz dominance theorem: one distribution X has a Lorenz curve everywhere inside of that of distribution Y with the same mean if, and only if, social welfare is higher in distribution X than in distribution Y. W(X) > W (Y), for all strictly quasi-concave social welfare functions. Dasgupta, Sen, and Starrett's theorem relaxed the assumptions of equal Ns and assumed only S-concavity (not strict concavity) but continued to assume equal means. Because this theorem will not rank distributions whose Lorenz curves intersect, its results still provide only a partial ordering of distributions from the Lorenz curve..

Four implications of these two theorems deserve emphasis. First, Lorenz curve dominance is equivalent to preference by all increasing S-concave (equality preferring) welfare functions. Second, for two distributions with equal means, distribution A will be preferred to distribution B if, and only if, the Lorenz curve for distribution A lies everywhere above the Lorenz curve for distribution B. Third, the Lorenz dominance result is restricted to distributions with equal means. It provides only a partial ordering of distributions, because Lorenz curves that cross cannot be ranked without a more specific welfare function. Fourth, the restriction to distributions with equal means implies that Lorenz dominance fails to capture any aspect of the trade-off between equality and efficiency (Okun, 1975).

Shorrocks (1983) more recently showed that, assuming strict quasi-concavity, distribution A is unambiguously more equally distributed than distribution B if its Lorenz curve is completely northwest of *and* its mean is higher than those of distribution B, because social welfare is higher. Even this method for ranking distributions is limited, however, because it requires satisfying both Lorenz dominance and higher mean income. We will return later to recent efforts to achieve a complete and unambiguous ranking of distributions, even when their ordinary Lorenz curves intersect.

The three measures in table 6-1 are based on the axioms of the social welfare function. Table 6-2 summarizes the performance characteristics of each of these three measures with respect to all the conceptual and technical criteria discussed in chapter two.

Table 6-1
Indexes Based on the Social Welfare Model

Atkinson's Index of Inequality (related to Champernown's and Jasso's measures, and to the coefficient of relative variation)

$$I_R = 1 - [\Sigma(Y_i / \overline{Y})^{1 - \alpha} (P_i)]^{1/(1 - \alpha)}$$

Kolm's Index of Inequality

$$I_L = (1/\alpha) \log [\Sigma_e \alpha * (\overline{x} - x_i)P_i)$$

Kaiser's Measure of Population Quality

$$b = 1 - \sqrt{1 - g^{2*}}$$

---

* g = geometric mean.

ATKINSON'S INDEX OF INEQUALITY (I_R)

The equation expressing Atkinson's (1970) index of inequality looks complicated at first. It is virtually impossible to express I_R in any simplified form that clearly demonstrates its definitional character. However, discussing two concepts—the equally distributed equivalent level of income and the inequality aversion parameter—in the context of the social welfare function, will help to clarify Atkinson's inequality formula:

$$I_R = 1 - [\Sigma(Y_i/\overline{Y})^{1 - \alpha} (P_i)]^{1/(1 - \alpha)}$$

The subscript R is used to designate Atkinson's measure. Kolm (1976a) argued that I_R makes a politically right-wing assumption because of its sensitivity to proportional and absolute increases, in contrast to Kolm's measure, which makes a left-wing assumption. These distinctions are treated below.

Atkinson began with Dalton's (1920) essentially conceptual definition of inequality as the ratio of the actual level of social welfare to that level which would be achieved if the income were equally distributed. He rejected it, however,

Table 6-2: Primary Properties of Indexes Based on the Social Welfare Model

	Polarity	Type of Index	Concentration	Comparative standard	Constant additions	Transfers	Scale invariance	Population symmetry	Lorenz dominance	Scale	Definition	Information use	Upper and lower limits	Simplicity
Atkinson's inequality (I_R)	inequality	relative, ANONC	yes	mean	increase	yes	yes	yes	yes	ordinal	yes	good	1, 0	poor
Kolm's inequality (I_L)	inequality	relative, ANONC	yes	mean	no change	yes	no (decreases)	no	no	ordinal	yes	good	>1, 0	poor
Kaiser's population quality (b)	inequality	relative, j-null-components	yes	mean	decrease	yes	yes	yes	yes	nominal	yes	good	1, 0	poor

because it requires measuring both social and individual welfare with a ratio scale and it is not invariant with respect to linear transformations. He substituted the idea of "equally distributed equivalent" levels of income (Y_{EDE}), defined as "the level of income per head which if equally distributed would give the same level of social welfare as the present distribution" (Atkinson, 1970:250). Behind the concept of equally distributed income equivalents is the fact that uniform distributions are ranked in the same order by their mean as by their social welfare. The mean income, therefore, can be used as an indicator of the level of welfare. Roughly, then, Atkinson's inequality measure can be defined as follows:

$$I_R = 1 - Y_{EDE}/\overline{Y}$$

or unity minus the ratio of the equally distributed equivalent income level to the mean of the actual distribution. The major advantage of using equally distributed income equivalents is that it assumes measurement of social welfare with only an ordinal scale. In other words, if we can rank societies in terms of their social welfare, we can rank them in terms of their inequality. Individual welfare must still be measured intervally (Schwartz and Winship, 1979). If this I_R declines, the distribution becomes more equal, that is, a higher level of equally distributed income is required (relative to the mean) to achieve the same level of social welfare as the actual distribution.

Atkinson offered the following interpretation of the numeric values of this conceptual definition. When $I_R = .30$, for example, it can be said that if incomes were equally distributed, only 70% of the existing total societal income is actually necessary to achieve the same level of social welfare. In other words, if society's total income were reduced by 30% and the remainder distributed equally, the result would produce the same amount of social welfare as before the reduction and redistribution.

The second important new concept is inequality aversiveness, designated by the parameter α in Atkinson's equation. It adds a normative dimension to the analysis because it allows the investigator to incorporate into the measurement a specified degree of dislike for inequality. As α increases from zero, more weight is attached to transfers at the lower end of the distribution and less weight is attached to transfers at the higher end. As α goes to infinity, only transfers at the bottom are taken into account (Atkinson, 1970). The larger the parameter, the greater the aversiveness to inequality.

Schwartz and Winship (1979) offered five related interpretations of the income inequality aversiveness parameter, three developed from welfare economics and two based on the need to rank distributions in terms of their inequality. First, α is the parameter of the individual welfare function that determines the rate at which social welfare increases in response to an increase in income. Second, the size of α indicates greater dislike of having people who are poor in comparison to the mean income. Larger α values will produce larger values of I_R, a signal that social welfare has decreased because of inequality in the distribution. For example, measuring income inequality in the United States using Kuznets' (1963) data with α set at 0.5, 1.0. 2.0, and 4.0 produced I_R values of 0.13, 0.24, 0.42, and 0.60. Measured inequality increases as the investigator's aversiveness to it increases.

The third social welfare interpretation of α involves the concept "transfer costs" (Atkinson, 1975:49), defined as the amount of a transfer that is lost in the process, possibly as an administrative cost for making the transfer. In other words, if we take ten dollars from a richer person to give to a poorer person, the transfer process itself might cost two dollars, so that only eight dollars might actually go to the recipient. This raises the question of how "efficient" a transfer must be before it is worthwhile. The investigator should make a decision about the proportion of a transfer that can be lost and still be a justifiable or desirable transfer. The answer determines the implied value of α from the formula $1/x = 2^{\alpha}$, where x is the proportion consumed by a transfer. If the analyst is willing to lose half the amount transferred, then α should be set at unity. If a 75% transfer cost is tolerable, α should be set at 2 (Atkinson, 1975:49). The formula $1/x = 2^{\alpha}$ can also be used to interpret a particular value of α.

Fourth, all non-intersecting Lorenz curves will rank the same regardless of the value of α, because I_R is consistent with the Lorenz criterion. Therefore, the value of α will affect only the comparisons among distributions whose Lorenz curves cross. Lower values of α weight the upper portion of the Lorenz curve more heavily; higher values weight the lower incomes more heavily. The analyst can set α in order to rank distributions with crossed Lorenz curves.

Fifth, setting α determines how strong the principle of diminishing transfers should be, because weighting different portions of the Lorenz curve differently is equivalent to deciding where transfers are most important. The marginal effect of a transfer to a recipient with income Y_i from a donor with income Y_j is proportional to:

$$Y_j^{-\alpha} - Y_i^{-\alpha} \quad \text{for } \alpha > 0,$$

$$\log(Y_i/Y_j) \quad \text{for } \alpha = 0,$$

$$Y_i^{-\alpha} - Y_j^{-\alpha} \quad \text{for } \alpha < 0.$$

Negative values of α violate the principle of transfers and the principle of diminishing transfers. Schwartz and Winship (1979), however, reformulated social welfare theory to include individual and social "decadence" as well as welfare, in order to accommodate negative values of α. Such a perspective is consistent with a strongly puritanical view in which income and wealth are seen as causing undesirable consequences for both individual and society. Money is seen as the root of all evil.

When $\alpha = -1$, I_R equals the coefficient of relative variation, and the effect of a transfer depends only on the absolute difference between donor and recipient, not on their positions in the distribution. This condition is called absolute transfer neutrality. The CRV has the largest (least negative) α that fails to satisfy the welfare economics assumption of diminishing transfers. When $\alpha < -1$, Atkinson's index is consistent with the principle of increasing transfers, stressing transfers from the rich rather than to the poor, presumably in order to reduce social decadence. When $\alpha > 0$, Atkinson's measure increasingly emphasizes transfers to the poor, as α increases, a situation of diminishing transfers.

If $\alpha = 0$, I_R equals Theil's entropy (chapter five), and the effect of a transfer depends only on the ratio of recipient's to donor's income, a property referred to as relative transfer neutrality. Values of $\alpha > 0$ are consistent with conventional welfare theory, and the resulting measures of inequality exemplify the principle of relative diminishing transfers. The effect of a transfer to one person from another person whose income is a fixed proportion higher (e. g., double) declines as the absolute level of their incomes increases. A $500 transfer from someone with $15,000 to someone with $7,500 reduces inequality more than a similar transfer from someone with $30,000 to someone with $15,000. Finally, when $-1 > \alpha < 0$, Atkinson's measure satisfies the principle of diminishing absolute transfers.

Setting α is a distinctly normative decision and should be based on the investigator's preference about the relative importance of different portions of the Lorenz curve in an inequality index or on how different types of transfers should affect the index value. Most analysts use several values of α (Bartels and Nijcamp, 1976; Sawyer, 1976; Williamson, 1977). Atkinson (1970) employed three values of the parameter: 1.0, 1.5, and 2.0. Schwartz and Winship (1979) argued that α should be between −0.5 and 2.5, probably between 0.5 and 0.75, but recommended that an investigator use several different values of inequality aversion.

The core of Atkinson's index is the ratio of a generalized mean to the standard arithmetic mean for a distribution. In the limit, when $\alpha \rightarrow 1$, I_R goes to $1 - (Y_g/Y_a)$, where Y_g equals the geometric mean and Y_a equals the arithmetic mean. The geometric mean is defined as the Kth root of the product of K terms in a series. For example, the fifth root of $(2 \times 4 \times 8 \times 16 \times 32) = 8$ (Mueller, Scheussler, and Costner, 1970:148-149). This is the procedure indicated whenever the symbol π appears in an inequality index.

For $\alpha > 0$, the geometric mean is always smaller than the arithmetic mean, except where income is equally distributed, in which case they will be equal and Atkinson's index will equal zero. Both Champernowne (1974) and

Jasso (1982) used unity minus the ratio of geometric to arithmetic means as a special case of Atkinson's index that arises when the marginal utility of income is inversely proportional to income. Champernowne also used the ratio of harmonic to arithmetic mean as a special case of Atkinson's measure when the marginal utility of income is inversely proportional to the square of income.

Atkinson's inequality equation is operationally more complicated than most, so a simple example will clarify what happens when this measure is applied to actual income data. I_R is applied to the following hypothetical income distribution using $\alpha = 2.00$. Assume ten income-earners with the following annual incomes: $5,000, $6,000, $7,000, $10,000, $10,500, $11,000, $11,500, $13,000, $18,000, and $19,000. Then arrange the individual incomes in ordinal classes as in table 6-3:

Atkinson's procedure weights the proportion of persons earning income in each ordinal class by the exponentiated proportion of income earned by each class and sums the products. It then exponentiates that sum. Choosing an alpha for Atkinson's index requires understanding a simple algebraic rule for simplifying negative exponents. A number taken to a negative exponent equals the reciprocal of that number to that positive exponent. For example, $\alpha^{-1} = 1/\alpha$, and $\alpha^{-3} = 1/\alpha^3$. Thus column four in table 6-3 is the reciprocal of column three. The exponent $1/(1 - \alpha)$, with $\alpha = 2$, equals -1.00. Consequently, we must compute the reciprocal of the sum of column six (1.78) to arrive at the index value (0.44).

The index value, $I_R = 0.44$, indicates that we could reach the same level of aggregate social welfare among these income earners with only about 56 percent of the present total income, if income were equally distributed. Or, alternatively, the gain from redistribution to bring about equality would be equivalent to raising total income by approximately 56 percent.

The polarity of Atkinson's I_R is toward inequality; increasing values of the index indicate increasing inequality. This measure is also sensitive to concentration because its core is exponentiated. Taagepera (1979) called it a measure of deprivation because of its sensitivity to poverty when $\alpha > 1$. It is a relative measure of inequality, because its values are independent of the number of income receivers. It is population symmetric, and it includes any number of null categories. It achieves its minimum value when all persons have equal income and its maximum when one person has all income. The rapidity with which I_R approaches its limits, however, depends on the value assigned to the inequality aversiveness parameter.

Table 6-3
Hypothetical Data and Computations
for Atkinson's Inequality Index ($\alpha = 2.0$)

1	2	3	4	5	6
i	f	$Y_i/\overline{Y}$	$(Y_i/\overline{Y})^{-1}$	P_i	$(Y_i/\overline{Y})^{-1}(P_i)$
$5,000 - $9,999	3	.162	6.2	.30	0.18
$10,000 - $14,999	5	.504	2.0	.50	1.00
$15,000 - $19,999	2	.333	3.0	.20	0.60
					1.78

$IR = 1 - .56 = 0.44$

Atkinson's measure is invariant with respect to multiplication of all shares by a positive constant. It declines, however, when a positive constant is added to each person's income. These two properties, in combination, provoked Kolm (1976a) to characterize Atkinson's index as a politically right-wing measure. He offered an incident from recent French history to illustrate this claim. Radical students and workers staged a massive general strike in France in 1968. Eventually, to settle the matter, French leaders agreed to a 13 percent increase in all payrolls. Thus laborers earning $100 per week received $13 more, while at the same time, executives earning $800 per week received $104 more. The students (who might have been lead by social science majors) were bitter rather than grateful, because they felt that the proportionate increase only exacerbated income inequality. I_R was the same before and after the increase, however, making it a rightist measure, in Kolm's perspective.

Its behavior with respect to transfers of income from a richer donor to a poorer recipient was discussed in detail earlier, in connection with setting the value of the inequality aversiveness parameter. Atkinson's index declines under this condition, but the nature of the decline depends on the value of the parameter. I_R assumes that individual welfare is measured on an interval scale and social welfare on an ordinal scale. In fact, income is measured on a ratio scale.

Atkinson's inequality index is defined for all possible distributions, makes full use of information, and is easily interpretable, because it is properly normed. In addition, it carries a straightforward social welfare interpretation discussed earlier. It is by no means a simple measure, but it offers extensive versatility and is well-grounded in economic theory.

KOLM'S INDEX OF INEQUALITY (I_L)

Kolm (1976a and 1976b) designed his index specifically in reaction to a certain characteristic of most inequality measures devised or used by economists. It assumes the following form:

$$I_L = (1/\alpha) \log [\Sigma_e \alpha \cdot (\overline{x} - x_i) (P_i)]$$

The subscript L attached to the I stands for "leftist." Kolm objected to the fact that most indexes based on social welfare theory, such as Atkinson's, are scale invariant with respect to proportional additions to each person's income and decline with equal additions to each person's income. He considered both of these properties to reflect politically right-wing assumptions, as indicated in the earlier discussion of Atkinson's index, and designed an index that makes leftist assumptions. Kolm's I_L, with inequality polarity, increases with a proportionate increase in the income of each person. In fact, when each person's income X_i is multiplied by the same number, I_L is multiplied by this number. When a positive constant is added to each person's income, I_L is unchanged. These major distinctions between Atkinson's I_R and Kolm's I_L underscore the importance of conceptual assumptions in selecting an index to measure a distribution.

Atkinson's I_R and Kolm's I_L have several other interesting similarities and differences (Kolm, 1976a). They are equal to each other if, and only if, their α parameters are zero. When the parameters tend to infinity, both measures classify distributions with equal means according to the minimum values. And when all incomes are equal, both measures equal zero regardless of the value of α (provided it is positive). In addition, Kolm's index contrasts with Atkinson's in terms of the Lorenz dominance criterion. Recall that with Atkinson's I_R as the measure, a distribution whose Lorenz curve is completely northwest of another distribution's is less unequal, regardless of their total or average incomes. The Kolm index, however, is lower if (a) the Lorenz curve is northwest, and (b) total or average income is not larger. Kolm's index resembles Atkinson's measure with respect to the other principles of inequality theory, including the principle of diminishing transfers and independence of number of components.

KAISER'S INDEX OF POPULATION QUALITY (b)

Kaiser (1968) devised his index as "a numerical measure which reflects the quality of the population apportionment in a legislative body," and concentrated his attention "only on the quality of apportionment in the particular, but important, sense of population equality" (298). Kaiser's measure assumes the following form:

$$b = 1 - \sqrt{1 - g^2}$$

where g is the geometric mean.

Although Kaiser's b is a relatively simple measure, the procedure from concept to final operational definition involves several steps and makes b look more complicated than it really is. It has no direct connection with social welfare in economic theory, but it is included in this section because it is based on the mathematical properties of the geometric mean, as is Atkinson's index.

The four steps involved in derivation of b are a) computing the population ratio, b) using a logarithmic transformation to correct for skewness, c) computing the geometric mean, and d) algebraic manipulation to arrive at the final equation (Kaiser, 1968). First, Kaiser wanted a measure of malapportionment that is independent of the average district population, so he divided each district population by the mean of all districts, creating population ratios. Subsequent analysis, therefore, produces a measure relative to the average. The ideal value for a population district is unity, because that indicates equality. The average population ratio is always unity.

A series of population ratios is also always positively skewed. The reason for this is straightforward. The minimum possible population ratio is zero. The maximum is K, the number of districts. For a system with K > 2, a much greater range of possible values exists for population ratios to deviate positively from their mean of unity than for their ratios to deviate negatively. Because the algebraic sum of deviations must be zero, the result is typically fewer, generally larger positive deviations, and generally smaller, negative deviations.

The second step in the procedure rids the population ratios of positive skew by taking the natural log of each value. Kaiser also argued that using the logs of population ratios substantively makes more sense than using raw population ratios. Assume, for illustration, a two-district system, one district of which has a population ratio of two, that is, a district with twice as large a population as ideal. What should be the population ratio of the other district that is equally malapportioned in the opposite direction? If the preferred answer is 0.50, implying that it is just as inequitable to have a district with half the ideal population as it is to have one with twice the ideal, then logs are appropriate. If the preferred answer is zero, implying that a district with no population is the same distance from the ideal (unity) as a district with twice the ideal population, then raw population ratios are appropriate. Kaiser preferred the logged values.

One technique for observing the sum of the logs of population ratios, without actually logging them, is to consider the product of the population ratios, because the log of a product is the sum of the logs (Spiegel, 1961:59-60). Assume a two-district system in which r_1 is the population ratio of the first district and r_2 is the population ratio of the second district. Then $r_2 = 2 - r_1$, because the sum of the two population ratios must equal two. The product, $r_1 r_2$, is largest when the two terms are equal at 1.0 (remember that they must sum to two). At that point, the product is 1.0. Other values of r_1 and r_2 produce smaller products; for example, $(0.8)(1.2) = 0.96$, $(0.4)(1.6) = 0.64$, and $(0)(2.0) = 0$. More generally, Kaiser recommended the product of the population ratios as a measure of the quality of apportionment, πr_i, where the symbol π indicates taking the product of the series of numbers.

However, this quantity is a function of the number of components or districts, K. The third step in the procedure takes the Kth root of the product (or raising it to the power of 1/K) in order to eliminate this undesirable characteristic. This step yields g, the following result:

$$g = (\pi r_i)^{1/K}$$

The quantity g is, in fact, the geometric mean, a measure of central tendency. When the sum of the numbers under consideration is a constant, however, the geometric mean serves as a measure of dispersion. As discussed earlier, the geometric mean is always smaller than or equal to the arithmetic mean. In this case, $g \leq 1.0$ and becomes increasingly smaller than 1.0 as malapportionment becomes worse.

Step four involves finding the relationship between the term g and Kaiser's measure b and rearranging the results to produce a computationally convenient equation. This step can be demonstrated with a simple example. In a two-component system, the geometric mean is the square root of the product of two population ratios:

$$g = \sqrt{(r_1)\,(r_2)}$$

This term may also be expressed as $g = r_1(2 - r_1)$, because the two population ratios must sum to 2.0. If r_1 is designated as the smaller of the two population ratios, $r_1 \leq 1.0$. It is also true that $b \leq 1.0$, so that we can say that $b = r_1$. Now, we can state that:

$$g = \sqrt{b(2 - b)}$$

This equation gives g as a function of b. We must find b as a function of g. Squaring both members of the equation gives $g^2 = b(2 - b)$, which may be rearranged to $b^2 - 2b + g^2 = 0$. Solving for b produces the final equation for Kaiser's b (taking the negative sign in solving the quadratic, because $b \leq 1.0$):

$$b = 1 - \sqrt{1 - g^2}$$

The polarity of Kaiser's b is toward equality. As apportionment grows more equal, b increases. It is sensitive to concentration because of its multiplicative nature and the squaring of the geometric mean. It is a measure of relative inequality, because it is independent of the number of components in the computation. Kaiser stipulated that a measure of malapportionment should indicate maximum inequality if any one district or component were completely unrepresented (i.e., were a null component), regardless of the distribution of population among the remaining districts. Thus, a predetermined number of null categories (1) constitutes maximal inequality, and b is a j-null-category type of inequality with $j = 1$ (Waldman, 1977). It has a maximum possible value of unity for total equality and an absolute minimum value of zero when any one district has zero population (the worst possible distribution).

A proportionate increase in the size of each district leaves the value of b unchanged; it is scale invariant. Adding a positive constant to each district increases the value of b, indicating greater equality of apportionment. A transfer of population from a larger to a smaller district increases b, reflecting greater equality. Kaiser's index assumes a nominal scale of measurement.

The measure is defined for all distributions and makes full use of information. Interpretability is excellent, because it varies from zero to unity. It is not a simple procedure.

GENERALIZED LORENZ DOMINANCE

The introduction to this chapter discusses the theory of welfare economics and two Lorenz dominance axioms. Until recently, using the ordinary Lorenz curve facilitated ranking distributions in terms of their inequality only if they did not intersect and had equal means, two rather serious limitations.

Shorrocks' (1983) theorem, however, provides a more powerful and versatile measure of ranking distributions. He proved that one income distribution A will have a generalized Lorenz curve (GLC) everywhere northwest of that of another distribution B (possibly with a different mean) if, and only if, social welfare is higher under A than B for all S-concave increasing social welfare functions.

The reader might want to refer to the relevant portions of chapters one and two that discuss the ordinary Lorenz curve (OLC). Figure 6-1 presents a generalized Lorenz curve based on the data in table 6-4.

Table 6-4
Generalized Lorenz Distribution

1	2	3	4	5
i	N_i	$C(N_i)$ cumulative percent of	$C_1(N_i)$ cumulative percent of	$(N/K)C_1(N_i)$ mean* times cumulative per-
person	income	people	income	cent of income
1	$ 15	.25	.075	3.75
2	25	.50	.200	10.00
3	50	.75	.450	22.50
4	110	1.00	1.000	50.00

* mean = N/K = \$50.

An OLC plots the cumulative proportion of people on the horizontal axis and the cumulative proportion of income on the vertical axis. The GLC also plots the cumulative proportion of people on the horizontal axis, but it plots dollars of income on the vertical axis. The mean of the income distribution is multiplied times each of the OLC's cumulative percentages of income to form a new series that becomes the vertical axis. The generalized Lorenz distribution data in figure 6-1 provide an example of the computations. The overall mean of the distribution (N/K = \$50) is multiplied times each of the "cumulative % of income" entries in column four. These products are recorded in column five and comprise the vertical axis in figure 6-1. The ordinate endpoint equals mean income, \$50 in the case of figure 6-1.

Shorrocks' innovative work improves inequality measurement in five ways. First, it enables ranking distributions with different means. Second, the GLC allows ranking distributions in terms of social welfare in a way that is sensitive to both equality and efficiency. The GLC captures the "tradeoff" between equality and efficiency (Okun, 1975), that is, both the preference for equality and the preference for higher incomes as dimensions of aggregate social welfare. Third, the height of the GLC reflects economic efficiency, because the ordinate endpoint equals mean income. Fourth, the curvature of the GLC (concave from above) reflects inequality. Fifth, the Shorrocks theorem permits social welfare inferences to be drawn in the same manner as OLCs, but with a possible advantage. Intersecting OLCs can be "uncrossed" if they have sufficiently large differences in mean income (Bishop and Thistle, 1987; Formby, 1987). Several economists (Beach and Davidson, 1983; Beach and Richmond, 1985) took this procedure one step farther by devising statistical significance tests for the differences between two GLCs. Significance testing provides an additional means by which to rank GLCs.

Figure 6-1
Generalized Lorenz Dominance*

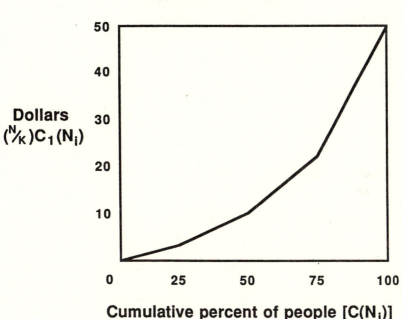

Dollars
$(^N\!/_k)C_1(N_i)$

Cumulative percent of people $[C(N_i)]$

*Based on data in Table 6-4

CONCLUSIONS

Atkinson's I_R and Kolm's I_L rest firmly on a social welfare interpretation, although they contrast significantly with respect to several important criteria. An index based on a conventional social welfare function can be interpreted as expressing the diminishing marginal utility of income for individual and social welfare. Increases in the incomes of higher-income recipients contribute less to social welfare than increases at lower-income levels. Kaiser's b can be interpreted in terms of the fact that the arithmetic mean is always larger than or equal to the geometric mean, also a mathematical feature of the Atkinson index. The larger the difference, the greater the inequality.

7

INTERGROUP INDEXES: INEQUALITY, SEGREGATION, AND INTERACTION

This chapter discusses intergroup indexes of inequality, segregation, and interaction, which comprise a conceptually different branch of inequality measurement, as chapter two indicated. Intergroup indexes measure inequality in the distribution of (a) members of two social groups among (b) geographical subareas of a jurisdiction or ordinal classes of some quantity such as income, education, or occupational prestige. Many of the conceptual and technical criteria discussed in chapter two also apply to both types of intergroup indexes in basically the same way that they apply to intragroup inequality. Some assume a slightly different meaning. Several additional criteria unique to intergroup measurement must be added.

CONCEPTUAL DEVELOPMENT

Intergroup index development began with an important publication by Jahn, Schmidt, and Schrag (1947), who fired the first shot in what became a ten-year "index war" (Peach, 1975:3). Advances in measuring intergroup inequality resulted from social scientists' professional concern about race relations in America. Today, the social groups between which inequality is measured include race, gender, and ethnicity. In this chapter, I use race in illustrative examples and in the statistical notation of intergroup equations wherever possible.

Indexes of racial segregation focus primarily on residential and school segregation. Residential segregation, a complicated, multidimensional concept, refers to "considerations of spatial pattern, unevenness of distribution, relative size of the segregated group, and homogeneity of sub-areas, among others" (Duncan and Duncan, 1955:217) with respect to peoples' homes in a jurisdiction such as a city. Investigators have sought to measure three distinct and important dimensions of residential segregation—racial unevenness and concentration among subareas and racial isolation. A particularly important conceptual and mensurative issue concerns whether an index is sensitive to composition as well

135

as to unevenness among subareas. Composition refers to the overall proportion of the minority group in question. We deal with that issue in detail later.

School segregation refers to "differential distribution of students to schools by race regardless of the overall racial proportions in the system concerned" (James and Taeuber, 1985:15). The resulting racial pattern of school attendance differs from either a random or an even distribution. We will also deal with this important conceptual and operational distinction in detail later.

Both residential and school segregation primarily involve differentiation, diversity, or dissimilarity in the spatial distribution of black and white individuals among neighborhoods or schools. In contrast, socioeconomic inequality in the distribution of units of some valued resource to black and white groups focuses on the distribution of income, occupational prestige, or educational attainment between blacks and whites. Operationally, this means examining inequality in the distribution of black and white persons among the ordered classes of a scale measuring income, occupation, or education.

CONFORMITY TO INEQUALITY THEORY

Basically, intergroup measures loosely conform to some of the same theoretical criteria and in approximately the same way as intragroup inequality measures. These criteria were discussed extensively in chapter two, so they will be mentioned at this point only if they apply differently to intergroup indexes. Several criteria unique to intergroup measures will also be introduced.

Unfortunately, social scientists only recently began to analyze intergroup measures in terms of principles of inequality theory, and knowledge in this area remains relatively restricted. We will consider specialized criteria for segregation and interaction measures separately from inequality measures, because they involve different assumptions. Because interpretation of several indexes of both types is intimately related to the principles of the Lorenz curve, we will first introduce the "segregation curve."

Segregation Curve

Duncan and Duncan (1955; see also Taeuber and Taeuber, 1965:202-204, and James and Taeuber, 1985) first adapted the Lorenz curve for graphically representing ecological segregation and called it the segregation curve. It applies equally well to residential and school segregation. Constructing a segregation curve is relatively easy. First, arrange all the geographical subareas (e.g., neighborhoods or schools) in order from highest to lowest on the basis of percentage black or minority. Second, compute two cumulative relative frequency distributions for the array, one for the per cent black living in each subarea and the other for the per cent white living in each subarea. Third, plot these two cumulative percentage distributions in the form of a Lorenz curve. Place cumulative per cent black along the horizontal axis and cumulative per cent white along the vertical axis. The segregation curve in figure 7-1 uses the hypothetical data contained in table 7-1, which illustrates computation of several intergroup measures.

Table 7-1
Hypothetical Example for
Constructing a Segregation Curve and
Computing Several Intergroup Measures

1	2	3	4	5	6	7	8	9
						Cumulative		Black %
		Frequency			Percent		Percent	of sub-
Subarea	Blacks	Whites	Total	Black	White	Black	White	area
A	120	40	160	.60	.05	.60	.05	.75
B	60	320	380	.30	.40	.90	.45	.16
C	20	240	260	.10	.30	1.00	.75	.08
D	0	200	200	.00	.25	1.00	1.00	.00
Total	200	800	1000	1.00	1.00			

If the composition and distribution of whites and blacks are completely even, then every subarea has an equal percentage black, each subarea proportion black equals the overall proportion black, every subarea has the same rank-order (all are tied), and the cumulative percentages of black and white will be equal. In this case, the segregation curve will coincide with the Lorenz diagonal in figure 7-1, indicating zero segregation. In contrast, if the distribution of whites and blacks is totally uneven (i. e., each subarea is either all black or all white), the segregation curve follows the horizontal axis from zero to 1.0 and then rises up the vertical axis from zero to 1.0, indicating complete segregation. For black-white distributions intermediate between these two extremes, the more the segregation curve sags beneath the diagonal, the greater the level of segregation. Some segregation indexes can be interpreted as alternative ways to measure the deviation of the curve from the diagonal. Their relationship to the segregation curve also demonstrates their relationships to each other (Duncan and Duncan, 1955).

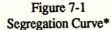

Figure 7-1
Segregation Curve*

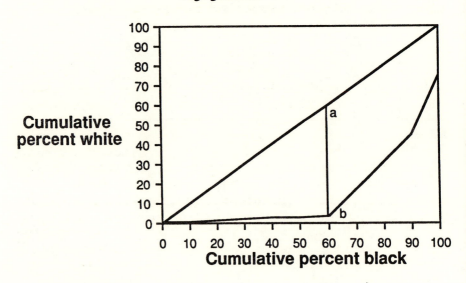

*Based on data in columns 7 and 8 of Table 7-1

Intergroup Segregation Indexes
    James and Taeuber (1985:11) pioneered the effort to "translate inequality measurement theory into terms suitable for segregation measurement." Three new conceptual criteria, with analogs in intragroup inequality theory, require definition: size invariance, composition invariance, and the Lorenz criterion. The organizational equivalence criterion is unique to segregation indexes. The transfers principle requires redefinition. Other familiar conceptual and operational criteria apply in a straightforward fashion.
    The principle of organizational equivalence has no analog in the theory of intragroup inequality measurement (James and Taeuber, 1985). It states that a segregation measure should permit comparison of jurisdictions (such as school districts) that differ in the number of subareas (such as schools) and the number of people (such as students). For example, consider a school district with two schools that have identical racial composition and number of students. The two schools are equivalent with respect to the distribution of students by race across all schools in the district, so both schools contribute equally to the measured level of segregation. According to the principle of organizational equivalence, the measured level of segregation would remain identical if these two schools are

combined into one school. If we relax the requirement that the schools be of equal size, the principle states that degree of segregation is unchanged if one school is divided into several small ones with identical racial composition or if several schools with the same racial composition are combined into a single school.

The organizational equivalence principle applies similar logic to entire school districts. If two districts are identical in all respects (including identical racial composition of schools), this principle requires that combining the two districts into a single district does not change the measured level of segregation. This principle allows combining identical schools into single schools that are twice as large as the corresponding schools in the original systems. The new district would be identical to each of the original districts in racial distribution among schools, except that each school contains twice as many students.

The principle of size invariance, whose analog in intragroup inequality measurement is population symmetry, states that the measured segregation level is unchanged if the numbers of black and white students are multiplied by a positive constant (James and Taeuber, 1985). This principle enables comparison of segregation in one district to segregation in a second district with r times as many students as the first, if the number of students of each race in each school in the second district is divided by r.

The transfers principle requires that measured segregation decline if black students move from schools of higher to lower black proportion or if white students move in the opposite direction (James and Taeuber, 1985). If the level of measured segregation of district A can be reduced to that of district B by transferring black students from schools of higher to lower proportion black, then district A is judged to be more segregated than district B.

The controversial principle of composition invariance, whose analog in intragroup measures is scale invariance, requires that proportional changes in the number of students of a given race enrolled in each school do not change the overall measured level of segregation (Jahn, Schmidt, and Schrag, 1947). James and Taeuber (1985) supported this principle because they understood segregation to refer to differential distribution of students to schools by race, regardless of the overall racial composition in the school district. Thus, following their definition, segregation measures must be insensitive to racial composition. Not all social scientists agree with this principle (cf., Coleman, Hoffer, and Kilgore, 1982). According to its supporters, nonetheless, conformity to the principle is important for a reason unrelated to the segregation curve: no segregation index value should have a built-in mathematical relationship with any variables that are studied as correlates of segregation (Jahn, Schmidt, and Schrag, 1947; Morgan and Norbury, 1981).

If the composition invariance principle is satisfied, however, doubling the number of black students in each school of a district would leave a measure of segregation unchanged. It would drastically change the degree of interracial exposure, however, a point to which we return later. Accepting the composition principle is equivalent to requiring that the segregation curve remain unchanged as the district's percentage of blacks changes.

The Lorenz principle incorporates the transfers, organizational equivalence, size invariance, and composition invariance principles through comparison of segregation curves (James and Taeuber, 1985). Any measure that conforms to all four of these principles also conforms to the Lorenz dominance criterion. According to this principle, if the segregation index value is lower for district A than for district B, then district A's segregation curve lies everywhere northwest of district B's segregation curve.

Segregation measures that satisfy the Lorenz criterion will rank pairs of districts identically, provided their segregation curves do not intersect. When two segregation curves do intersect, unambiguous segregation ranking of two school districts is impossible.

Intergroup Inequality Measures

One new conceptual criterion, directionality, must be defined, and one criterion discussed in chapter two must be redefined for application to intergroup inequality measures (Fossett and South, 1983). The other conceptual criteria apply in the usual fashion. First, the principle of directionality concerns the implied feature of inequality that differences between two groups may favor one group or the other. A directional measure has some value that represents complete equality between the groups, with values above this point indicating an advantage for one group and values below this point indicating an advantage for the other group. If an index does not have directionality, it cannot indicate which of two groups is relatively better off.

Intergroup indexes should also be properly bounded not only for interpretability but also for additional reasons. The logical range of a properly bounded measure's values is a symmetrical distribution around zero with an upper limit of positive unity and a lower limit of negative unity. Thus if two groups exchanged income distributions, the sign of the index would change, but the value would remain the same. Satisfying this criterion produces three desirable properties of intergroup measures. First, the sign of the index reveals the direction of advantage. Second, the value of the measure indicates how far the actual inequality is from its maximum. A score of + 0.5, for example, indicates that one group enjoys half the maximum possible advantage it could enjoy. Third, comparing values above and below the point of equality permits determining whether they are equally unequal (Fossett and South, 1983).

Equations for the six intergroup indexes discussed in this chapter appear in table 7-2. The statistical notation used in these indexes has been standardized only to the extent of indicating white (W) and black (B) groups as prime examples. The separate discussion of each index explains the notation in detail. The segregation indexes refer to distribution of the populations of two social groups (e.g., blacks and whites) among numerous geographical subareas (e.g., neighborhoods, census tracts, city blocks, schools) of a larger jurisdiction (e.g., city, school district, metropolitan area) that contains the total population. Interaction indexes measure probability of contact between the populations of two groups primarily in terms of one group's isolation from or exposure to the other. Inequality indexes compare the distribution of two social groups among ordinally or intervally ranked classes in a total population.

To facilitate quick assessment of any of these intergroup measures, table 7-3 presents a summary of their conceptual and technical characteristics. In addition to explaining the equations, the remainder of this chapter discusses the indexes' characteristics in detail.

Table 7-2
Intergroup Indexes

1. Duncan and Duncan's Index of Dissimilarity

$$ID = 1/2 \, \Sigma \, | \, W_i - B_i |$$

2. Lieberson's Index of Diversity

$$A_b = 1 - \Sigma P_i Q_i$$

3. Bell's Indexes of Interaction Probability

a) $_bP^*_w = \Sigma \, (b_i/B) \, (w_i/t_i)$

b) $_bP^*_b = \Sigma \, (b_i/B) \, (b_i/t_i)$

c) $_wP^*_w = \Sigma \, (w_i/W) \, (w_i/t_i)$

d) $_wP^*_b + \Sigma \, (w_i/W) \, (b_i/t_i)$

4. Correlation Ratio Squared

$$eta^2 = \frac{\Sigma t_i b_i^2}{TWB} - \frac{B}{W}$$

5. Lieberson's Index of Net Difference

$$ND_{wb} = \sum_{i=2}^{I} W_i \left(\sum_{j=1}^{i-1} B_j\right) - \sum_{i=2}^{I} B_i \left(\sum_{j=1}^{i-1} W_j\right)$$

6. Fossett and South's Index of Average Relative Advantage

$$ARA = \sum_{i=1}^{I} \sum_{j=1}^{J} (X * W_i * B_j)$$

DUNCAN AND DUNCAN'S INDEX OF DISSIMILARITY (ID)

Duncan and Duncan (1955) unquestionably won the index war with their index of dissimilarity. So many sociologists have used it so often, for so many years of decennial census data, describing so many American cities and school systems, that abandoning ID for even a much better measure would involve substantial losses in continuity and comparability. Even Lieberson (1981:61), originator and champion of several competing indexes, admitted that "the index of dissimilarity (ID) has been the most widely used measure of residential segregation in sociology for nearly 25 years." The ID equation assumes the following form:

$$ID = 1/2 \; \Sigma \, | \, W_i - B_i \, |$$

where W_i =   proportion of whites in the subarea, and
        B_i =   proportion of blacks in the subarea

Calling it the "non-white section index," Jahn, Schmidt, and Schrag (1947) actually originated the index of dissimilarity. The Duncans' (1955) subsequent methodological analysis of several segregation measures, however, was so insightful and influential that their name for the index, dissimilarity, became permanent, and the index became permanently identified with them. Their

Table 7-3: Primary Properties of Intergroup Indexes

	Polarity	Type of Index	Mathematical model	Concentration	Comparative standard	Constant additions	Transfers	Composition invariance	Organizational equivalence	Size invariance	Lorenz dominance	Directionality	Scale	Definition	Information use	Upper and lower limits	Simplicity
Duncan and Duncan's dissimilarity (ID)	inequality	relative, ANONC	deviations	no	mean	decrease	no	yes	yes	yes	no	no	nominal	yes	good	0, 1	good
Lieberson's diversity (A_w)	inequality	relative, ANONC	combin-atorics	yes	all inter-group pairs	increase	yes	yes	yes	yes	yes	no	nominal	yes	good	0, 1	good
Bell's Interaction (P*)	depends	relative, ANONC	combin-atorics	yes	all pairs	appropriate change	yes	no	yes	yes	no	no	nominal	yes	good	1, 0	good
Correlation ratio squared (eta²)	inequality	relative, ANONC	combin-atorics	yes	all pairs	decrease	yes	no	yes	yes	no	no	nominal	yes	good	1, 0	fair
Lieberson's net difference (ND)	inequality	relative, ANONC	combin-atorics	yes	cumula-tive pairs	no	no	yes	N/A	yes	no	yes	ordinal	yes	good	+1, -1	poor
Fossett and South's average rel. adv. (ARA)	inequality	relative, ANONC	combin-atorics	yes	cumula-tive pairs	decrease	no	yes	N/A	yes	no	yes	interval	yes	good	+1, -1	poor

seminal paper analyzed five other indexes, but most of them became casualties in the index war and virtually disappeared.

Interpreting the equation is simple. It involves computing one-half the sum of the absolute differences between two proportions—the proportion of the area's blacks who live in each subarea and the proportion of the area's whites who live in each sub-area. The sum of the positive differences equals the sum of the negative differences, so their absolute sum must be divided by two; otherwise, differences would be double-counted. The conventional interpretation of an ID value is that it indicates the proportion in one group that must be moved in order to achieve an even distribution, defined as no difference in proportions for the two groups in each subarea and in the jurisdiction as a whole (Fossett and South, 1983; Sakoda, 1981; Lieberson, 1981).

Duncan and Duncan (1955) were the first to demonstrate a geometric interpretation of ID through its relationship with the segregation curve. ID equals the maximum vertical distance between the segregation curve and the diagonal, represented by the dotted line ab in figure 7-1. The reader might also want to refer to the discussion of the Schutz index in chapter three, because it is algebraically and geometrically similar to ID. Because ID involves two groups, however, an example of its calculation aids understanding.

Table 7-1 is a computational table based on hypothetical data for the distribution of one thousand black and white residents among four neighborhoods of a city. Columns one, two, and three contain the number of black, white, and all residents, respectively, in each subarea. Columns four and five contain the proportions of black and white in each subarea. Following the equation, ID = 1/2 $|0.60 - 0.05| + |0.30 - 0.40| + |0.10 - 0.30| + |0 - 0.25| = 0.55$. Fifty-five percent of either group would have to be relocated in order to achieve an even distribution of black and white residents, in other words, to desegregate totally.

A brief word about ID's denominator is in order. The sum of the absolute differences between black and white proportions is divided by two, because positive differences equal negative differences, and either indicates the proportion of residents who must be moved to reduce segregation to zero. The denominator two (operationalized by multiplying the numerator by one-half) is an accurate approximation for systems with a large number of subareas but is technically incorrect. The correct denominator is $2(1 - minW_i)$, where $minW_i$ is the smallest W_i. It can also be shown that corrected ID is one form of Coulter's generalized index of inequity (chapter eight) with its exponent set at unity.

ID's polarity is toward inequality; the greater an ID value, the more spatially segregated or racially unequal a jurisdiction is. It captures inequality but not concentration in the distribution because it sums absolute proportional differences. Based on a deviations model, ID uses total proportion black in the jurisdiction as the comparative standard against which to assess proportion black in each subarea. This comparative standard of evenness addresses whether each subarea has the same proportion black as the city as a whole (Taeuber and Taeuber, 1965). And "the basic notion of unevenness is symmetrical; if Negroes are segregated from whites, whites are equally segregated from Negroes" (Taeuber and Taeuber, 1965:243). Cortese, Falk, and Cohen (1976) argued that evenness is a less useful comparative standard than randomness, which they accepted as a more appropriate representation of the opposite of segregation.

The index of dissimilarity satisfies the principle of transfers under only one condition (James and Taeuber, 1985: Fossett and South, 1983; White, 1983). It does decrease if a black person from a subarea with a black proportion greater than that of the whole jurisdiction is exchanged with a white person from a subarea with a black proportion less than the overall black percentage. And, exchanges in the opposite direction will increase values of ID. However, these changes in the values of ID result only if the transfer occurs between two subareas both of which are above (or below) the overall proportion black. All exchanges that move the segregation curve closer to the diagonal do not necessarily reduce the values of ID (Winship, 1978). If one is interested in the principle of diminishing transfers, ID also fails, because changes produced by transferring people is the same for subareas near the jurisdictional proportion as for subareas that differ extremely from that proportion.

Many social scientists have used ID to measure segregation because they understood that the Duncans' measure is composition invariant, indicating that values of ID are insensitive to the proportion black in the total population (Taeuber *et al.*, 1981; James and Taeuber, 1985). Others (e.g., Cortese, Falk, and Cohen, 1976) criticized ID, arguing that under certain conditions it is influenced by the overall proportion of the black population. Still others showed that any such relationship between ID and per cent black is kept at a bare minimum or occurs only under rare circumstances (Lieberson and Carter, 1982). Taeuber and Taeuber (1965:218), for example, correlated ID values and per cent black for one hundred and eighty-eight cities and found no association.

ID satisfactorily meets the standards of organizational equivalence and size invariance. It permits comparison of jurisdictions with different numbers of subareas and population sizes, and it is unchanged if the number of persons of each race is multiplied by a positive constant (James and Taeuber, 1985).

Satisfying the principles of organizational equivalence, size invariance, composition invariance, and transfers means that if the segregation curve of jurisdiction A is everywhere above and nowhere below that of jurisdiction B, the former is characterized by less segregation. Because ID fails to satisfy the transfers criterion fully, it does not conform to the Lorenz criterion.

The dissimilarity index declines with addition of a positive constant to the frequency of each social group (e.g., black and white) in each subarea. This behavior indicates a decline in the amount of measured segregation.

Among technical criteria, ID is simple to compute, defined for all distributions, and uses distributional information well. It is properly bounded, varying from zero to unity and yielding an easy interpretation. An ID value equals zero when the black population is distributed evenly, that is, when all subareas have the same racial composition as the city and the city is maximally integrated. It equals unity when all subareas are racially homogeneous, that is when no mixed subareas exist, and the jurisdiction is maximally segregated.

ID assumes that the subareas are nominal categories and, consequently, should not be used on ordinal classes such as income or education (Lieberson, 1981; Fossett, Galle, and Kelly, 1986). It is properly an index of nominal heterogeneity, not ranked inequality, because it measures the number of people of one race who would have to be redistributed in order make each subarea's racial ratio equal to that of the total population of the jurisdiction (Fossett and South, 1983; Blau, 1977:77, 118).

Several additional characteristics potentially reduce the value of Duncan and Duncan's index of dissimilarity. Cortese, Falk, and Cohen (1976) showed not only that the expected value of the index is greater than zero, but also that it bears an inverse relationship with both the size of the subarea on which the computation is based and the proportion of the population belonging to the minority. In addition, White (1983) complained that ID fails to take into account the spatial proximity of subareas. ID ignores the difference between ten relatively homogeneous subareas that are widely scattered throughout a jurisdiction and ten such subareas that are contiguous.

Considering all of ID's deficiencies, it would be reasonable to assume that the index of dissimilarity lacks respect among social scientists. Even its critics, however, feel compelled to praise ID. White (1983:1008) stated that it "has come to be the principle statistic for measuring segregation . . . ." Cortese, Falk, and Cohen (1976:630) admitted that ID has "achieved preeminence in the measurement of segregation." Lieberson and Carter (1982: 297) declared that ID "is a noteworthy exception to the difficulty social science has in generating standardized measurement." ID continues to occupy a respected position in social science measurement.

LIEBERSON'S INDEX OF DIVERSITY (A_b)

Chapter three discussed Lieberson's index of diversity designed to measure inequality within a population, based on the combinatorics model. Lieberson (1964, 1969) also elaborated his index to measure diversity between two populations. The formula for his between-populations diversity index is expressed as follows (Agresti and Agresti, 1977):

$$A_b = 1 - \Sigma P_i Q_i$$

where P_i = proportion of the category in population P, and
Q_i = proportion of the category in population Q

P and Q represent two population groups of any type, for example, two cities, nation-states, races, legislatures, genders, etc. The index of intergroup diversity comparatively examines the distribution of population group members among nominal categories of some attribute within each of the two populations. Lieberson (1969) interpreted this simple but efficient measure as the probability of obtaining individuals from different social groups if persons from each of the two populations are randomly paired together. If all possible pairs are formed that include one individual from population P and one individual from population Q, in what percentage of the pairs will the individuals be classified differently on the nominal variable of interest? Whereas Duncan and Duncan's index of dissimilarity measures distribution of the members of two racial groups among several subareas of a jurisdiction, Lieberson's A_b measures distribution of the members of several categories of a social group between two populations.

For example, assume two cities whose populations are divided among four racial groups: white, black, Hispanic, and other. City P's proportions for these four groups are 0.20, 0.40, 0.30, and 0.10; city Q's proportions are 0.40, 0.05, 0.50, and 0.05, respectively. Multiplying each group's two proportions and summing them equals 0.255, the probability of randomly selecting one person from population P and one from population Q who come from the same racial/ethnic category (e. g., two Hispanics). This figure must be subtracted from unity, $A_b = 1 - 0.245 = 0.745$, in order to measure diversity between the two populations. In other words, the probability is 0.745 that randomly selecting one person from each of the two cities will produce a pair of people from two different racial/ethnic groups, an ethnically heterogeneous pair.

Lieberson's index can be used to measure the diversity between two populations for any number of nominal categories of a social group variable (e. g., religion, race, ethnicity, political party, occupation, etc.). It compares a social groups' proportions within each of two populations rather than the spatial location of members of two groups and is, therefore, not a conventional segregation index.

This measure's polarity is toward equality, specifically the absence of concentration, because higher index values indicate greater diversity or less concentration. The standard with which the A_b procedure compares each intergroup pair is every other intergroup pair. A set of group proportions from one population is compared to the equivalent set of group proportions from another population, one intergroup pair at a time. In this respect, Lieberson's index resembles inequity measures (chapter eight).

The principle of transfers applies but not in a straightforward manner. Applied to Lieberson's intergroup diversity, it holds that diversity decreases if members of category i of population P are moved to category i of population Q, provided $P_i > Q_i$, and assuming that the size of the transfer (T) is smaller than the difference between the two populations' equivalent categories (i.e., $T < [P_i - Q_i]$). Diversity increases for an opposite transfer of individuals. Lieberson's measure does conform to this principle. Transfers from a larger category in P to a smaller equivalent category in Q tend to equalize the sizes of all proportional categories between the two populations. The product of two more equal proportions is greater than that of two less equal proportions. Subtracting this function from unity then produces a decline in the measured diversity for such a transfer. Proportional increases of all categories leave A_b unchanged. Adding a positive constant to all categories increases diversity. A_b is also consistent with the size invariance criterion.

Lieberson's index of diversity is insensitive to the number of categories in each population and is, therefore, a measure of relative inequality. It reaches its maximal value, indicating maximum diversity between the two populations, if $P_i = 0$ whenever $Q_i > 0$, and $P_i > 0$ whenever $Q_i = 0$. In other words, the categories into which the observations in the first population fall are mutually exclusive of the categories into which the observations of the second population fall. Intergroup diversity reaches its minimum when $P_i = Q_i = 1.0$ for some category i, that is, when all the members of each population fall in the same category (Agresti and Agresti, 1977).

Two other interesting features of Lieberson's index merit attention. If each category in the first population is identical in proportion to each equivalent category in the second population, that is, when $P_i = Q_i$, $i = 1 ... K$, $A_b = 1 - \sum P_i Q_i = 1 - \sum P_i^2 = 1 - \sum Q_i^2$. Observe that $1 - \sum Q_i^2$ is identical to or the complement of several intragroup inequality indexes such as Herfindahl and Hirschman's concentration index (HH) and Lieberson's index of diversity (D) (chapter four). In addition, when $P_i = Q_i = 1/K$ for all i, then $A_b = 1/K$. If each population has an equal distribution among equivalent groups, Lieberson's diversity index equals the mean proportion.

Lieberson's index of intergroup diversity conforms to all four Lorenz-related criteria. Therefore, if the intergroup distribution in system A has a lower diversity index value than the intergroup distribution in system B, then system A is less diverse than system B, and A's segregation curve lies everywhere above and nowhere below that of system B.

From a technical standpoint, A_b is defined for all distributions, uses all distributional information well, and is simple to compute and understand. It is properly bounded, and its upper and lower limits are insensitive to number of population categories. Maximum diversity is achieved and the index equals unity when all P_i are zero when equivalent Q_i contain observations, and all Q_i are zero when equivalent P_i contain observations. A_b achieves zero when all members of both populations are classified in the same category. As mentioned earlier, this index assumes that the members of each population are divided into nominal categories.

BELL'S INTERACTION PROBABILITY INDEX (P*)

Bell's (1954) index of interaction probability, a revision of Shevky and Williams' (1949) isolation index, actually involves four separate procedures, when considered for two groups such as blacks and whites. Two of the procedures measure extent of racial isolation (black interaction with blacks and white interaction with whites), and two measure extent of interracial contact or exposure (whites to blacks and blacks to whites). They will be introduced as a group and their common statistical features discussed.

Duncan and Duncan's index of dissimilarity apparently won the index war of 1947-55 and ruled supreme in segregation studies for about a quarter of a century as a result. However, Lieberson's revision of Bell's P* measures in the early 1980s seriously challenged ID's predominance and initiated a series of new index battles.

Bell's interaction probability index is actually four separate equations, each expressing interaction of members of one group with members of another group or with themselves. They are:

$$(1) \quad _bP^*_w = \Sigma(b_i/B)(w_i/t_i)$$

$$(2) \quad _bP^*_b = \Sigma(b_i/B)(b_i/t_i)$$

$$(3) \quad _wP^*_w = \Sigma(w_i/W)(w_i/t_i)$$

$$(4) \quad _wP^*_b = \Sigma(w_i/W)(b_i/t_i)$$

where b_i = number of blacks in the subarea,
w_i = number of whites in the subarea,
B = total number of blacks in city,
W = total number of whites in city, and
t_i = total population of the subarea

The subscripts preceding and following P* indicate, respectively, the group from whom and to whom interaction is directed. For example, $_bP^*_w$ indicates the probability of black interaction with whites. When the subscripts are different, black with white or white with black, the interaction probability is defined as interracial contact or exposure of the members of one group to the members of the other group. If the subscripts are identical, black interaction with black or white interaction with white, the interaction probability is defined as the isolation of one group from the other. Hence, "P^*-type indexes have a distinctive meaning in terms of describing the isolation within a group and the level of interaction across group lines" (Lieberson and Carter, 1982: 303).

Bell (1954:357-358) defined his original measure as follows: the "numerator is an approximation to the probability P that the next person a random individual from group 1 will meet is also from group 1. The denominator is an approximation to the hypothetical probability P_h that the next person a random individual from group 1 will meet is also from group 1 assuming group 1 is homogeneously mixed in all census tracts of the city." Bell called the numerator P^*. As will be demonstrated, the indexes can be calculated to determine the probability that an individual from either group will interact with a member of his/her own group or a member of the other group. In any case, P^* measures are based on a combinatorics model.

Bell's indexes can also be interpreted as measures of central tendency, rather than as measures of dispersion, in the strict statistical sense (James and Taeuber, 1985). This definition can be stated in several ways. For example, the value of $_bP^*_w$ indicates the percent of white residents living in the subarea of the average black resident in the city. Similarly, it indicates, for a randomly selected black in the city, the probability that someone else selected from the same residential subarea will also be black (Lieberson, 1981).

On the other hand, $_bP^*_b$ refers to the isolation experienced by black residents. For a randomly selected black resident, it measures the probability that someone else chosen from the same residential subarea will also be black. The equation for $_bP^*_b$ is composed of the sum of the average proportion that blacks are of the population in each subarea, weighted by the number of blacks residing in each of these subareas (Lieberson, 1981; Farley and Taeuber, 1968).

Interaction probability, either isolation or exposure, differs from unevenness as an aspect of conventional segregation for several reasons. Lieberson and Carter (1982) claimed that P^*-type measures are superior to the index of dissimilarity on such problems as the consequences of residential segregation, the actual impact of residential contact, and the responses of one group to another. Similarly, Stearns and Logan (1986) stressed three important social phenomena that are especially affected by interaction frequency: intermarriage, rate of linguistic assimilation, and occupational composition.

Bell's four measures share two important but controversial characteristics. P^* indexes violate the principle of composition-invariance, and they are asymmetrical. Composition refers to the percentages of groups in the total population, a distributional characteristic to which these indexes are sensitive, as mentioned earlier. They are asymmetrical because normally the isolation of blacks from whites differs from the isolation of whites from blacks and the same with contact probabilities (Blau, 1977:20-26). The reason for the difference is that P^*

takes into account both racial composition and dissimilarities in their spatial distribution (Lieberson, 1980:254-258; 1981; Lieberson and Carter, 1982). According to Lieberson and Carter (1982), Bell's original failure fully to appreciate the asymmetry of the P^*-type measures is a major reason they were underutilized during the twenty-five years of ID predominance. Both characteristics give conceptual distinctiveness to the interaction probability indexes.

P^*-type measures are a "direct and simple way of describing the combined effects of composition and non-random residential patterns on the isolation of ethnic or racial groups from either the remainder of the population or specific subgroups" (Lieberson, 1981:66). They merge in a single index the two forces most likely to produce isolation—differences in spatial distribution and relative numbers. Using the hypothetical data in table 7-1 to compute the index of black isolation produces the following results:

$$_bP^*_b \;=\; \Sigma(b_j/B)(b_j/t_j) = (120/200)(120/160)$$

$$+ (60/200)(60/380) + (20/200)(20/260)$$

$$+ (0/200)(0/200) = .51$$

The average black resident lives in a subarea where .51 of the residents are black, a group isolation value derived by weighting the black proportion in each subarea population by the number of blacks. Black interaction with whites can be similarly computed, but this time by weighting the black proportion in each subarea by the number of whites:

$$_bP^*_w \;=\; \Sigma(b_j/B)(w_j/t_j) = (120/200)(40/160)$$

$$+ (60/200)(320/380) + (20/200)((240/260)$$

$$+ (0/200)((200/200) = .49$$

The average black resident lives in a subarea where .49 of the residents are white, an intergroup interaction index value. Black interaction with whites and white interaction with blacks are asymmetric. These pairs will be equal only in the rare instance in which the two groups have exactly the same number of residents in the area (Lieberson, 1980:256). Lieberson and Carter (1982:309) argued that "the asymmetrical quality of P^* indexes allows us to understand how the same process, residential isolation, may appear radically different to the groups involved because, in fact, the situation and the trends are different."

To complete the computations, $_wP^*_w = .92$, and $_wP^*_b = .08$. These values indicate that the average white has a .92 probability of exposure to fellow whites, whereas the average black resident has eight chances in one hundred to interact with white residents.

Rather than compute each of the four P^* values separately, it is possible to take advantage of the interrelationships among the four indexes (Stearns and Logan, 1986; Lieberson, 1980:257). White exposure to blacks and white isolation are complementary; black exposure to whites and black isolation are complementary. Therefore, $_wP^*_b = 1 - {_wP^*_w}$, and $_bP^*_w = 1 - {_bP^*_b}$. In a similar fashion, black isolation can be defined in terms of white isolation, and vice versa: $_bP^*_b = 1 - [(W/B)(1 - {_wP^*_w})]$, and $_wP^*_w = 1 - [(B/W)(1 - {_bP^*_b})]$.

Actual interaction potential between groups is affected by their relative numbers as well as the pattern of spatial segregation (Lieberson, 1980: 254). The effect of composition on the values of Bell's measures can be demonstrated through their interrelationships. Because $_wP^*_b = ({_bP^*_w})(B/W)$, one equation and index value can be derived from the other as long as the relative size of overall proportion black and white is known. But a change in one P^* of a given magnitude will have a different effect on the other index value. The difference is a function of the ratio between white and black populations in the city. If $_w\Delta_b$ represents a change in $_wP^*_b$, it follows that the change in the $_bP^*_w$ index, $_b\Delta_w$, will be a function of the ratio of black to white population, as follows: $_b\Delta_w = {_w\Delta_b}/(B/W)$. The greater the difference between the two groups in their total numbers in the city, the greater will be the differential consequence of a change in segregation (Lieberson, 1981).

The polarity of one of Bell's measures depends on the identity of the two subscripts (i.e., the direction of interaction); greater group isolation represents greater inequality, and more intergroup exposure represents more equality. Interaction indexes also represent concentration, however, not just inequality.

The sensitivity of P^* to transfers is complicated but consistent with the transfers principle. A transfer of black residents from a subarea with a higher proportion black to a subarea with a lower proportion black increases the exposure of each group to the other and results in a decline in the isolation of each group.

Adding a positive constant to the number of black residents in each subarea affects P^* measures in the same way that a transfers does. If one hundred black residents are added to each of the four subareas in table 7-1, for example, black interaction with whites and white interaction with blacks both increase; black isolation and white isolation both decline. Adding the positive constant to black residents moves the measures toward greater equality.

Similarly, multiplying the number of minority students in each subarea or school by a positive constant does not affect P^* values; the measures are size invariant. They are also characterized by organizational equivalence. A P^* value does not change if each of a city's subareas is split in half or if the city is merged with an identical one.

As mentioned earlier, however, Bell's interaction probability measures violate the criterion of composition invariance. They are sensitive to the proportion black in school system or city. For this reason, James and Taeuber (1985:4) eliminated them from consideration as segregation indexes, arguing that "interracial exposure (contact) refers to the racial composition of an individual's environment. Racial exposure indexes for schools describe the average or typical school racial composition encountered by students or a particular race." They declared P^*-type indexes to be compositional measures of central tendency rather than measures of dispersion. Because of P^*-type measures' failure to satisfy the compositional invariance principle, they fail to meet the Lorenz standard.

These four nominal-scale indexes are defined for all distributions and make good use of information about the distribution (some would say they use too much information, i.e., overall proportion black). P^* measures are not properly bounded between zero and unity, making interpretation more difficult. If a population distribution is characterized by no segregation whatsoever, neither of the two P^* measures of white interaction with blacks and black interaction with whites equals zero, as ID does. Rather, for a condition of no segregation, $_wP^*_b = {}_bP^*_b = P_b$ or proportion black, and $_bP^*_w = {}_wP^*_w = P_w$ or proportion white. It is easy, incidentally, to standardize P^* values in terms of these limits, so that they vary from zero to unity. The two remaining isolation measures are complements of the two interaction measures: $_wP^*_w = 1 - P_b$ and $_bP^*_b = 1 - P_w$. All the P^* measures are simple to compute.

One indicator of an index's utility is the number of times it is reinvented or rediscovered under other names and in algebraically different forms. In fact, it was the Shevky and Williams index (1949) that Bell (1954) modified. Since then, the P^*-type measure has found reincarnation in Zoloth's (1976) segregation index, Coleman, Kelly, and Moore's (1975) standardized segregation measure, Burstein's (1976) dominance index, and Schnare's (1977) standardized P^*. Nor was standardizing P^* new, because Bell (1954) and Bell and Willis (1957) had earlier standardized P^* to eliminate compositional influence. About standardizing P^*, however, Lieberson and Carter (1982:308) argued that "it would seem pointless to give up the attractive interaction qualities of P^* for a measure which still does not fully eliminate compositional influences."

BELL'S CORRELATION RATIO SQUARED (ETA^2)

Bell (1954) adopted the square of a conventional statistical measure, the correlation ratio, as his "revised index of isolation." It is expressed as follows:

$$\text{eta}^2 = \frac{\Sigma t_i b_i^2}{TWB} - \frac{B}{W}$$

where b_i = black population in the ith neighborhood,
$\underline{b}_i$ = percentage black in the ith neighborhood,
T = total population,
$\underline{B}$ = overall proportion black, and
$\underline{W}$ = overall proportion white

As a segregation index, eta^2 is "a variance-based measure, which can be understood as the ratio of the variance in racial composition between neighborhoods to the total variance in racial composition" (Stearns and Logan, 1982: 127). The numerator in the first term on the right-hand side of the equation is the sum of the square of the percent black in each neighborhood, weighted by total black population in each neighborhood. The denominator is the product of the overall percentages black and white weighted by overall population. Subtracted from that ratio is the ratio of overall percent black to overall percent white.

Two prominent features of eta^2 are its measurement of composition, resembling P^*, and its sensitivity to concentration. Summing the square of each subarea's black population makes eta^2 particularly sensitive to racial concentration. An increase of ten percentage points in a subarea with sixty percent black population counts much more than an identical change in a subarea with five percent black population. The square of percent black in the former subarea changes from .36 to .49, whereas it changes from .0025 to .0225 in the latter subarea (Stearns and Logan, 1982). For this reason, Stearns and Logan (1982) recommended eta^2 especially for measuring succession, that is, changes in residential patterns brought about by increasing black concentration in majority black neighborhoods.

Relationships between eta^2 and each of the four P^* measures can be derived from the following equation:

$$eta^2 = [_bP^*_b - P_b]/P_w = [_wP^*_w - P_w]/P_b$$

Solving this equation for each of the four P^* measures produces the following definitions of interaction probability measures in terms of eta^2 (Stearns and Logan, 1982):

$$_bP^*_b = (eta^2)(P_w) + P_b$$

$$_wP^*_w = (eta^2)(P_b) + P_w$$

$$_bP^*_w = P_w - (eta^2)(P_w)$$

$$_wP^*_b = P_b - (eta^2)(P_b)$$

Eta^2 is related to the P* measures but differs substantially from the index of dissimilarity. It has a segregation or inequality polarity and is a relative measure that includes any number of null components. Based on a combinatorics model, it uses all possible pairs as the comparative standard. Both constant additions and transfers (as defined earlier in this chapter) decrease the value of eta^2. It is not composition invariant, of course. It does comply with the organizational equivalence and size invariance axioms. And of course, it fails to satisfy the Lorenz dominance criterion.

It is defined for all distributions and makes good use of information. Eta^2 is a nominal-scale index that reaches its upper limit, unity, only under the condition of complete segregation, in other words, when each geographical subarea contains population of only one race. It reaches its minimum, zero, when each subarea's percent black equals that of the whole jurisdiction. It is a simple measure to compute and interpret.

LIEBERSON'S INDEX OF NET DIFFERENCE (ND$_{wb}$)

Lieberson's (1975) index of net difference has recently gained acceptance as a measure of intergroup income inequality (Riedesel, 1979; Villemez, 1978; Fossett, Galle, and Kelly, 1986), and it could be used to measure the inequality of other units. The definitional equation for this measure assumes the following form:

$$ND_{wb} = \sum_{i=2}^{I} W_i \left(\sum_{j=1}^{i-1} B_j \right) - \sum_{i=2}^{I} B_i \left(\sum_{j=1}^{i-1} W_j \right)$$

where i = the class of a ranked distribution,
W_i = proportion of whites in the class,
B_i = proportion of blacks in the class,
ΣB_j = cumulated percent of blacks ranked below the class, and
ΣW_j = cumulated per cent of whites ranked below the class

This equation is more difficult to comprehend and compute than most, partly because ND$_{wb}$ is an ordinally-scaled index. Using a modified version of an example provided by Lieberson (1975:280) helps to clarify the statistical procedure. Table 7-4 contains ranked income classes in ascending order and the proportions of whites and blacks earning incomes in each class.

The procedure for Lieberson's ND$_{wb}$ is based on comparison of two cumulative relative frequency distributions, for example populations W and B in table 7-4, ranked with respect to some ordinally classified characteristic I, such as income. If individuals in the populations of W and B are randomly paired together, three probabilities are possible: the probability that W will exceed B, $pr(W > B)$; that B will exceed W, $pr(B > W)$; and that W and B are tied, $pr(W = B)$. These three probabilities are exhaustive and sum to unity. Lieberson's index, expressed as ND_{wb}, simply subtracts $pr(B > W)$ from $pr(W > B)$, disregarding ties or $pr(W = B)$. The order of the subscripts indicates the direction of the probability difference.

Table 7-4
Procedure for Computing Index of
Net Difference for Grouped Data

Income classes (i) in $1000s		Cumulative Proportional Frequency Distributions	
		Whites (W)	Blacks (B)
$0 - $5		0.000	0.001
5 - 10		0.001	0.001
10 - 15		0.001	0.002
15 - 20		0.004	0.007
20 - 25		0.008	0.021
25 - 30		0.033	0.108
30 - 35		0.085	0.373
35 - 40		<u>0.864</u>	<u>0.487</u>
	Total	1.000	1.000

Using the data in table 7-4 to demonstrate the net difference procedure provides the following results:

(1) $pr(W > B) = \Sigma W_i (\Sigma B_j) = (0.868)(0.513) + (0.085)(0.140) + \ldots$
       $(0.001)((0.001) = 0.458$

(2) $pr(B > W) = \Sigma B_i (\Sigma W_j) = (0.487)(0.132) + (0.373)(0.047) + \ldots$
       $+ (0.001)(0.000) = 0.084$

(3) $ND_{wb} = pr(W > B) - pr(B > W) = 0.458 - 0.084 = 0.374$

In computing pr(W > B), the procedure first multiplies the largest W proportion (0.864) times the largest B proportion (0.487) subtracted from unity (0.513). Then, the second largest W proportion (0.085) is multiplied times the sum of the largest (0.487) and second largest B (0.373) proportions subtracted from unity (0.140). The process continues, cumulating the B proportions and subtracting them from unity for multiplication by the appropriate W proportion. To compute pr(B > W), the procedure is simply reversed, multiplying the largest B proportion times the largest W proportion subtracted from unity, and so on.

A positive value for ND_{wb} indicates the probability that white income is greater than black income, for a randomly selected black and white. A negative value indicates the probability that black income is greater than white income.

The definitional equation exposes the probability logic underlying ND_{wb}, comparing two cumulative relative frequency distributions, but it is unnecessarily complicated for computational purposes. Fortunately, Fossett and South (1983) developed a simpler computational formula:

$$ND_{wb} = \sum_{i=1}^{I} \sum_{j=1}^{I} (X * W_i * B_j)$$

where, if $i > j$, $X = +1$,
   if $i = j$, $X = 0$,
   if $i < j$, $X = -1$, and
   * indicates multiplication

This formula reveals that ND_{wb} is the average of an inequality score assigned to each pairwise comparison between individuals in the two groups. The inequality score assigned assumes three values: positive unity when an individual from the second group has a higher value (e.g., income), zero when the individuals are tied, and negative unity when the individual from the first group has a higher value than the individual from the second group.

ND_{wb} indicates both the direction and magnitude of group advantage. It is positive or negative, depending on which group has advantage, and zero only if the two groups are equal. It has a logical range of negative unity to positive unity. And its equation assumes that the characteristic in terms of which two groups are compared (e.g., income, occupation, or education) is ordinally scaled.

The polarity of Lieberson's index follows its directional characteristic and its notation, ND_{wb}. It varies from total negative inequality (complete advantage of whites over blacks) through equality (neither group has an advantage), to complete positive inequality (complete advantage of blacks over whites). As a multiplicative function, it is sensitive to relative concentration of the ordinal characteristic.

The index of net difference, applied to any two groups, generally satisfies the principle of transfers. The exception comes when the minimum and maximum incomes in the ordinal distribution for group W are higher than the corresponding minimum and maximum values in the ordinal distribution of group B. Under these conditions, ND_{wb} is insensitive to transfers from donors in B with incomes below the minimum in W to recipients in W with incomes above the maximum in B, even though these transfers favor group W. In a similar fashion, ND_{wb} is insensitive to transfers in the opposite direction between the same donor and recipient, unless they cause the donor in W to fall to or below the maximum in B, or cause the recipient in B to rise to or above the minimum in W, even though such a transfer favors group B. Such empirical conditions are relatively rare (Fossett and South, 1983).

Lieberson's index also fails to satisfy the principle of equal additions, because it measures rank advantage rather than relative advantage (Fossett and South, 1985). The computational formula for ND_{wb} clearly indicates this characteristic. It weights a minor difference between two paired individuals identically to a very large difference. It does, however, satisfy the principle of proportionate increases. Because it does not satisfy the transfers principle, it fails to conform to the Lorenz criterion.

ND is defined for all distributions and makes good use of information in the distributions. It is easily interpretable, because it varies from negative to positive unity. It is not a simple measure to compute.

FOSSETT AND SOUTH'S INDEX OF AVERAGE RELATIVE ADVANTAGE (ARA)

Lieberson's index of net difference represents an improvement over Duncan and Duncan's index of dissimilarity, because the former corrects the latter's violations of the principles of directionality and transfers (with the rare exception noted). However, ND_{wb}, like the index of dissimilarity, violates the equal additions criterion, because it fails to reflect the size of relative income differences between the two groups. Fossett and South's (1983) index of average relative advantage modifies ND_{wb} to make it appropriately sensitive to equal additions. Their computing formula is as follows:

$$ARA = \sum_{i=1}^{I} \sum_{j=1}^{J} (X * W_i * B_i)$$

where if $w_i > b_j$, x = $(w_i - b_j)/w_i$,
    if $w_i = b_j$, x = 0,
    if $w_i < b_j$, x = $(w_i - b_j)/b_j$, and
    * indicates multiplication

The index of average relative advantage measures "the difference between two opposing probabilities of group advantage, where the probability of advantage is weighted by the relative magnitude of the income advantage involved" (Fossett and South, 1983:865). ARA assigns inequality scores or weights to all pairwise comparisons, but, unlike Lieberson's index of net difference, an ARA weight is the difference in actual income between the two individuals as a proportion of the larger of the two incomes, not just a positive or negative unity or zero. Therefore the weight reflects the relative magnitude of the advantage involved.

Fossett and South's procedure takes advantage of the fact that the ordinal classification of a variable such as income has interval properties. In that sense, ARA intervalizes the ordinal net difference index, and thereby makes ARA consistent with the equal additions criterion, distinguishing it from ND_{wb}. Using ARA to measure intergroup inequality on ordinal characteristics such as occupational prestige or alienation should probably be avoided, unless the investigator is willing to assume that the ordinal classes represent an implicit underlying interval scale. In every other way, ARA's conformity to the criteria of inequality theory resembles that of Lieberson's index of net difference.

CONCLUSIONS

If the investigator wants to measure social differentiation over a geographical area, Duncan and Duncan's index of dissimilarity is appropriate. If probability of interaction among people between or within social groups in a geographical area is important, Bell's interaction index and the squared correlation ratio can be used. Lieberson's diversity index is probably the best comparative measure of the distribution among nominal groups between two geographical areas or populations. Both Lieberson's net difference and Fossett and South's average relative advantage measure distributions between two groups, such as blacks and whites; the former assumes distribution among ordinal classes and the latter index assumes interval qualities of a distribution among ordinal classes. One of the indexes is based on the deviations model; the other five are derived from a combinatorics model.

8

INDEXES OF INEQUITY

What if uniformity is judged to be unreasonable or unfair in some distribution? What if components of the system are judged to vary in their merit or the degree to which they deserve the units, in terms of some specific standard of equity? Such a case calls for distribution of unequal amounts to each component.

Inequity indexes are designed to measure distribution under this condition, that is, when some form of inequality is assumed to be normatively preferable. Equity is defined as the extent to which an actual distribution to individuals, places, or groups conforms to a specific distributional standard other than complete equality.

Inequity measurement is a relatively recent addition to social science methodology. Interest in distributional inequality among social philosophers can be traced back in history to Aristotle in approximately 350 B.C. The earliest known successful effort to measure inequality mathematically is credited either to Max Lorenz in 1905 or Corrado Gini in 1912. But statistical indexes of inequity did not appear in the social science literature until the early 1980s. They represent the latest in social scientists' enduring efforts to measure and explain who gets what. This chapter discusses the conceptual logic of inequity, examines the statistical procedures of three inequity indexes, and evaluates the indexes with respect to their consistency with the conceptual and operational criteria.

THE LOGIC OF INEQUITY

In measuring inequity, each share of an actual distribution is compared to the share of an entirely different, independent distribution (Coulter, 1980 and 1983b; Nagel, 1984:69-71), called the standard distribution or equity standard. Thus the extent of inequity characterizing a distribution is measured with respect to its divergence from some other distribution among the components of the same system.

The equity standard represents the investigator's normative choice of what is equitable. It also involves the implicit assumptions not only that a given distribution should not be equal, but also that units should be redistributed in order to make the distribution conform to the equity standard. It is explicity normative and implicitly interventionist.

Inequity analysts originally developed several equity criteria in this context (Cf. Lineberry, 1977; Lucy and Mladenka, 1978; Jones et al., 1980; Hochschild, 1981; Levy, 1974) that apply equally well to virtually any sort of distributional problem. Five of them have achieved prominent status in empirical distributional analysis: equality, need, economic market forces, demand, and social status.

The equality criterion resembles the primary assumption in inequality measurement, that is, that every component should receive identical shares. In some cases of inequity measurement, if this is the assumption, then one of the simpler inequality indexes should probably be used instead. However, such is not always the case.

The key to understanding equality as an equity standard lies in the difference between distribution to individuals as components and distribution to spatial aggregates of individuals as components. Assume, for example, that every individual should receive the same amount of some benefit, but that population is unequally distributed throughout a system of geographical subareas, and that the benefit must be delivered to subareas rather than to individuals. If the benefit is to be distributed across unequally populated subareas of the system, it is necessary to distribute unequal amounts of the benefits to the subareas in order to achieve a uniform per capita distribution. In such a case, spatial inequality would be interpersonally equitable. In other words, units would be unequally distributed to subareas in terms of their unequal population sizes. Examples of equity criteria based on individual equality are population for distributing police protection (Coulter, 1980) and number of structures (households and businesses) for distributing fire hydrants (Coulter, 1983a) among unequally populated subareas in a city.

The second normative standard, need, stipulates that units should be distributed to components in proportion to the intensity of their need for the units (Rae, 1981:99-101). According to this standard, in an anti-poverty program, more assistance should be given to poorer persons. In an anti-crime program, more police protection should be given to higher crime areas. Components with less need should receive less. Examples of an equity standard based on need are using crime incidence statistics to distribute preventive police patrol (Nagel, 1984:71-72) and incidence of fires to distribute fire hydrants (Coulter, 1983a) among subareas.

The third inequity criterion reflects the economic marketplace; it is the willingness and ability of components to pay for the units. In other words, the units of some valued resource should be distributed in terms of people's willingness and ability to pay market prices for them. Those who can and want to pay more should receive more. Those who cannot or will not pay more should receive less. Presumably, those who cannot or will not pay at all should receive none. Using average neighborhood property values in a city as a basis for distributing police protection among neighborhoods (Boyle and Jacobs, 1982) is an example of an equity standard based on the marketplace criterion.

The demand criterion states that a system is equitable if units are distributed to the components who request them and withheld from those who do not. This standard is also known as the "Adam Smith rule" (Levy, Meltsner, and Wildavsky, 1974) because of its similarity to economists' supply and demand principles. It has nothing to do, however, with willingness and ability to pay. The criterion simply requires that those who ask shall be given (provided they are legally entitled), and those who do not ask shall be left alone. Examples of demand as an equity criterion are distributing street repair crews and material to fill potholes in city streets on the basis of pothole complaints received from citizens (Sharp, 1986; Coulter, 1988).

Finally, social status can be used as an equity standard. This usually means that persons with higher social status should receive more and better of what is being distributed, and those with lower social status should receive less and worse, a standard usually referred to as the "underclass hypothesis" (Lineberry, 1977). High status is usually defined in terms of one or more of the following ascriptive characteristics: income, wealth, education, occupation, or political power. Status can also be defined in terms of characteristics such as sex and race. Persons of low status tend to be left out. An example of using an equity standard based on social status is distributing more city services to white, wealthier neighborhoods (Jones, 1982).

Social scientists use inequity indexes to measure the extent to which a given actual distribution is identical to a normative standard, usually defined in terms of equality, need, market forces, demand, or social status. Inequity is present to the extent that discrepancies exist between the actual shares and the values that the shares should assume, based on an appropriate equity standard. An alternative definition of equity standard is a minimum level of decency below which a component should not be allowed to fall (Nagel, 1984:73). According to this definition, inequity is the extent to which the shares of a given distribution fall below the minimum decency level.

Equations for inequity measures are more complicated than those of inequality and segregation measures, because they involve comparison of two independent distributions. Only three inequity indexes exist in the literature. Table 8-1 presents their formulae. Table 8-2 presents a synoptic evaluation of the main properties of three inequity indexes. The investigator may use it as a quick guide to selecting a particular index, once the research problem is identified as inequity.

Table 8-1
Equations for Inequity Indexes

---

1. Coulter's Generalized Index of Inequity

$$I_\alpha = \frac{[\Sigma| P_i - Q_i|^\alpha]^{1/\alpha}}{[(1 - minQ)^\alpha - (minQ)^\alpha + \Sigma Q_i{}^\alpha]^{1/\alpha}}$$

2. Nagel's Equity

$$EQ = 1 - \frac{\Sigma(A_i - M_i)^2}{\Sigma(Z^* - M_i)^2}$$

3. Nagel's Proportionality

$$PR = 1 - \frac{\Sigma(A_i - P_i)^2}{\Sigma(Z^* - P_i)^2}$$

---

* Z indicates zero allocation.

COULTER'S GENERALIZED INDEX OF INEQUITY (I_α)

Coulter's (1980, 1983b; Coulter and Pittman, 1983) generalized index of inequity was the first inequity measure. It operationalizes Aristotle's conception of "proportional equality" (Barker, 1958:205) or distribution to individuals, places, or groups on the basis of what they deserve in terms of some equity standard. Although its underlying logic is simple, the generalized equation in table 8-1 appears complicated. It is a generalized equation because it contains a parameter, α or alpha, whose value must be set by the investigator. The parameter's value determines the extent to which the index is sensitive only to inequality or is also sensitive to concentration, a point discussed in detail later.

The index of inequity is essentially based on the deviations model, although it also relies on additional, more complex mathematics. It uses as a comparative standard the proportionate share that each component should receive, based on its merit defined by the equity standard. When the investigator sets the alpha parameter at unity or two, the generalized equation reduces to a considerably simpler form. Different alphas produce different forms of the equation. In

Table 8-2: Primary Properties of Inequity Indexes

	Polarity	Type of Index	Concentration	Comparative standard	Constant additions	Transfers	Scale invariance	Population symmetry	Lorenz dominance	Scale	Definition	Information use	Upper and lower limits	Simplicity	Mathematical model
Coulter's generalized inequity (I_1)	inequality	absolute, type B	no	independent distribution	decrease	no	yes	no	no	nominal	yes	good	1,0	good	deviations
Coulter's generalized inequity ($I_{>1}$)	inequality	absolute, type B	yes	independent distribution	decrease	yes	yes	no	no	nominal	yes	good	1,0	fair	deviations
Nagel's equity (EQ)	equality	relative, ANONC	yes	independent distribution	increase	no	no	yes	no	nominal	yes	good	1,0	good	deviations
Nagel's proportionality (PR)	equality	relative, ANONC	yes	independent distribution	increase	yes	yes	yes	yes	nominal	yes	good	1,<1	good	deviations

addition to selecting an equity standard (Q), the investigator must also select a value for the parameter. The mechanics of the procedure are described first, and then the underlying conceptualization. If we set alpha at unity, the generalized equation reduces to the following form:

$$I_1 = \frac{\Sigma \mid P_i - Q_i \mid}{2(1 - minQ)}$$

where P_i = proportional share of the component,
Q_i = proportional share that should be received by the component; the equity standard distribution
$minQ$ = smallest Q value

A much simpler computational equation, Coulter's I_1 provides a convenient means to explain the logic underlying the general procedure. The numerator computes the sum of the absolute differences between two sets of proportional shares, the actual distribution (P) and the equity standard distribution (Q). The denominator divides the numerator by the maximum value it could attain, given the equity distribution.

A discrepancy exists whenever a share in the actual distribution does not equal the equivalent share in the standard distribution, that is, some $P_i \neq Q_i$. The sum of the positive differences (when some $P_i > Q_i$) represents a surplus, which always equals the sum of the negative differences (when some $P_i < Q_i$), which represents a deficit. The sum of the absolute differences must be divided by two; otherwise, each discrepancy would be double-counted.

The denominator not only divides the numerator by two to correct for double-counting absolute differences. It also divides by the maximum value that the numerator can take, specifically the difference between the standard distribution and the most inequitable possible distribution (called the malimum distribution), given the equity standard distribution. An example, based on hypothetical data contained in table 8-3, will help to clarify the procedure.

Table 8-3 includes the actual P distribution and the Q equity standard distribution with which P is to be compared. For purposes of illustration, the P distribution can be thought of as representing the actual distribution of hours of police patrol among four neighborhoods of a city, and the Q distribution can be considered to represent the hours of police patrol that should have been distributed, based on a need standard of street crime incidence. For example, the first neighborhood had forty per cent of the preventive patrol and ten per cent of the crime. With the alpha parameter set at unity, the equation's numerator calls for the sum of the absolute differences between actual and standard distributions,

0.80, as is contained at the bottom of column three of table 8-3. The denominator is $2(1 - \text{min}Q) = 2(1 - 0.10) = 1.8$; Therefore, $I_1 = .80/1.8 = .44$.

Table 8-3
Hypothetical Data for Computing
Coulter's I_α with $\alpha = 1$ and 2

1	2	3	4	5	6
					malimum
P_i	Q_i	$|P_i - Q_i|$	$(P_i - Q_i)^2$	Q_i^2	distribution
.40	.10*	.30	.09	.01	1.00
.30	.20	.10	.01	.04	0.00
.20	.30	.10	.01	.09	0.00
.10	.40	.30	.09	.16	0.00
1.00	1.00	0.80	0.20	.30	1.00

* = minQ

The parenthetical expression in the denominator, $(1 - \text{min}Q)$ operationalizes the concept of the malimum distribution, as presented in column six of table 8-3. The worst possible actual distribution or most inequitable distribution possible, given the equity standard, is represented by the distribution in column six. The malimum distribution involves giving all the P units to the component with the smallest Q value and zero P units to every other component. In the case of table 8-3, the malimum distribution is $P_1 = 1.0$ and all other $P_i = 0.00$. The formula's denominator automatically computes this malimum distribution, whatever the value of the alpha parameter (Coulter and Pittman, 1983).

The numerator of I_1 is mathematically identical and conceptually equivalent to the numerator of Duncan and Duncan's index of dissimilarity (chapter seven). It is mathematically identical because it requires summing the absolute differences between two sets of proportions, each of which sums to unity. It is conceptually equivalent because ID measures difference between two groups' distributions, and I_α measures the difference between an actual distribution and a hypothetical standard distribution. The two indexes differ in their denominators, however. Duncan and Duncan's ID denominator is two (operationalized by multiplying the numerator by one-half); the denominator of Coulter's I_1 is $2(1 - \text{min}Q)$. When the number of components is small, the difference between the two denominators can be critical. Differences tend to be trivial for systems with a large number of components. Both are intended mathematically to norm their respective indexes from zero to unity by dividing the numerator by its maximum possible value. The ID denominator is technically incorrect. Coulter's I_α, when $\alpha = 1.00$, can be interpreted as a properly normed version of Duncan and Duncan's ID.

If the parameter of the generalized equation is set at two, for example, the inequity equation becomes:

$$I_2 = \sqrt{\frac{\Sigma (P_i - Q_i)^2}{1 - 2(minQ) + \Sigma Q_i^2}}$$

With alpha set at two, the equation carries out the same logic but under different operational rules. Its numerator sums the squared differences between actual and standard distributions. Its denominator still represents the difference between the standard distribution and the most inequitable possible actual distribution, the malimum, given the equity standard expressed in Q and given that differences are squared in the denominator. Finally, the procedure requires extracting the square root of the ratio, in order partially to return the value to its original numerical units. Using the hypothetical data in table 8-2, the numerator of $I_2 = \sqrt{.20}$, as indicated at the bottom of column four. The denominator equals $1 - 2(0.1) + 0.3 = 1.1$. Thus:

$$I_2 = \sqrt{(.20/1.1)} = \sqrt{.182} = .43.$$

Setting the parameter value depends on the investigator's conceptualization of inequity. The greater the parameter, the disproportionately more heavily are larger discrepancies weighted in comparison to smaller ones. When α equals unity, all discrepancies are weighted equally. That is, ten discrepancies of 0.01 weigh the same as one discrepancy of 0.10. As alpha increases beyond unity, however, larger differences are weighted disproportionately more heavily than smaller ones, due to the exponent, α, in the generalized equation. This means that a final index value is disproportionately more heavily influenced by components with the largest differences between actual and standard distributional shares. The simplified distribution in table 8-3 contains little concentration of discrepancies, in terms of the particular equity standard. Half of all components are tied for the largest discrepancy.

Setting $\alpha = 2$, for example, reduces very small discrepancies to virtually zero, because it involves squaring small proportions. A discrepancy of .02 squared equals .0004. a discrepancy of 0.20 squared is .04. The ratios of the discrepancies and their squares illustrate the diminishing marginal value of smaller discrepancies between actual and equity distribution. The ratio of .20 to .02 is ten to one. The ratio of their squares, .04 to .0004, is one hundred to one.

The generalized exponent, α, determines the index's sensitivity to concentration. It allows the investigator to choose a form of I_α that is sensitive only to inequality or that is also sensitive to concentration in various degrees, relative to the available amount of inequality. In the case of inequity indexes, inequality refers to the aggregate discrepancy between actual and standard distribution. Concentration refers to the extent to which the total sum of discrepancies is scattered among many components or clustered in only a few (Coulter, 1983b; Smithson, 1979). Exponentiation with alpha increasingly greater than unity produces an index that is increasingly sensitive only to concentration, relative to the available amount of inequality in the distribution. Coulter's I_α is firmly grounded in the theory of convexity in mathematical analysis and optimization (Coulter and Pittman, 1983).

The polarity of I_α is toward inequality or concentration; the larger an index value, the greater the inequity of the distribution. I_1 reflects inequality only, because its summational core does not involve any multiplicative function. Inequity indexes with $\alpha > 1.0$ are increasingly sensitive to concentration.

Regarding the principle of transfers, inequity measures require special interpretation. The important point is the effect of a transfer on the size of the aggregate discrepancy between actual and standard distributions, rather than on the sizes of donor's and recipient's shares. Applied to inequity measurement, the transfer principle requires that measured inequity decrease if a transfer decreases the aggregate discrepancy in the system.

Different forms of the generalized inequity index (i.e., with $\alpha = 1.0$ or $\alpha > 1.0$) behave differently when units of an actual distribution are transferred from one component to another. I_1, for example, resembles both the Schutz coefficient (chapter three) and Duncan and Duncan's index of dissimilarity (chapter seven) with respect to the transfers principle. It conforms only partially to that principle, due to the fact that it sums absolute differences. For I_1, only a transfer of units from a component whose actual share exceeds its standard share to a component whose actual share is smaller than its standard share (or vice versa) reduces aggregate discrepancy and produces a decrease in the inequity index score. Subtracting Q_i from P_i produces positive and negative discrepancies, the signs of which are, of course, ignored in computing I_1. I_1 complies with the transfers principle only if units are transferred from a component that has a positive discrepancy to one that has a negative discrepancy. Therefore I_1 does not fully comply with the transfers criterion.

In contrast, forms of the index with $\alpha > 1.0$ are consistent with the principle of transfers. A transfer of units from a donor with a larger discrepancy to a recipient with a smaller discrepancy decreases the inequity score. The effect of the transfer depends on the size of the alpha as well as the size of the transfer.

Except for sensitivity to concentration and transfers, inequity indexes with any alpha equal to or greater than unity behave the same way. Specifically, multiplying every component's share by a positive constant leaves the value of I_α unchanged, so it comports with the scale invariance principle. Adding a positive constant to every component causes the inequity score to decline, reflecting decreased inequity. The generalized index fails to conform to the population symmetry criterion when K is small; if two identical distributions are merged, for example, I_α for the merged system differs from that of either of the parts that comprise it. However, when K grows larger (e.g., K > 10), I_α increasingly approximates conformity to population symmetry. For large systems, it does.

The index of inequity also presents a special case of interpretation regarding its sensitivity to number of components and, therefore, which type of measure it is. Neither its upper nor its lower limit depends on the number of components. The values of I_α range from a minimum of zero for total equity, when all $P_i = Q_i$, to a maximum of unity in the case in which the component that should receive the smallest share (according to the equity standard) actually has all units. Inequity's scores (but not its range) are affected by number of components, regardless of alpha's value, and it is for that reason a type B absolute index.

The inequity index score declines when system size increases, due to the mathematical correctness of the denominator that norms the index. The denominator uses the smallest share in the equity distribution, minQ. Increasing the number of components decreases the size of minQ, so number of components affects the inequity index value. I_1 generally declines only slightly when number of components increases, whereas I_α with a larger exponent experiences a larger decrease, due to disproportionately reducing the importance of smaller discrepancies between actual and equity distributions.

The I_α procedure takes all null components into account, regardless of whether they occur in the actual or standard distribution. By definition, a null component in the standard distribution will appear as minQ in the denominator and make the index value larger. However, in all other ways, I_α omits from consideration any component that is null in both actual and standard distributions, because neither number of components (K) nor mean proportional share (1/K) appears in the equation. For this reason, increasing the number of "double-null" components beyond one does not affect index scores.

I_1 satisfies the principle of scale invariance but violates the population symmetry and transfers criteria. Therefore, it is inconsistent with the Lorenz dominance criterion. When the alpha parameter is greater than unity, however, the index of inequity satisfies the transfers and scale invariance axioms, but violates the population symmetry criteria. Therefore, it does not conform to the Lorenz dominance principle.

The index of inequity is defined for all distributions, uses all distributional information well, and is bounded from zero to unity. Inequity is a more complicated concept than inequality, and the generalized index of inequity is a complicated measure. When reduced to its appropriate forms with alpha set at unity or two, however, it is computationally simple. Finally, Coulter's I_α assumes that components are nominally scaled categories.

Political scientists have used Coulter's index to measure inequity in several kinds of empirical distributions, including distribution of public services among subareas of a jurisdiction (Coulter, 1980 and 1983a; Buczko, 1982; Jones, 1982). Other researchers have used the index to analyze the distribution of business contributions to United Way among seven sectors of the economy (Miller and Collins, 1985) and changes in the distribution of physicians by type among subareas of a state (Knopke, Hartman, and Coulter, 1988).

NAGEL'S INDEX OF EQUITY (EQ)

Nagel's (1984) index offers a different but potentially useful conceptualization of inequity. He defined equity as "allocating societal or governmental benefits or costs to places, groups, or people in such a way as to provide each of them with a minimum level of benefits and costs in light of their needs and resources" (Nagel, 1984:73). In this definition, he conceptualized equity as a minimum constraint regarding benefits that persons should receive, such as income or services, or as a maximum constraint on detriments that persons should receive, such as taxes or crime.

Nagel operationalized his "minimum decency level" conceptualization of equity with the following equation:

$$EQ = 1 - \frac{\Sigma(A_i - M_i)^2}{\Sigma(Z - M_i)^2}$$

with A_i = actual frequency distribution to the component,
M_i = minimum decency level frequency for the component,
Z = zero allocation (most inequitable), and
when $A_i > M_i$, $A_i - M_i$ = 0

The ratio in the equation measures inequity, but it is subtracted from unity, giving EQ an equity polarity. Note that the formula operates on raw frequencies rather than on proportions. The numerator of the ratio sums the squared differences between the actual distribution to each component and the number of units each component must have to attain a minimum level of decency, but only if the actual share is below the minimum standard. The operational procedure requires that whenever an actual share's frequency exceeds its minimum decency level, the difference is scored zero, "since inequity occurs only when people are allowed to fall below the minimum decency level" (Nagel, 1984:78). In other words, according to Nagel's conceptualization, inequity means having too little and does not include having too much. It is evident, also, that Nagel's EQ is based on a deviations model and that the minimum decency level serves as the comparative standard.

The denominator of the ratio sums the squares of the differences between the lowest possible distribution to a component (nothing) and the minimum decency level. This sum represents the maximum possible deviations, because by definition, components cannot be given less than nothing. Dividing the numerator by this denominator norms the ratio and yields the percentage of maximum possible inequity achieved by the actual distribution. Subtracting the ratio from unity yields Nagel's equity score.

Because it is so subjective, selecting a minimum decency level for analyzing any particular distribution is difficult. Determining biological needs, such as the minimum number of calories a person requires to remain alive or achieve a certain level of work, is relatively easy. The question becomes considerably more subjective when we move from biology to economics: how many dollars (or appropriate units of currency) must a person have in order to purchase the least expensive food that will supply the minimum number of calories to sustain life? It becomes even more subjective when translated into its political form: what exactly should the government do in order to assure that all its citizens can meet their minimum economic or biological needs? The answers vary across time and societies, depending primarily on custom and what the society thinks it can afford (Nagel, 1984:79-80).

A brief example will demonstrate how the index of equity works, based on Nagel's minimum decency conceptualization. Table 8-4 includes hypothetical data and the necessary computation.

$EQ = 1 - 14/207 = 1 - .07 = .93$. The actual distribution is ninety three per cent of perfect equity, based on a minimum decency concept of equity (column two of table 8-4) and the particular frequencies and sum of the minimum standard selected by the investigator. The sum of differences in column five is divided by the sum of differences in column six, and the difference is subtracted from unity to arrive at a value for Nagel's EQ.

Nagel designed EQ to be sensitive to concentration as well as to inequality, but of course only for those components whose shares are below the minimum decency level. He stipulated that "the deviation between the actual allocation to a person, group, or place and the minimum is squared, rather than just using the absolute difference, because squaring accentuates extreme cases. Thus a deviation of 1 for each of two people is not as bad as a deviation of 2 for one person . . . (when) squaring is done" (Nagel, 1984:78).

Table 8-4
Computation of Nagel's Indexes of Equity
and Proportionality Based on Hypothetical Data*

1 A_i	2 M_i	3 P_i	4 $A_i - M_i$	5 $(A_i - M_i)^2$	6 $(Z - M_i)^2$	7 $(A_i - P_i)^2$	8 $(Z - P_i)^2$
5	1	1	0	0	1	16	1
6	8	8	2	4	64	4	64
9	6	6	0	0	36	9	36
2	5	5	3	9	25	9	25
7	9	9	2	4	81	4	81
			Total	14	207	42	207

*For an explanation of the notation, refer to the equations for Nagel's EQ and PR.

EQ does not completely satisfy the principle of transfers. Specifically, a transfer between two components, both of whose actual shares exceed their minimum levels, leaves Nagel's EQ value unchanged. Nor does EQ satisfy the scale invariance axiom; multiplying each actual value by a positive constant increases equity measured by EQ. In fact, if the positive constant is large enough, all components' actual shares would be larger than any of their minimum-decency-level shares, and equity would equal unity. Consistent with expectation, however, and for the same reason, adding a positive constant to each actual share increases Nagel's equity value. EQ does conform to the principle of population symmetry. For example, if two identical systems are merged, measured equity remains the same for the combined distribution as it was for each of the parts.

Neither EQ's upper and lower limits, unity and zero, nor its values depend on the number of components, so it is a properly bounded measure in that sense. Its logical range goes from zero for perfect equity, when each component's actual share equals or exceeds its minimum decency share, to unity when each component possesses no units. It is a relative measure that includes any number of null components. Because EQ is inconsistent with the transfers and scale invariance principles, it fails to satisfy the Lorenz dominance criterion. The fact that the Lorenz curve of distribution A is everywhere northwest of the Lorenz curve of distribution B does not necessarily mean that an EQ score for distribution A is larger (more equitable) than an EQ score for distribution B.

EQ is defined for all distributions. From a technical standpoint, Nagel's equity does not necessarily make good use of all distributional information. Specifically, it omits consideration of the differences between actual and minimum standard shares when the actual exceeds the minimum. I rate EQ's information use as good, however, because it conforms to Nagel's conceptual definition of equity. Its interpretation is quite clear because zero represents total inequity and unity represents total equity, and its computation is simple. Finally, it assumes that shares are defined as nominal categories.

Unfortunately, EQ has not been used to examine an empirical distribution in published research. Despite EQ's failure to satisfy several important principles of inequity theory, it innovatively operationalizes a useful conceptualization of equity based on the minimum decency standard.

NAGEL'S INDEX OF PROPORTIONALITY (PR)

Nagel (1984:82-85) also operationalized the Aristotelian concept of proportional equality or equity in the following form:

$$PR = 1 - \frac{\Sigma (A_i - P_i)^2}{\Sigma (Z - P_i)^2}$$

where A_i =   actual frequency distribution to the component,
P_i =   distribution of A to each i in proportion to its merit, and
Z =   zero allocation (most inequitable)

Nagel's index of proportionality has an equity polarity; the larger the index value, the greater the level of proportional equity. The ratio of the equation actually computes inequity, but it is subtracted from unity to produce an equity index. Based on a deviations model, the index operates on raw frequencies.

The numerator sums the squared differences between the frequencies of the actual distribution (A_i) and the frequencies of the standard distribution (P_i) or the shares that would occur if the units were distributed in proportion to an equity standard such as merit. The term "proportionate distribution" or "proportionate share" used in this context refers to the frequencies that each component would receive if the A_i were distributed in proportion to the P_i. The proportionate distribution based on merit serves as the comparative standard. Recall that the numerator of Nagel's index of equity (EQ) differs from this numerator in that it subtracts the minimum decency levels (rather than proportionate shares) from actual shares, and omits the difference if the actual exceeds the minimum decency level.

The denominator of PR sums the squares of the differences between each proportionate share and zero, that is, the differences between what the equity standard indicates each component should receive and nothing. Nothing is as far away as one can get from the proportionate shares, assuming by definition that one cannot distribute negative units. PR's denominator resembles that of Nagel's EQ, except that the latter subtracts the minimum from zero rather than subtracting the proportionate share from zero.

The ratio in the PR formula represents dividing the sum of the actual squared differences by the sum of the maximum squared differences that could occur under the condition of maximum proportional inequity, as Nagel defined it. It measures inequity; subtracting it from unity yields the proportionality index.

Table 8-4 presented earlier contains the data and computations necessary to obtain a PR score. Reference to the PR equation and appropriate columns in table 8-4 will clarify the procedure. The equation calls for dividing the sum of column seven by the sum of column eight and subtracting that ratio from unity: $PR = 1 - 42/207 = 1 - .20 = .80$, a value indicating that the distribution is eighty per cent of perfect proportionate equality. Note that in table 8-4, the same equity standard distribution was used to evaluate the same actual distribution with both of Nagel's equity indexes, EQ and PR. They produce substantially different results as expected ($EQ = .93$, and $PR = .80$), because they operationalize different conceptualizations of inequity. EQ dismisses component actual share excesses above the standard share as irrelevant, whereas PR considers them to be inequitable.

Because PR squares the discrepancies between actual and equity standard, it is sensitive to concentration of units as well as to inequality. It is also sensitive to transfers. A PR value increases with a transfer from a component with a larger discrepancy to a component with a smaller discrepancy. Otherwise, a transfer that increases the aggregate squared discrepancy increases the PR score.

Nagel's proportionality conforms to the principle of scale invariance. Multiplying each actual share by a positive constant does not change the size of a PR value or measured equity. Its behavior is also consistent with the constant additions criterion. When a positive constant is added to each actual share (and the frequencies in the standard distribution are adjusted appropriately so that each component's standard frequency remains the same proportion of the total), the value of PR increases, indicating an increase in measured equity.

PR also obeys the population symmetry rule. Therefore, it is consistent with the Lorenz dominance criterion. The fact that distribution A has a larger PR value (indicating greater equity) than distribution B means that distribution A has a Lorenz curve that is everywhere above and nowhere below that of distribution B.

The values of this index demonstrate no sensitivity to number of components. For instance, if each component's actual and standard shares are split in half, doubling the number of components and halving the size of each, the PR score remains the same. It is a relative measure that includes any number of single-null components but excludes all double-null components. Nagel's proportionality is defined for all distributions and makes good use of distributional information.

Unfortunately, PR suffers from a conceptual flaw that is operationalized in the procedure and results in a technical difficulty that limits its usefulness. Keep in mind that PR operates on raw frequencies. Nagel indicated that the index ranges from zero to unity. However, because of its conceptualization, it is not properly bounded. It reaches zero, Nagel's definition of maximum inequity, when the actual distribution is null for all components. It can also reach zero under different conditions. It reaches unity, according to Nagel's definition of maximum equity, when the actual distribution is identical to the standard or proportional distribution. PR can also assume negative values under some distributional conditions.

Consider a simple, two-component system in three distributional situations. In the first situation, each component should receive ten units, but each actually receives none. In this case, PR = 0, maximum inequity. In the second situation, each component should receive ten units, but one unit actually receives twenty and the other none. In this extremely different second case, PR also equals zero. In the third situation, component A should receive twenty units and component B should receive none, but component A receives none and component B twenty. In this third case, PR = 1 − 2 = −1.0. Proportionality can assume even larger negative values; for example, PR can equal −1.23 in a four-component system sharing twenty units.

The difficulty lies in conceptualizing maximum inequity as each component receiving nothing, regardless of what each should receive according to the equity standard. In this conceptualization, maximum inequity exists only if there is no actual distribution at all. Which is, in fact, more inequitable: (a) all components receiving nothing or (b) one component receiving all, regardless of the equity standard? Nagel stated that "giving everybody nothing is the worst allocation in terms of equity" (Nagel, 1984:81). The conceptualization is imaginative and interesting, but its operationalization in PR simply does not work under some distributional conditions.

The index of proportionality is fairly simple to compute and assumes that the components of the actual distribution are nominally scaled. No examples of application of PR to the study of actual distributions yet exists in the published literature.

CONCLUSIONS

Inequity logic provides a context for interpreting the results of inequity indexes. The model stipulates that an index value represents the difference between an actual distribution and an independent, standard distribution that the investigator stipulates as appropriate or equitable. The particular conceptualization of inequity, the equity standard chosen, and the way in which the differences are statistically treated (including whether the summational core uses absolute or squared discrepancies) determine the differences among inequity index values. Relatively few choices confront the researcher who wants to measure inequity. All the indexes are based on a deviations model and use some form of an independent distribution as the comparative standard.

9

SUMMARY AND CONCLUSIONS

In this final chapter I return to two simple themes introduced in the first chapter, namely, that distribution is an important social science concept that we should measure well, and that good measurement requires careful conceptual and operational definition of the problem. Next, to illustrate use of the conceptual and technical criteria to define the problem and to select an appropriate measure, I briefly critique Judith Treas's work on income inequality. Finally, I conclude with a brief discussion of six methodological improvements that should be made on inequality measurement in order to enhance future research in this field.

THE IMPORTANCE OF DISTRIBUTION

In chapter one, I argued the importance of the generic concept distribution, its primary derivative inequality, and its many secondary derivatives that provide variations on the primary theme. The distribution of political power stands at the center of polity and political science. The distribution of social status stands at the center of society and sociology. The distribution of income and economic class stands at the center of the economy and economics. Polity, society, and economy are social systems, and all social systems form and continue because units are distributed among a set of components. In fact, one definition of a social system is any set of components united by sharing a distribution of units of power, status, or class. A social system can vary in size from the international economy to the family. Components can be people, places, or groups. Units can be any measurable manifestation of power, status, or class.

The concept distribution not only defines the idea of the social system but also gives meaning to it. Most non-trivial social behavior can legitimately be interpreted in terms of efforts by people, places, or groups to preserve or change the distribution of units among them. Frequently, they exert such an effort simply to preserve or increase the size of their own share of the units, not intentionally to change the overall distribution among all components within the system. If they succeed, however, their behavior does serve to change the overall distribution or to preserve it in the face of challenges. Both maintenance and change within a social system, then, can be interpreted as the result of the dy-

namics created by individuals' and groups' behavior directed toward maintaining
or increasing their share of units.

Why should social scientists measure distribution? Because it constitutes
perhaps the most important dimension of the existence and dynamics of social
behavior. Adequate description and explanation of any important social phenomenon require direct reference to distributional concepts. Try to describe or
explain the behavior of a family, legislative body, business, ethnic or racial
group, university, etc., without reference to distributional concepts. It is very
hard to do and produces rather insipid results.

APPROPRIATE CONCEPTUALIZATION AND MEASUREMENT

That we should measure distribution seems clear enough. More complicated and less clear is how we should measure distribution. The correct general
answer is that we should appropriately link our particular conceptualization of
distribution with a particular set of statistical procedures. This admonition,
however, assumes prior resolution of an invariably difficult problem, that is,
forming an appropriate conceptualization of inequality, given the particular empirical properties of the distributional problem we confront.

Chapter two offers advice on conceptualizing inequality. How we should
measure inequality depends on the objective distributional properties of the research problem that interests us and on how we conceptualize those properties.
As we contemplate a particular distributional research problem, we should answer a series of conceptual and technical questions that comprise a checklist for
inequality measurement. The answers have both theoretical and practical significance. Appropriate reference to the summary tables near the beginning of chapters three through eight helps to link theoretical conceptualizations of inequality
to specific indexes of inequality. These tables indicate which indexes incorporate
which conceptual and technical assumptions about inequality in their operational
equations.

Understanding the principles of inequality theory and the technical properties of inequality measures enables the investigator properly to conceptualize a
given distributional research problem. These principles and properties will also
help us correctly to translate our conceptualization of inequality into an operational definition by indicating which index(es) might be most appropriate. One
way to draw some useful conclusions from this book is to examine an example
of inequality research with respect to its conformity to the norms suggested in
chapter two. The purpose of such an exercise is to demonstrate how the investigator used the principles of inequality theory to conceptualize the problem and to
select an appropriate measurement index.

To measure the relative effects of social welfare benefits and business cy-
cles on family income inequality, sociologist Judith Treas (1983) consciously

made many correct decisions. She carefully conceptualized the problem, reviewed several principles of inequality theory, and selected an index that operationalized her conceptualization appropriately. Although she might have used inequality theory even more thoroughly, her attempt to link concept and measure, on the whole, appropriately represents excellent methodological decisions.

Treas (1983:549) summarized her theoretical interest as follows: "Improved employment opportunities are a plausible explanation of reductions in income inequality, because economic booms may trickle down, transforming some poor families into middle-income ones. Similarly, the expansion of public welfare programs seems a force for greater equality to the extent that these programs benefit less well-off families." She choose inequality as the dependent variable and employment levels and public welfare programs as the explanatory variables.

Based on this theoretical interest, she preferred a measure with several specific theoretical and technical characteristics. First, "theoretical concerns . . . argue that inequality is best guaged with reference to the entire distribution of income, rather than a single point on the distribution (i.e., the poverty line)" (Treas, 1983:549). Thus she wanted a measure that fully uses distributional information. Second, she wanted a measure that will "decline when income is transferred from a high-income to a low-income person without changing their rankings" (Treas, 1983:550), that is, one that conforms to the principle of transfers.

Third, because she tested her hypotheses using a dataset describing income distribution over the period 1947-77, she preferred a measure that would be impervious to the constant proportional increases occasioned by inflation over the 30 years, that is, a scale invariant measure. Fourth, she needed a measure that would "weight changes in the bottom tail more heavily," (Treas, 1983:550), because that was "in accord with our normative notions that such changes are of greater consequence to social welfare." Fifth, she obviously wanted to measure inequality, not inequity. Sixth, she wanted to focus on intragroup inequality rather than intergroup inequality.

Treas considered but rejected the Gini coefficient (chapter three), and then chose Theil's H (chapter five). She did so largely because Gini is disproportionately sensitive to distributional changes near the mean and because Theil's absolute entropy is disproportionately sensitive to distributional changes among the smaller components or poorest individuals. Theil's H also conforms well to her other theoretical preferences: transfers, scale invariance, and intragroup inequality (not inequity nor intergroup inequality).

That Treas deliberately made these methodological decisions and made them correctly clearly sets her work apart from most inequality research. However, by deciding to use absolute entropy, Treas also either implicitly or unintentionally made several additional theoretical assumptions, some of which might be inappropriate. Theil's absolute entropy a)measures concentration rather than just inequality, b) uses the mean as an implicit comparative standard (as all entropy-based indexes do), c) reflects decreased concentration with constant additions, d) is a measure of absolute inequality that excludes null components, e) fails the population symmetry test, f) is, therefore, not a Lorenz-dominant measure, and g) assumes that the components are nominally scaled.

By now, the reader should detect that at least two of these properties of Theil's H might be disadvantages in the Treas analysis. First, because income categories are ordinally rather than nominally scaled, she might have more appropriately selected an index that assumes that components are ordinal classes, as her income categories are. Second, an increase in Theil's H, from one year to the next, does not necessarily mean increased equality (unless both years' distributions have identical means and numbers of components), because their Lorenz curves may intersect. Three other potential flaws are fortunately of little concern in Treas's analysis. Interpretability is not a serious problem, even though both H values and the H upper limit are dependent on number of components, and excluding null categories means excluding society's most destitute group. However, the number of income components, K, was constant throughout the 30-year period. In addition, the best dataset she was able to use, drawn from the Current Population Survey, simply did not include persons with no income, so her chosen index excluded no null components.

Treas's study illustrates methodological rigor superior to that of most social science investigations of inequality. It's results appear valid and reliable. However, she could have conceptualized inequality even more thoroughly and, therefore, possibly selected an even more appropriate index for her conceptualization. Which index might have been more appropriate? Atkinson's I_R (chapter six), with the alpha parameter set at two or three, probably operationalizes the Treas conceptualization of inequality better than Theil's entropy. Atkinson's inequality index replicates the Theil measure with respect to all of Treas's explicit criteria except that it assumes ordinally-scaled components (such as Treas's income categories), a clear improvement.

Finally, we should not forget that many indexes have certain important idiosyncratic characteristics because of their peculiar statistical treatments of the basic information about the distribution. We should consider these peculiarities before choosing an index, either because we want to avoid or to guarantee the peculiarities, given the nature of the distributional problem. Some of these peculiarities make an index unique or at least different from most others.

FURTHER METHODOLOGICAL DEVELOPMENT

We know a lot about the theoretical and technical properties of measuring inequality, as this book documents. However, further methodological research on inequality indexes would probably strengthen our ability to make more precise and reliable causal inferences. Five methodological problems seem most in need of solution: aggregation bias, decomposability, sampling distribution, distributional characteristics, and stability.

Aggregation Bias

Waldman (1977:238) is virtually the only inequality researcher to express concern over aggregation bias, which he defined as "under- or overestimation of the true value that occurs when our interest is in data originally for separate categories but available in combined categories." Investigators often confront aggregation bias in measuring income inequality. Both the U. S. Census and U.S. Internal Revenue Service report the incomes of millions of people in as few as 10 to 14 categories. Sample surveys usually report respondents' incomes in even fewer categories. In using this kind of aggregated data, it is important to know how much bias the aggregation introduces and the possible differential sensitivity of indexes to aggregation bias.

Waldman's (1977) preliminary research into aggregation bias suggests two distinct possibilities. First, most indexes are subject to extensive aggregation bias and, second, indexes demonstrate little variability in the aggregation bias to which they are subject. Regarding the second point, he surmised that indexes using logarithmic transformations, such as the entropy measures, substantially distort even slight aggregations, in comparison with other treatments of the summational core.

Decomposability

Decomposition refers to determination of the contribution of each of several constituent parts to the total. Constituent parts might be subsets of components or geographic regions. According to social scientists (Theil, 1967 and 1972; Waldman, 1975) who have investigated this methodological problem, only the entropy measures are decomposable without bias. Theil (1967) decomposed entropy measures of per capita income inequality among 54 countries into within-regional and between-regional components. Waldman (1975) decomposed entropy measures of vote inequality among Italian political parties into sets of parties and geographic components. Further methodological research might devise additional indexes that are decomposable.

Sampling Distribution

In many cases of inequality measurement based on sample data, it might be important to know if a particular index value differs significantly from unity or from some other value of the same index. Similarly, it might be important to estimate confidence intervals for an index value. In order to accomplish either of these tasks, the sampling distribution of the statistic must be known (Wilcox,

1973; Waldman, 1977). Little or nothing is known about the sampling distributions of most inequality measures. If more were known, investigators could take this into account in selecting a measure.

Distributional Characteristics

This property refers to the behavior of an index when it is computed for all distributions with given number of units (N) and number of components (K). Wilcox (1973) argued that such a distribution should be symmetrical, preferably normal. If so, interpreting an index value between the upper and lower limits becomes easier and more reliable. Numerous interpretation problems occur in the absence of information about a measure's distribution. For example, some measures appear to reach their upper or lower limit rather quickly, some have great trouble reaching their limits, and some demonstrate a large range in the upper limits reached (Waldman, 1977).

Waldman (1977) made preliminary estimates of distributional characteristics of 20 indexes using N = 50 and K = 2, while varying P_1 from 0.1 to 0.5. Almost all indexes reached zero as a minimum value, but maximum values varied widely. In addition, means and standard deviations of values also differed considerably. It would appear that most measures do not conform to Wilcox's desideratum that their distributions should be normal or at least symmetrical.

Stability

Finally, Wilcox (1973) argued for further investigation into the stability of indexes, that is, the extent to which they change with the addition of components with few units. If a researcher is uncertain about whether to include or omit such components, an index whose value depends little on whether they are included or excluded may be preferable. Such indexes are less likely to distort conclusions based on them.

Presumably, adding these six criteria to the others detailed in chapter two would enhance an investigator's ability to select the most appropriate index. That is, an investigator might also want an index that has minimal aggregation bias, is decomposable, has a known set of procedures for computing statistical significance of index values, has a normal distribution, and is quite stable. Establishing these six properties as technical criteria for evaluating inequality indexes represents a major set of measurement problems for methodologists to solve in the future.

Rae (1981:150) concluded that "equality is the simplest and most abstract of notions, yet the practices of the world are irremediably concrete and complex . . . . We are always confronted with more than one practical meaning for equality and equality itself cannot provide a basis for choosing among them." Measuring inequality is tricky business, requiring a creative combination of science, craft, and art. When done well, it produces both truth and beauty. This book is intended to help us all do it better.

REFERENCES

Alker, Haward R., Jr. and Bruce M. Russett (1964). "On Measuring Inequality," *Behavioral Science*, 9 (July): 207-218.

Agresti, Alan and Barbara F. Agresti (1977). "Statistical Analysis of Qualitative Variation," in Karl F. Schuessler, ed., *Sociological Methodology, 1978*. San Francisco: Jossey-Bass Publishers.

Allison, Paul D. (1978). "Measures of Inequality," *American Sociological Review*, 43 (December): 865-880.

Amemiya, E. C. (1963). "Measurement of Economic Differentiation," *Journal of Regional Science*, 5 (Summer): 84-87.

Atkinson, A. B. (1975). *The Economics of Inequality*. London: Oxford University Press.

Atkinson, A. B. (1970). "On the Measurement of Inequality," *Journal of Economic Theory*, 2, 244-263.

Attneave, Fred (1959), *Applications of Information Theory to Psychology*. New York: Holt-Dryden.

Bailey, Kenneth D. (1985). "Entropy Measures of Inequality," *Sociological Inquiry*, 55 (Spring): 200-211.

Barker, Ernest, ed. (1958). *The Politics of Aristotle*. New York: Oxford University Press.

Bartels, C. P. A. and P. Nijcamp (1976). "An Empirical Welfare Approach to Regional Income Distributions," *Socioeconomic Planning Sciences*, 10, 244-263.

Beach, C. M. and R. Davidson (1983). "Distribution-Free Statistical Inference with Lorenz Curves and Income Shares," *Review of Economic Studies*, 50 723-735.

Beach, C. M. and J. Richmond (1985). "Joint Confidence Intervals for Income Shares and Lorenz Curves," *International Economic Review*, 26 (June): 439-450.

Bell, Wendell (1954). "A Probability Model of the Measurement of Ecological Segregation," *Social Forces*, 32: 357-3644.

Bell, Wendell and Ernest M. Willis (1957). "The Segregation of Negroes in American Cities," *Social and Economic Studies*, 6 (March): 59-75.

Bishop, John A. and Paul D. Thistle (1986). "Income Inequality and Economic Welfare Among the States," paper prepared for the annual meeting of the Southern Economic Association, November, 1986.

Blau, Peter M. (1977). *Inequality and Heterogeneity*. New York: The Free Press.

Boadway, Robin and Neil Bruce (1984). *Welfare Economics*. Oxford, England: Basil Blackwell, Inc.

Boyle, John and David Jacobs (1982). "The Intra-City Distribution of Services: A Multivariate Analysis," *American Political Science Review*, 76 (June): 371-380.

Brams, Steven J. (1968). "Measuring the Concentration of Power in Political Systems," *American Political Science Review*, 62 (June): 461-475.

Buczko, William (1982). "Measures of Inequity, Distribution Standards, and Municipal Expenditures," *Social Science Quarterly*, 63 (December): 661-673.

Burstein, Alan M. (1976). "Patterns of Segregation and the Residential Experience," *Historical Methods Newsletter*, 9, 105-113.

Carnap, Rudolf (1977). *Two Essays on Entropy*. Berkeley, Cal.: University of California Press.

Champernowne, David (1974). "A Comparison of Measures of Inequality of Income Distribution," *The Economic Journal*, 84 (December): 787-816.

Chiang, Alpha C. (1984). *Fundamental Methods of Mathematical Economics*. New York: McGraw-Hill Book Co.

Coleman, James S. (1960). "The Mathematical Study of Small Groups," in Herbert Soloman, ed., *Mathematical Thinking in the Measurement of Behavior*. Glencoe, Ill.: The Free Press, 1-151.

Coleman, James S., T. Hoffer, and S. Kilgore (1982). "Achievement and Segregation in Secondary Schools: A Further Look at Public and Private School Differences," *Sociology of Education*, 55, 162-182.

Coleman, James S., S. D. Kelly, and J. A. Moore (1975). *Trends in School Segregation*, 1968-1973. Washington, D.C.: Urban Institute.

Coleman, Stephen (1975). *Measurement and Analysis of Political Systems.* New York: John Wiley and Sons.

Cortese, Charles F., R. F. Falk, and Jack Cohen (1976). "Further Considerations on the Methodological Analysis of Segregation Indices," *American Sociological Review*, 41 (August): 630-637.

Coulter, Philip B. (1980). "Measuring the Inequity of Urban Public Services," *Policy Studies Journal*, 8 (Spring): 683-698.

Coulter, Philip B. (1981). "Measuring Distributional Inequity," *Policy Studies Journal*, 10 (December): 395-405.

Coulter, Philip B. (1983a). "Inferring the Distributional Effects of Bureaucratic Decision Rules," *Policy Studies Journal*, 12 (December): 347-356.

Coulter, Philip B. (1983b). "Distinguishing Inequality and Concentration," *Political Methodology*, 10: 323-337.

Coulter, Philip B. (1988). *Political Voice, Citizen Demand for Urban Public Services.* Tuscaloosa: The University of Alabama Press.

Coulter, Philip B. and Terry Pittman (1983). "Measuring Who Gets What: A Mathematical Model of Maldistribution," *Political Methodology*, 9: 215-234.

Cowell, F. A. (1977). *Measuring Inequality, Techniques for the Social Sciences.* New York: John Wiley and Sons.

Dahl, Robert A. (1984). *Modern Political Analysis.* Englewood Cliffs, NJ: Prentice-Hall, Inc.).

Dahl, Robert A. (1956). *A Preface to Democratic Theory.* Chicago: The University of Chicago Press.

Dahrendorf, Ralf (1986). *Essays in the Theory of Society.* Stanford, CA: Stanford University Press.

Dalton, Hugh (1920). "The Measurement of the Inequality of Incomes," *The Economic Journal*, 30 (September): 348-361.

Dasgupta, P., A. K. Sen, and D. Starrett (1973). "Notes on the Measurement of Inequality," *Journal of Economic Theory*, 6: 180-187.

David, H. A. (1968). "Gini's Mean Difference Rediscovered," *Biometrica*, 55, 573-575.

Denbigh, K G. and J. S. Denbigh (1985). *Entropy in Relation to Incomplete Knowlege*. Cambridge, England: Cambridge University Press.

Duncan, Otis D. and Beverly Duncan (1955). "A Methodological Analysis of Segregation Indexes," *American Sociological Review*, 20 (March): 210-217.

Easton, David (1981). *The Political System*, 2d ed. Chicago: The University of Chicago Press.

Farley, Reynolds and Karl E. Taeuber (1968). "Population Trends and Residential Segregation Since 1960," *Science*, 159: 953-956.

Feld, S. and B. Grofman (1980). "The Class Size Paradox and Conflict of Interest Among Faculty, Students, and Administration," *Frontiers of Economics*, 3.

Formby, John (1987). "Income Inequality and Economic Welfare," unpublished manuscript, Department of Economics, Finance, and Legal Studies, University of Alabama.

Fossett, Mark and Scott J. South (1983). "The Measurement of Intergroup Income Inequality: A Conceptual Review," *Social Forces*, 61 (March): 855-871.

Fossett, Mark, Omer R. Galle, and William R. Kelly (1986). "Racial Occupational Inequality, 1940-1980: National and Regional Trends," *American Sociological Review*, 51 (June): 421-429.

Galtung, Johan (1967). *Theory and Methods of Social Research*. New York: Columbia University Press.

Gerth, Hans and C. Wright Mills (1946). *From Max Weber: Essays in Sociology*. New York: Oxford University Press.

Gini, Corrado (1912). *Variabilita e Mutabilita*. Bologna, Italy.

Gini, Corrado (1936). "On the Measure of Concentration with Especial Reference to Income and Wealth," Cowles Commission.

Greenberg, J. (1956). "The Measurement of Linguistic Diversity," *Language*, 32, 109-115.

Hall, Marshall and Nicholas Tideman (1967). "Measures of Concentration," *Journal of the American Statistical Association*, 62 (March): 162-168.

Hammond, K. R. , J. E. Householder, and N. John Castellan, Jr. (1970). *Introduction to the Statistical Method.* New York: Alfred A. Knopf, Inc.

Helmert, F. R. (1876). "Die Berechnung des Warscheinlichen Beobachtungfehlers aus den ersten Potenzen dur Differenzen Gleichgenauer Directer Beobachtungen," *Astronomische Narhrichten*, 88 127-132.

Herfindahl, O. C. (1950). "Concentration in the Steel Industry," Ph.D. dissertation, Columbia University.

Hexter, J. Lawrence and John W. Snow (1970). "An Entropy Measure of Relative Aggregate Concentration," *The Southern Economic Journal*, 36 (January), 236-143.

Hirschman, A. O. (1945). *National Power and Structure of Foreign Trade.* Berkeley, Cal.: University of California Press.

Hochschild, Jennifer L. (1981). *What's Fair?* (Cambridge, MA: Harvard University Press).

Horowitz, Ira (1970). "Employment Concentration in the Common Market: An Entropy Approach," *Journal of the Royal Statistical Society*, 133 (part 3), 463-479.

Horvath, J. (1970). "Suggestion for a Comprehensive Measure of Concentration," *Southern Economic Journal*, 36 (April): 446-452.

Jackman, Robert W. (1975). *Politics and Social Equality: A Comparative Analysis.* New York: John Wiley and Sons.

Jahn, Julius, Calvin F. Schmid, and Clarence Shrag (1947). "The Measurement of Ecological Segregation," *American Sociological Review*, 12 (June): 293-303.

James, David R. and Karl E. Taeuber (1985). "Measures of Segregation," in Nancy Brandon Tuma, ed., *Sociological Methodology 1985.* San Francisco: Jossey-Bass, Inc., 1-32.

Jasso, Guillermina (1982). "Measuring Inequality Using the Geometric Mean/Arithmetic Mean Ratio," *Sociological Methods and Research*, 10 (February): 303-326.

Jasso, Guillermina (1981). *Proceedings of the American Statistical Association*, 350-355.

Jones, Bryan D. *et al* (1980). *Service Delivery in the City*. New York: Longman Publishers.

Jones, E. Terrence (1982). "The Distribution of Urban Services in a Declining City," in Richard C. Rich, ed., *The Politics of Urban Public Services* Lexington, MA: Lexington Books, 103-112.

Kaiser, Henry F. (1966). "A Measure of the Population Quality of Legislative Apportionment." *American Political Science Review*, 62 (March): 208-215.

Kendall, Maurice G. (1952). *The Advanced Theory of Statistics*. New York: Hafner Publishing Co.

Kendall, Maurice G. and Alan Stuart (1977). *The Advanced Theory of Statistics*. Vol. 1, 4th ed., New York: Macmillan.

Kesselman, Mark (1966). "French Local Politics: A Statistical Examination of Grass Roots Consensus," *American Political Science Review*, 60 (December): 963-974.

Kinchin, A. I. (1957). *Mathematical Foundations of Information Theory*. New York: Dover.

Kittel, C. (1956). *An Introduction to Solid State Physics*. New York: John Wiley.

Kittel, C. (1958). *Elementary Statistical Physics*. New York: John Wiley.

Knopke, Harry, Julia Hartman, and Philip B. Coulter (1988). "Where Have All the Physicians Gone?" unpublished manuscript, College of Community Health Sciences, The University of Alabama, Tuscaloosa, Alabama.

Kolm, Serge-Christophe (1976a). "Unequal Inequalities, I," *Journal of Economic Theory*, 12, 416-442.

Kolm, Serge-Christophe (1976b). "Unequal Inequalities, II," *Journal of Economic Theory*, 13, 82-111.

Kravis, I. (1962). *The Structure of Income*. Philadelphia: University of Pennsylvania Press.

Kuznets, Simon (1963). "Quantitative Aspects of Economic Growth of Nations: VIII. Distribution of Income by Size," *Economic Development and Cultural Change*, 11 (January): 1-80.

Laakso, Markku (1977). "Proportional Methods of Representation and Fragmentation of the Finnish Political Sysktem," (in Finnish) *Politiikka*, No. 3: 225.

Laakso, Markku and Rein Taagepera (1979). "'Effective' Number of Parties: A Measure with Applications to West Europe," *Comparative Political Studies* 12 (April): 3-27.

Labovitz, S. and J. P. Gibbs (1964). "Urbanization, Technology, and the Division of Labor: Further Evidence," *Pacific Sociological Review*, 7 (Spring): 3-9.

Lasswell, Harold D. (1935). *World Politics and Personal Insecurity*. New York: McGraw Hill.

Leik, Robert K. (1966). "A Measure of Ordinal Consensus," *Pacific Sociological Review*, 9 (Fall), 85-90.

Levy, Frank, Arnold Meltsner, and Aaron Wildavsky (1974). *Urban Outcomes: Schools, Streets, Libraries*. Berkeley: University of California Press.

Lieberson, Stanley (1964). "An Extension of Greenberg's Linguistic Diversity Measures," *Language*, 40 (November): 526-531.

Lieberson, Stanley (1969). "Measuring Population Diversity," *American Sociological Review*, 34 (December): 850-862.

Lieberson, Stanley (1975). "Rank-Sum Comparisons Between Groups," in David Heise, ed., *Sociological Methodology 1976*. San Francisco: Jossey-Bass, Inc.

Lieberson, Stanley (1980). *A Piece of the Pie: Blacks and White Immigrants Since 1880*. Berkeley: University of California Press.

Lieberson, Stanley (1981). "An Asymmetrical Approach to Segregation," in Ceri Peach *et al.* (eds.), *Ethnic Segregation in Cities*. Athens, GA: The University of Georgia Press.

Lieberson, Stanley and Donna K. Carter (1982). "Temporal Changes and Urban Differences in Residential Segregation: A Reconsideration," *American Journal of Sociology*, 88 (September): 296-310.

Lineberry, Robert L. (1977). *Equality and the Distribution of Urban Services*. Beverly Hills, CA: Sage Publications.

Lorenz, Max C. (1905). "Methods of Measuring the Concentration of Wealth," *Publications of the American Statistical Association*, 9, 209-219.

Lucy, William H. and Kenneth R. Mladenka (1978). *Equity and Urban Service Distribution*. Washington, DC: The National Training and Development Service.

Machlup, Fritz (1952). *The Political Economy of Monopoly*. Baltimore: The Johns Hopkins University Press.

Martin, J. David and Louis N. Gray (1971). "Measurement of Relative Variation: Sociological Examples," *American Sociological Review*, 36 (June), 496-502.

Marx, Karl (1976). *Capital: a Critique of Political Economy.*, tr. Ben Fowkes, New York: Vintage Books.

Marx, Karl and Frederich Engels (1963). New York: Russell and Russell.

Mayer, Lawrence S. (1972). "An Analysis of Measures of Crosscutting and Fragmentation," 4 (April): 405-415.

Michaely, M. (1962). *Concentration in International Trade*. Amsterdam: North Holland.

Miller, Mark J. and Judith Collins (1985). "Coulter's Index: An Application to the Nonprofit Sector," *Policy Studies Journal*, 14 (December): 223-230.

Morgan, Barrie S. and John Norbury (1981). "Some Further Observations on the Index of Residential Differentiation," *Demography*, 18 (May): 251-256.

Mosteller, Frederick, Robert E. K. Rourke, and George B. Thomas, Jr. (1961). *Probability with Statistical Applications*. Reading, Mass.: Addison-Wesley Publishing Company, Inc.

Mueller, John H., Karl F. Scheussler, and Herbert L. Costner (1970). *Statistical Reasoning in Sociology*. Boston: Houghton Mifflin Company.

Nachmias, David and David H. Rosenbloom (1973). "Measuring Bureaucratic Representation and Integration," *Public Administration Review*, 33, 590-597.

Nagel, Stuart S. (1984). *Public Policy: Goals, Means, and Methods.* New York: St. Martin's Press.

Newberry, D. M. G., (1970),"A Theorem on the Measurement of Inequality," *Journal of Economic Theory*, 2: 264-266.

Ostwalt, Martin, tr. (1962). *Aristotle's Nichomachean Ethics.* Indianapolis: The Bobbs-Merril Company.

Pareto, Vilfredo (1972). *A Manual of Political Economy.* A. S. Schweir and A. N. Page, eds., London: Macmillan.

Peach, Ceri (ed.) (1975). *Urban Residential Segregation.* London: Longman Publishers, Inc.

Pen, Jan (1971). *Income Distribution.* New York: Praeger Publishers.

Pigou, A. C. (1920). *Wealth and Welfare.* London: Macmillan.

Pinard, Maurice (1971). *The Rise of a Third Party: A Study in Crisis Politics.* Englewood Cliffs, N. J.: Prentice-Hall.

Przeworski, Adam (1975). "Institutionalization of Voting Patterns, or is Mobilization the Source of Decay?" *American Political Science Review*, 69 (March), 49-67.

Rae, Douglas W. (1981). *Equalities.* Cambridge, MA: Harvard University Press.

Rae, Douglas W. (1967). *The Political Consequences of Electoral Laws.* New Haven, Conn.: Yale University Press.

Rae, Douglas W. (1971). "Comment on Wildgen's 'The Measurement of Hyperfractionalization,'" *Comparative Political Studies*, 4 (July): 244.

Rae, Douglas W. and Michael Taylor (1970). *The Analysis of Political Cleavages.* New Haven: Yale University Press.

Ray, James Lee and J. David Singer (1973). "Measuring the Concentration of Power in the International System," *Sociological Methods and Research*, 1 (May): 403-437.

Riedesel, P. L. (1979). "Racial Discrimination and White Economic Benefits," *Social Science Quarterly*, 60 (June): 120-134.

Rothschild, Michael and Joseph E. Stiglitz (1973). "Some Further Results on the Measurement of Inequality," *Journal of Economic Theory*, 6:188-204.

Sakoda, James M. (1981). "A Generalized Index of Dissimilarity," *Demography*, 18 (May): 245-250.

Samuelson, Paul A. (1970). *Economics*. New York: McGraw-Hill.

Sawyer, Malcolm (1976). *Income Distribution in OECD Countries, Occasional Studies*. Paris: Organization for Economic Cooperation and Development.

Schnare, Ann B. (1977). *Residential Segregation by Race in U.S. Metropolitan Areas: An Analysis Across Cities and Over Time*. Washington, D.C.: Urban Institute.

Schutz, R. R. (1951). "On the Measurement of Income Inequality," *American Economic Review*, 41:107-122.

Schwartz, Joseph (1978). "Three Studies in Stratification," Unpublished doctoral dissertation, Harvard University.

Schwartz, Joseph and Christopher Winship (1979). "The Welfare Approach to Measuring Inequality," in Karl F. Schuessler, ed., *Sociological Methodology 1980*. San Francisco: Jossey-Bass Publishers.

Scott, Robert Haney and Nic Nigro (1982). *Principles of Economics*. New York: Macmillan Publishing Company.

Sen, Amartya (1973). *On Economic Inequality*. London: Clarendon Press.

Shannon, Claude E. and Warren Weaver (1971). *The Mathematical Theory of Communication*. Urbana, Ill.: University of Illinois Press.

Sharp, Elaine B. (1986). *Citizen Demand-Making in the Urban Context*. Tuscaloosa, AL: The University of Alabama Press.

Shevky, E. and M. Williams (1949). *The Social Areas of Los Angeles, Analysis and Typology*. Berkeley: The University of California Press.

Shorrocks, Anthony F. (1983). "Ranking Income Distributions," *Economica*, 50, 3-17.

Simpson, E. H. (1949). "Measurement of Diversity," *Nature*, 163 (April): 8.

Smithson, Michael (1979). "The Taagepera-Ray Generalized Index of Concentration," *Sociological Methods and Research* , 2 (November): 123-142.

Spiegel, Murray R. (1961). *Theory and Problems of Statistics*. New York: Schaum Publishing Company.

Sraffa, P. ed. (1951-1973). *The Works and Correspondence of David Ricardo*. London: Cambridge University Press.

Stearns, Linda Brewster and John R. Logan (1986). "Measuring Trends in Segregation, Three Dimensions, Three Measures," *Urban Affairs Quarterly*, 22 (September): 124-150.

Taagepera, Rein (1979). "Inequality, Concentration, Imbalance," *Political Methodology*, 6: 275-291.

Taagepera, Rein and Bernard Grofman (1981). "Effective Size and Number of Components," *Sociological Methods and Research*,10 (August): 63-81.

Taagepera, Rein and James Lee Ray (1977). "A Generalized Index of Concentration," *Sociological Methods and Research*, 5 (February): 367-383.

Taeuber, Karl E. and Alma F. Taeuber (1965). *Negroes in Cities, Residential Segregation and Neighborhood Change*. Chicago: Aldine Publishing Co.

Taeuber, Karl F. *et al* (1981). "A Demographic Perspective on School Desegregation in the USA," in Ceri Peach *et al*, eds., Athens, GA: The University of Georgia Press, 83-109.

Theil, Henri (1967). *Economics and Information Theory*. Amsterdam: North Holland.

Theil, Henri (1969). "The Desired Political Entropy," *American Political Science Review*, 63 (June): 521-525.

Theil, Henri (1972). *Statistical Decomposition Analysis*. Amsterdam: North Holland Publishing Company.

Treas, Judith (1983). "Trickle Down or Transfers? Postwar Determinants of Family Income Inequality," *American Sociological Review*, 48 (August): 546-559.

Väyrynen, Raimo (1972). "Analysis of Party Systems by Concentration, Fractionalization, and Entropy Measures," *Scandinavian Political Studies*, vol. 7/72, New York: Columbia University Press, 137-155.

Villemez, W. J. (1978). "Black Subordination and White Economic Well-Being: Comment on Szymanski," *American Sociological Review*, 43 (October): 772-776.

Waldman, Loren K. (1975). "Statistical Decomposition of Measures of Party Systems' Properties," *Political Methodology*, 2 (February): 189-219.

Waldman, Loren K. (1976). "Measures of Party Systems' Properties: The Number and Size of Parties," *Political Methodology*, 3: 199-214.

Waldman, Loren K. (1977). "Types and Measures of Inequality," *Social Science Quarterly*, 58 (September): 229-241.

White, Michael J. (1983). "The Measurement of Spatial Segregation," *American Journal of Sociology*, 88 (March): 1007-1018.

Wilcox, Allen R. (1973). "Indices of Qualitative Variation and Political Measurement," *Western Political Quarterly*, 26 (June): 325-343.

Wildgen, John K. (1971). "The Measurement of Hyperfractionalization," *Comparative Political Studies*, 4 (July): 233-243.

Williamson, Jeffrey G. (1977). "'Strategic' Wage Goods, Prices, and Inequality," *American Economic Review*, 66, 29-41.

Winship, Christopher (1978). "The Desirability of Using the Index of Dissimilarity or Any Adjustment of It for Meauring Segregation: A Reply to Falk, Cortese, and Cohen," *Social Forces*, 57: 717-720.

Yntema, D. B. (1933). "Measures of the Inequality in the Personal Distribution of Wealth and Income," *Journal of the American Statistical Association*, 28 (December): 423-433.

Zoloth, B. S. (1976). "Alternative Measures of School Segregation," *Land Economics*, 52:278-298.

INDEX